EASTERN CANADA
TRAVEL ✦ SMART®

W9-BMN-813

EASTERN CANADA
TRAVEL ✦ SMART®

Third Edition

Felicity Munn

John Muir Publications
A Division of Avalon Travel Publishing

John Muir Publications
A division of Avalon Travel Publishing
5855 Beaudry Street, Emeryville, CA 94608

Printed in the United States of America.
Third edition. First printing March 2000.

ISSN 1097-0479
ISBN 1-56261-521-1

Editors: Peg Goldstein, Lizann Flatt
Graphics Editor: Bunny Wong
Production: Marie J.T. Vigil
Design: Marie J.T. Vigil
Cover Design: Janine Lehmann, Marie J.T. Vigil
Typesetting: Janet Shade
Map Style Development: American Custom Maps—Jemez Springs, NM
Map Illustration: Julie Felton, Kathy Sparkes
Printing: Publishers Press
Front Cover: *small*—© Bob Krist/Leo de Wys., Inc.
              large—© Bill Terry/Photo Network (Rose Blanche, Newfoundland)
Back Cover: © Gene Ahrens

Distributed to the book trade by
Publishers Group West
Berkeley, California

EASTERN CANADA TRAVEL•SMART: A GUIDE THAT GUIDES

Most guidebooks are primarily directories, providing information but very little help in making choices—you have to guess how to make the most of your time and money. *Eastern Canada Travel•Smart* is different: By highlighting the very best of the region and offering various planning features, it acts like a personal tour guide rather than a directory.

TAKE THE STRESS OUT OF TRAVEL

Sometimes traveling causes more stress than it relieves. Sorting through information, figuring out the best routes, determining what to see and where to eat and stay, scheduling each day—all of this can make a vacation feel daunting rather than fun. Relax. We've done a lot of the legwork for you. This book will help you plan a trip that suits you—whatever your time frame, budget, and interests.

SEE THE BEST OF THE REGION

Author Felicity Munn has lived in Eastern Canada her whole life. She has handpicked every listing in this book, and she gives you an insider's perspective on what makes each one worthwhile. So while you will find many of the big tourist attractions listed here, you'll also find lots of smaller, lesser known treasures, such as L'Anse aux Meadows in Newfoundland and the Reversing Falls in Saint John, New Brunswick. And each sight is described, so you'll know what's most—and sometimes least—interesting about it.

In selecting the restaurants and accommodations for this book, the author sought out unusual spots with local flavor. While in some areas of the region chains are unavoidable, wherever possible the author directs you to one-of-a-kind places. We also know that you want a range of options: One day you may crave fresh crab or lobster, while the next day you would be just as happy (as would your wallet) with a hamburger. Most of the restaurants and accommodations listed here are moderately priced, but the author also includes budget and splurge options, depending on the destination.

CREATE THE TRIP YOU WANT

We all have different travel styles. Some people like spontaneous weekend jaunts, while others plan longer, more leisurely trips. You may want to cover as much ground as possible, no matter how much time you have. Or maybe you prefer to focus your trip on one part of the region or on some special interest, such as skiing, hiking, or whale-watching. We've taken these differences into account.

Though the individual chapters stand on their own, they are organized in a geographically logical sequence, so that you could conceivably fly into Toronto and travel chapter by chapter to each destination in the book. Of course, you don't have to follow that sequence, but it's there if you want a complete picture of the region.

Each destination chapter offers ways of prioritizing when time is limited: In the Perfect Day section, the author suggests what to do if you have only one day to spend in the area. Also, every Sightseeing Highlight is rated, from one to four stars: ★★★★—must see; ★★★—highly recommended; ★★—worthwhile; and ★—see if you have time. At the end of each sight listing is a time recommendation in parentheses. User-friendly maps help you locate the sights, restaurants, and lodging of your choice.

And if you're in it for the ride, so to speak, you'll want to check out the Scenic Routes described at the end of several chapters. They take you through some of the most scenic parts of region.

In addition to these special features, the appendix has other useful travel tools:

- The Planning Map and Mileage Chart help you determine your own route and calculate travel time.
- The Special Interest Tours show you how to design your trip around any of five favorite interests.
- The Calendar of Events provides an at-a-glance view of when and where major events occur throughout the region.
- The Resource Guide tells you where to go for more information about national and provincial parks, individual cities and counties, local bed-and-breakfasts, and more.

HAPPY TRAVELS

With this book in hand, you have many reliable recommendations and travel tools at your fingertips. Use it to make the most of your trip. And have a great time!

WHY VISIT
EASTERN CANADA?

Canada is just across the border. It's so close and so similar in so many ways—and yet so different. You'll find wide-open spaces and pristine natural beauty, European-flavored cities and awesome restaurants, Old World charm and limitless outdoor activities. For nature lovers, history buffs, big-city afi-cionados, gourmands, and kids—there's something for everyone. From the heady rush of Niagara Falls to the craggy appeal of tiny fishing outposts along the rocky Newfoundland coast; from the bustle of big cities to the soothing serenity of oceanside vistas, Eastern Canada holds the promise of infinite dis-coveries.

The great outdoors usually springs to mind when you think of Canada, with good reason. This country is justifiably renowned for its splendid natural attractions. For starters, you can explore Prince Edward Island's gently rolling hills and sweeping beaches, cruise the Thousand Islands in Ontario, whale-watch on Quebec's Saguenay River, hike Newfoundland's unmatched Gros Morne National Park, or kayak in the stunning Bay of Fundy (home to the highest tides in the world). The Cabot Trail on Nova Scotia's Cape Breton Is-land provides so many wondrous vistas of cliffs and ocean that you may be in danger of scenic overdose.

Simultaneously, Canadian cities are cultured and cosmopolitan enough to suit the most sophisticated tastes, with the added advantage of being safer than American cities. Toronto, for instance, likes to think of itself as New York City without the crime and grime (that's why some wags call it "the Big Lemon"). Ottawa, the nation's capital, boasts 29 museums. Montreal, the so-called Paris of North America, offers wall-to-wall summer festivals and a dizzying range of restaurants, all spiced with French-Canadian joie de vivre. Visiting Quebec City even lets you "do" Europe without crossing the Atlantic.

History buffs find themselves strolling through the past. The cobblestone streets of Montreal and Quebec City are suffused with the ambience of bygone centuries. Signs of Halifax's colorful seafaring history include the world's largest number of *Titanic* grave sites. In St. John's, you can raise a glass in a city that boasted more than 80 pubs before the Americans began their battle for independence. At L'Anse aux Meadows on the other side of Newfoundland, at the only authenticated Viking site in North America, you can chat with interpreters acting as if they're the Norse adventurers who created a settlement there one thousand years ago.

Diversions for kids are plentiful as well. Everyone, no matter his or her age, is amazed by Niagara Falls. Children also invariably love Magnetic Hill in Moncton, New Brunswick, where visitors' cars are seemingly pulled up a hill by a giant, invisible hand. Kid-friendly museums abound in Eastern Canada's cities, including the new Children's Own Museum in Toronto, conceived especially for kids six and under.

Add to all these attractions a big bonus—low cost. The Canadian dollar is almost the weakest it's ever been against the U.S. buck, so American visitors these days stretch the worth of their money by 45 to 50 percent. Small wonder that the number of U.S. visitors to Canada in the past year or so has shattered all previous records.

THE LAY OF THE LAND

With a total land area of 9,922,330 square kilometers (3,831,033 square miles), Canada is the second-largest country in the world, behind only Russia. It also contains more lakes and inland waterways than any other country—the legacy of a massive glacier that once covered nearly the whole country and left in its wake many thousands of lakes. In fact, the lakes are so numerous that nobody, it is said, has ever been able to count them all.

Lake Ontario and Lake Huron, two of the Great Lakes, provide enormous outdoor playgrounds in Ontario. Eastern Canada's great rivers include the St. Lawrence, which runs from the Great Lakes to the Gulf of St. Lawrence; the Saguenay, which drains into the St. Lawrence; and the Saint John, which empties into the Bay of Fundy between Nova Scotia and New Brunswick.

All of Labrador and much of Quebec are made up of the Canadian Shield, a region of ancient granite rock sparsely covered with soil. Newfoundland, Nova Scotia, New Brunswick, and Prince Edward Island, as well as Quebec's Gaspé Peninsula, are all part of the Appalachian-Acadian region, which runs into the Appalachian mountain system that also includes the Green Mountains in Vermont and New Hampshire's White Mountains. The St. Lawrence and Lower Lakes region, covering much of southern Quebec and Ontario, is a level plain with a large expanse of arable land.

Eastern Canada doesn't have the mountains that Western Canada does, but the Laurentian Mountains in Quebec are high enough to accommodate the best skiing east of the Rockies.

FLORA AND FAUNA

Forests—endless acres of everything from spruce, balsam fir, and jack pine to maple, beech, walnut, oak, elm, poplar, aspen, and birch—blanket much of Eastern Canada. Flowering plant species include the aster, buttercup, goldenrod, trillium, and violet; Nova Scotia is particularly known for its wildflowers. The forests are populated with wolf, black bear, caribou, deer, and moose among other species. Red fox, marten, muskrat, otter, mink, squirrel, and rabbit are also numerous. So are beavers, but you're more likely to see a beaver dam than you are an actual beaver because they're rather shy. In cities, it's not unusual to spot raccoons. In Toronto, in fact, they're a real problem because they can cause damage to houses. Hunters are attracted by such game birds as duck, goose, ruffled grouse, and partridge. Other bird species include heron, woodpecker, warbler, finch, and loon—another creature you may never see but whose haunting call you will always remember, should you be lucky enough to hear it on a quiet woodland lake.

In the four provinces of Atlantic Canada, shorebirds include the gull, tern, gannet, kittiwake, cormorant, and puffin. Coastal waters are inhabited by lobsters, oysters, scallops, and salmon. Folks who like to fish are lured by the inland freshwater fish, which include trout, pickerel, pike, and bass. Few snakes are found in Canada, and those that can be found tend to be of the harmless garter variety.

HISTORY

Indians and Inuit (Eskimo) peoples lived in Canada for many thousands of years before the arrival of the first Europeans—namely the Vikings, who set up a community in Newfoundland one thousand years ago. That settlement was abandoned fairly quickly, thanks to a climate even the Norse found harsh. But in the 1400s another wave of Europeans began to arrive. John Cabot, an Italian explorer commissioned by the English, landed in Newfoundland (or possibly Nova Scotia) in 1497. Several decades later, French explorer Jacques Cartier sailed up the St. Lawrence River, claiming the land for France.

The rivalry between the British and the French continued off and on until Quebec fell to the British at the Battle of the Plains of Abraham in 1759, and Montreal surrendered to the British fleet one year later. As a result, under the Treaty of Paris (1763), New France came under British rule. Chiefly because it enabled them to govern more effectively, the British guaranteed that the French could keep their traditional language, civil law, and Roman Catholic religion. In the War of 1812, the United States decided to invade British North America, specifically Upper Canada (now Ontario). But the Upper Canadians forged an alliance with the chief of the Native American nations, who were already fighting the Americans on their own turf, and ultimately repelled the invaders.

In 1867, with confederation, Canada achieved self-government without leaving the British Empire. The new nation was a federation of Nova Scotia, New Brunswick, Quebec (Lower Canada), and Ontario (Upper Canada). Later, Prince Edward Island, Newfoundland, and the western provinces (British Columbia, Alberta, Manitoba, and Saskatchewan) joined.

More recently, the issue of French-Canadian separatism has ebbed and flowed, sometimes languishing but always eventually erupting again. The situation reached something of a boiling point in the 1960s, when extremist separatists set off bombs in Montreal. In the autumn of 1970, in what came to be known as the October Crisis, some of the extremists kidnapped the British trade commissioner. He was later released; however, another cell of the group kidnapped and murdered a provincial cabinet minister.

The issue has quieted down a lot since then, but the Quebec-Canada wrangling continues endlessly. In 1980 a referendum was proposed in Quebec to decide whether the province should separate from the rest of the country; the vote was against separation, but only by a 60 to 40 margin. In the autumn of 1995, with the pro-separation Parti Québecois political party in power again in the province, another referendum was held (or "neverendum," as some called it) on the same issue. The vote, once again, was for Quebec to remain a part of Canada—but only by a razor-thin margin of less than two percentage points. Another referendum seems inevitable within the next few years, but public opinion polls suggest that support for independence has ebbed.

For those interested in Canada's history, National Historic Sites, operated by Heritage Canada (which also oversees the national parks), can be found around almost every corner. The best of them, such as the Fortress of Louisbourg in Nova Scotia, sweep visitors away to another era.

CULTURES

Canada's total population, according to the 1996 census, is 28.8 million. About three-quarters of that number live in a fairly narrow band along the U.S. border. The overall population density is approximately three people per square kilometer (or 7.8 people per square mile).

Canadians are a polyglot lot. In fact, Toronto has been designated the world's most ethnically diverse city by the United Nations. The largest share of Canada's population consists of people of British (about 35 percent) and French (about 25 percent) descent. The remainder of the population consists of people of various ethnic origins, ranging from Greek and Italian to Chinese and Vietnamese. Native peoples and Inuit collectively account for less than 2 percent of the population. African Americans, who make up less than 1 percent of the population, are largely descendants of early immigrants from the United States—mainly runaway slaves. Canada abolished slavery early on, and many slaves escaped via the Underground Railroad.

The vast majority of French Canadians live in the province of Quebec, but sizable numbers also live in New Brunswick and Ontario. New Brunswick is the only officially bilingual province in Canada. French is the official language in Quebec, whereas English is the official language in the rest of the country. The federal government has long had a bilingualism policy, meaning that all government services are supposed to be available in both English and French.

Language may cause much bickering within Canada, but for English-speaking visitors, it shouldn't be a problem. Quebec is the one place visitors may hit snags because most traffic and commercial signs, among other things, are written only in French. Some merchants around Montreal post "F/E" stickers in their shop windows, indicating that they will serve you in French or English, whichever you prefer. In most situations, someone should be available to translate. Quebec City is such a tourist mecca that people working in the tourism industry routinely speak English to visitors from elsewhere in Canada and from the United States. When driving in Quebec, try to remember that est is east, ouest is west, sud is south, and nord is north.

THE ARTS

Toronto is the third-largest English-language theater city in the world, after London and New York City. Toronto loves to boast about its culture, but major theater, opera, and dance groups are found in other big cities, too. The National Ballet of Canada and Les Grand Ballets Canadiens, based in Montreal, are the major ballet companies, and the best-known orchestras are the Montreal Symphony and the Toronto Symphony.

If you still think Canada's a cultural backwater, drop in on one of the country's numerous festivals. Montreal and Toronto both host world-class film festivals late every summer. In Montreal, the Just for Laughs Comedy Festival attracts comics from around the globe. The city's jazz festival, much of it held outdoors with free admission, is hugely popular. Ottawa also hosts a big jazz festival every summer. Not to be missed are the Stratford Festival in Stratford, Ontario, devoted to the works of Shakespeare, and the Shaw Festival in Niagara-on-the-Lake, Ontario, showcasing the works of George Bernard Shaw and his contemporaries.

Megastar songstress Celine Dion is Canadian, as are Alanis Morissette and Shania Twain. So, it would seem, is half of Hollywood, including Jim Carrey, Pamela Anderson Lee, Keanu Reeves, Leslie Nielsen (whose brother was a senior cabinet minister with the federal government for years), Alex Trebek, Dan Akroyd, and Donald and Kiefer Sutherland.

Lovers of the visual arts will find plenty to see as well. The focus, to some extent, is on Canadian art, especially at places like the National Art Gallery in Ottawa and the Confederation Centre Art Gallery in Charlottetown. But the collections at these and other major art museums also include extensive international works, and a blockbuster international touring exhibit is invariably appearing in a Canadian venue at any given time.

For those with a literary bent, Toronto has been the setting for novels by Margaret Atwood and Robertson Davies, among others, and Mordecai Richler sets some of his books in his hometown of Montreal. Writer/musician Leonard Cohen, born and bred in Montreal, sometimes uses the city as a backdrop in his work. In *Barometer Rising,* Hugh MacLennan wrote about the Halifax Explosion. Farley Mowat set *The Boat Who Wouldn't Float* on Newfoundland's Avalon Peninsula, and National Book Award winner E. Annie Proulx also chose Newfoundland as a backdrop for *The Shipping News*. Prince Edward Island, for its part, was the setting of that perennial favorite of children's literature, *Anne of Green Gables.*

CUISINE

Canada's cultural diversity is reflected in its eclectic cuisine. The variety is a good thing, too, because aside from a few items such as maple syrup, rainbow trout, and Atlantic Canada's fresh seafood and fiddleheads, Eastern

Canada's indigenous dishes aren't much to write home about. Especially in the big cities, you'll find something for virtually every taste, from hot dogs sold by street vendors to U.S.-based fast-food outlets to the finest and most expensive French fare. Popular ethnic cuisine runs the usual gamut, from Mexican and Chinese to Italian and Greek. In recent years, Thai and Cajun restaurants have also been gaining in popularity. Toronto's large Caribbean population supports a wider selection of Bahamian and other Caribbean-themed restaurants than you'll find in other cities. In fact, in Toronto you can feast on dishes from literally every country around the world because the city is so ethnically diverse. (Don't forget to try the local wines when you're in Ontario.) Montreal has several Vietnamese restaurants operated by immigrants who chose Quebec because of the language. As for indigenous dishes in French Canada, the most notorious is probably *poutine,* sold in many Quebec greasy spoons and elsewhere. It consists of French fries and cheese curds smothered in gravy. As noted, fresh seafood is the way to go in Atlantic Canada, especially lobster. Prince Edward Island is also known for Island Blue mussels and Malpeque oysters.

Starbucks outlets have been sprouting up like mushrooms in Canada, but a Canadian chain, Second Cup, serves equally good if not better coffee.

OUTDOOR ACTIVITIES

Someone once said that people in New Zealand look disgustingly fit and healthy because they're all so outdoorsy. It's not quite that way in Canada—some of the residents are still pasty-faced and indolent—but anyone who relishes biking and hiking adventures will no doubt find Canada to be something of a paradise.

With a gazillion lakes and rivers, boating and water sports are extremely popular. For those in search of real thrills, several rivers in the Laurentian Mountains, accessible from either Montreal or Ottawa, are considered among the best white-water rafting rivers on the continent. Much the same goes for fishing; you haven't lived until you've had fresh rainbow trout out of the lake and into the frying pan. The Miramichi River in New Brunswick is world famous for its salmon fishing.

The hiking possibilities are endless; all you have to do is head for the nearest national or provincial park. Bicycle paths (on which at least as many in-line skaters can be found as cyclists) are available even in big cities, and increasingly you'll find them in the countryside, too, as unused railroad-track beds are converted into recreation trails and the TransCanada Trail takes shape. The trail isn't slated for completion until sometime in 2000, or possibly even later, but meanwhile, more and more sections of it are open for walking, cycling, horse-back riding, cross-country skiing, and snowmobiling. When completed, it will be the longest recreation trail in the world, snaking from St. John's to Victoria, British Columbia, with a branch heading north to the Northwest Territories.

Naturally, ecotourism-type activities are extremely popular, and plenty of opportunities to pursue them are available throughout Eastern Canada. Bird-watchers flock to Atlantic Canada, particularly Newfoundland. Whale-watch-ers are virtually guaranteed sightings in the St. Lawrence River, the Bay of Fundy, and around Newfoundland.

If you're brave enough to visit Eastern Canada in winter, you must try both skiing and ice skating. Ski hills are usually within an hour of the major cities. Or, if you prefer cross-country skiing, you can do that almost anywhere, any time, including in city parks. Outdoor skating rinks appear all over the place once the cold weather sets in, including in the very heart of the cities (one rink is lo-cated smack in front of Toronto City Hall, for example). In some places, you can go dogsledding—a fascinating experience because of the dogs, who seem to live for tearing at top speed across the frozen landscape. Or, you might consider snowshoeing. Probably the easiest winter activity of all, snowshoeing can take you deep into winter wonderlands and, unlike snowmobiling, it's en-vironmentally friendly.

PLANNING YOUR TRIP

Before you set out on your trip, you'll need to do some planning. Use this chapter in conjunction with the tools in the appendix to answer some basic questions. First of all, when are you going? You may already have specific dates in mind; if not, various factors will probably influence your timing. Either way, you'll want to know about local events, the weather, and other seasonal considerations. This chapter discusses all of that.

How much should you expect to spend on your trip? This chapter addresses various regional factors you'll want to consider in estimating your travel expenses. How will you get around? Check out the section on local transportation. If you decide to travel by car, the Planning Map and Mileage Chart in the appendix can help you figure out exact routes and driving times, while the Special Interest Tours provide several focused itineraries. The chapter concludes with some reading recommendations, both fiction and nonfiction, to give you various perspectives on the region. If you want specific information about individual cities or counties, use the Resource Guide in the appendix.

WHEN TO GO
Given the Canadian climate, June, July, and August are the best months in which to visit. But in southern Ontario, for example, April and May are pretty

9

good as well. September and October, when the autumn colors kick in, are generally a safe bet—except maybe in Newfoundland, which can have variable and unpleasant weather.

Summer is peak season, of course, but that doesn't mean you should avoid visiting at that time. Some of the natural attractions can get awfully busy, such as Niagara Falls or the Cabot Trail, so it can be more rewarding to visit such areas in spring or autumn when the crowds are a lot thinner. Remember, however, that in certain sparsely populated areas such as Western Newfoundland and the Gaspé Peninsula in Quebec, most of the hotels are only open during peak tourist season. That consideration aside, plenty of space is available in this country to accommodate everyone. Some cities are almost a must in peak season—Montreal, with its famous jazz and comedy fests, for instance.

Visually, the most stunning period in Eastern Canada is late September and early October, when the changing leaves paint a sublime tableau of scarlet, yellow, and orange as far as the eye can see. It's been called the greatest natural show on earth, and it's worth seeing. The height of the colors varies depending on several factors, but Canadian Thanksgiving, the first Monday after the first Tuesday in October, is often when they peak. As a bonus, the peak summer travel season is over by this time, so tourist facilities are less crowded and prices may even be lower. Lately, Canadian tourism officials have been heavily promoting autumn getaways, trying to spread the wealth around.

Winter is characterized by subzero temperatures and bone-numbing cold—time to dress warmly and indulge in some winter sports. Most cities also host winter festivals of one sort or another. Among the best are Ottawa's Winterlude and Quebec City's Winter Carnival. Winterlude is centered on the frozen Rideau Canal, billed as the longest skating rink in the world. The Quebec City event focuses on a massive ice palace and features hoards of merrymakers warding off the cold with copious amounts of an alcoholic concoction called caribou.

The one exception to the cold and snow is Toronto. Thanks to its location on Lake Ontario, it almost never has snow at Christmas, for instance, and some years it barely snows at all throughout the winter. Winter is also the time when many of the city's theaters and hotels offer their best deals, so it's worth investigating.

Canadian temperatures are measured in Celsius, not Fahrenheit. To convert Celsius to Fahrenheit, multiply the Celsius figure by 9, divide the result by 5, and add 32 (don't forget your pocket calculator, eh?). Or, to figure out the approximate temperature in Fahrenheit, double the Celsius temperature and add 30; 20 degrees C, for example, becomes roughly 70 degrees F.

HOW MUCH WILL IT COST?

All prices in this book are given in Canadian dollars. The Canadian dollar varies in value against U.S. currency, but lately $1 U.S. has been worth around $1.45 Canadian. No question: American visitors get a lot more bang for their buck in Canada.

Canadian money comes in a couple of denominations that may seem strange to Americans—the $1 coin, which has a loon on it and is known as a "loony," and the $2 coin (the "two-nie"). Bills are printed in $5, $10, $20, $50, and larger denominations, and each is a different color.

On the other hand, prices for just about everything in Canada tend to be higher than in the United States. If you're a budget traveler, expect to spend about $50 a night for a motel room or $75 a night for a hotel room for two people. In the moderate range, figure on about $100 a night. Upscale hotel rooms cost anywhere from $100 to $200. Bed-and-breakfasts start at around $50 a night. Camping rates generally range from about $15 to $20, as do youth hostel rates.

To calculate food costs, figure inexpensive restaurant meals at under $20 per person for dinner, moderate establishments at $20 to $40, and pricey places at $40 and up. Budget about $10 per person for breakfast and lunch. Admission prices to parks, museums, and attractions vary widely. To be on the safe side, figure an average of $5 to $8 per person.

If you're driving and plan to visit every destination in this book, base gas estimates on approximately 2,500 miles. If you are flying or taking the train to Canada, expect to pay about $300 per week for a small rental car.

In addition to the the prices, Canada has the GST, the federal goods-and-services tax. Canadians loathe the GST and grit their teeth whenever they have to pay the 7 percent tax—as they do on virtually everything, whether it's a haircut, hotel room, or toothbrush. Visitors have to pay it, too, but at least they can get a rebate for GST paid on goods transported out of the country within 60 days of purchase. Tax charged on hotel and motel accommodations is also eligible for a refund.

You can apply for a rebate as long as the GST paid is $7 or more; in other words, you need only buy $100 worth of goods to be eligible for the rebate. Remember to keep all original receipts, which must clearly show that the GST was paid. You have one year from the date of purchase to claim the rebate. GST rebate application forms are available at participating Canadian duty-free shops, tourist information centers, and, in other countries, Canadian embassies and consulates. The easiest way to get a rebate is to hand in the form at a participating duty-free shop, where you'll get a cash rebate on the spot. Or you can mail the form, with receipts, to Revenue Canada, Customs and

Excise, Visitor Rebate Program, Ottawa, Ontario K1A 1J5. Proof that you are not a Canadian resident and a sample signature are required. For more information, call 800/668-4748 from within Canada or 613/991-3346 from outside Canada; or write to Revenue Canada at the aforementioned address.

Ontario, Quebec, and Prince Edward Island each has its own separate sales tax as well, whereas Nova Scotia's, New Brunswick's, and Newfoundland's provincial sales taxes are "harmonized," or folded in with, the GST. Again, rebates are available for visitors. Call provincial tourism departments for more information. The phone numbers are listed under Resources in the Appendix.

A trip to Canada, by the way, provides cigar smokers with a rare chance to find out whether the mystique surrounding Cuban cigars is justified. Specialty smoke shops sell them individually or in boxes; prices begin at $4 per cigar.

ORIENTATION AND TRANSPORTATION

To get the most from your trip, traveling by car is the best bet; that way, you can noodle along at your own pace, exploring and lingering as you please. Driving in Canada shouldn't hold any surprises, but you should keep a few things in mind. Distance is measured in kilometers, so a speed limit of 100 kph does not give you license to floor it. The 100 kph highway speed limit is roughly 60 miles an hour. In town, the 50 kph speed limit is roughly 30 miles an hour.

Roads in Ontario, Prince Edward Island, and Nova Scotia tend to be slightly better maintained than in the other three provinces. In the Newfoundland countryside, you also have to beware of wandering animals. Generally speaking, however, the road system across all six provinces is extensive and well maintained. If traveling by car isn't feasible, virtually all the cities and towns en route are accessible by public transportation.

Air Canada and Canadian Airlines International are the major air carriers (although it looks like the two might merge). Each is affiliated with several regional airlines serving smaller centers. In summer, several charter airlines such as Canada 3000 and Air Transat also offer discount flights on domestic routes; to book your flight, see a travel agent.

If you love train travel, look to Via Rail, the national passenger railway service. Trains runs frequently between Toronto, Ottawa, Montreal, and Quebec City, which collectively form the busiest railway corridor in the country. The express train between Toronto and Montreal makes the trip in four hours flat, and the Montreal–Quebec City express service takes less than three hours. From Montreal, Via also runs trains to the scenic Gaspé Peninsula and to Halifax. Via offers both coach-class and first-class travel. Coach passengers who book at least five days ahead get 35 percent off (40 percent if you're a student or senior) on off-peak days, meaning any day except Friday, Sunday, and public holidays. Between Toronto and Montreal, for example, an adult one-way first-class ticket costs $139, whereas full economy fare is $92, and the off-peak discount fare is $69. Via also offers discounted rates for kids under age 12. Most Via trains are wheelchair accessible.

For extensive train travel, consider the Canrailpass, valid for any 12 days of travel in a 30-day period throughout Via's network. The 1999 peak-season rates were $589 for adults and $529 for youths and seniors, for travel between June 1 and October 15, whereas low-season rates were $379 for adults and $345 for youths and seniors. Via has ticket offices in all the major cities on this itinerary, or you can see a travel agent.

Towns served by neither Via nor any airlines are invariably on the network of intercity bus routes. Buses are operated by different companies depending on the area. In Ontario, the major bus lines are Greyhound Canada and Voyageur Colonial; in Quebec it's Voyageur Colonial; in Nova Scotia the company is Acadian Lines; and in New Brunswick and Prince Edward Island, S.M.T.

If you're into the idea of traveling in a home-away-from-home, call 888/467-8464 from Canada or 800/467-8464 from the United States for information on renting recreational vehicles.

RECOMMENDED READING

A Short History of Canada (McClelland & Stewart, 1997) is written by a professional historian. But don't let that put you off—it's both entertaining and informative. Author Desmond Morris covers a lot of ground in what is, indeed, a fairly short book. The history lesson is easily digestible, thanks to the author's storytelling talents. It was first published in 1983 but has been updated a couple of times since then; the latest edition takes us into the 1990s.

The Spirit of Canada (Malcolm Lester Books, 1999), edited by Barbara Hehner, is aimed at kids but will doubtless delight their parents as well. Subtitled *Canada's Story in Legends, Fiction, Poems and Songs*, it deals with everything from First Contact to exploration in the North to the Great Depression and includes old favorites like "The Cremation of Sam McGee" and new classics like Gordon Lightfoot's "The Railroad Trilogy."

Niagara—A History of the Falls (McClelland & Stewart, 1992) is by Pierre Berton, a prolific writer and well-known Canadian personality. Berton's use of memorable characters—stuntpeople, explorers, artists, power brokers, suicide victims, love-sick bridegrooms—makes for a lively social history of the famous falls.

On the practical side, the *Canadian Bed and Breakfast Guide,* by Gerda Pantel (Penguin Books, 1999) is billed as the most comprehensive guide available to the rapidly growing B&B scene in Canada and is updated every year. For outdoorsy types, *Canada's National Parks: A Visitor's Guide* (Prentice Hall Canada, 1997), by Marylee Stephenson, features a wealth of information on national parks across the country, including park services and campgrounds.

For current suggestions on restaurants, shows, and galleries, check local dailies such as the *Toronto Star,* the *Globe and Mail,* the *National Post,* or the *Toronto Sun,* all in Toronto, and the *Kingston Whig-Standard,* the *Ottawa Citizen,* the *Montreal Gazette,* the *Halifax Herald,* and the *St. John's Evening Telegram* in the various provinces.

1
TORONTO

Toronto is sometimes called "Toronto the Good," a nickname arising from the city's strict Puritanism in the late nineteenth century. Perhaps out of envy, other Canadians have tended to view Toronto with some suspicion—it works too well; something must be wrong—and its residents as uptight and driven, motivated mainly by money. But the anti-Toronto jokes are mostly in the past because Toronto has evolved into a truly vibrant metropolis. Perched on the edge of Lake Ontario, it is picturesque, clean, and safe. It is also one of the most ethnically diverse cities in the world. Originally settled by English and Scottish immigrants, today Toronto is home to more than 80 different ethnic groups speaking 100 different languages. The city has the third-largest theater industry in the English-speaking world, behind New York and London.

With a population of more than 4.2 million, Greater Toronto is Canada's largest metropolitan area. It lies farther south than most of Michigan and all of Minnesota, at the same latitude as the northern California border. Huge Lake Ontario keeps the climate temperate; summers are clear and hot, winters cool with little snow.

MORE TORONTO HISTORY

Toronto is the Huron Indian word for "meeting place," which is how Canadian Indians used the site before a French fur-trading post was established here in

TORONTO

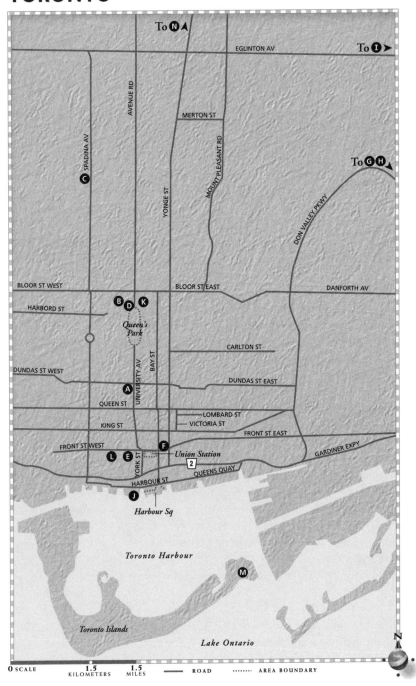

To N

EGLINTON AV

To I

AVENUE RD

MERTON ST

MOUNT PLEASANT RD

SPADINA AV

C

YONGE ST

To G H

DON VALLEY PKWY

BLOOR ST WEST

BLOOR ST EAST

DANFORTH AV

HARBORD ST

B D K

Queen's Park

CARLTON ST

UNIVERSITY AV

BAY ST

DUNDAS ST WEST

A

DUNDAS ST EAST

QUEEN ST

KING ST

LOMBARD ST

VICTORIA ST

FRONT ST EAST

FRONT ST WEST

F

Union Station

2

L E

YORK ST

GARDINER EXPY

QUEENS QUAY

HARBOUR ST

J

Harbour Sq

Toronto Harbour

M

Toronto Islands

Lake Ontario

N

0 SCALE   1.5   1.5   —— ROAD   ········ AREA BOUNDARY
         KILOMETERS MILES

1750. The British colonized the area in 1793 and named the town York, but the name reverted to Toronto when the city was incorporated. During the War of 1812, an American force of ships raided York, burned the parliament buildings, and ransacked the village. In retribution, the British invaded Washington and tried to burn down the president's residence. The building remained intact, but its scorched outside walls had to be whitewashed— hence, the White House.

At Canada's confederation in 1867, Toronto was the capital of Upper Canada, now Ontario. The seat of government is located at Queen's Park, on land once used as an asylum for the mentally disturbed.

A PERFECT DAY IN TORONTO

Start at the Toronto Islands, a world away from the city bustle, yet practically within shouting distance of the downtown waterfront. These islands are small oases that sit in the harbor, and they're always worth a visit. After the islands, by way of contrast, wander through the heart of downtown to engage in some serious window-shopping, followed by a dose of culture and history at the Royal Ontario Museum and the Bata Shoe Museum. Then head off to spend the evening at The Beaches, a lively neighborhood east of downtown that boasts a two-mile boardwalk along the beach, with lots of restaurants, cafés, bars, and boutiques.

ORIENTATION

Traffic is dense in metropolitan Toronto and a nightmare at rush hour. Parking can be hard to find and expensive when you do find it. The city has a strict ticketing and tow-away policy. Leave your vehicle at the hotel and use the efficient public transit system of subway, buses, and streetcars—or walk. The major sights and activities are mostly downtown within walking distance of

SIGHTS

- **A** Art Gallery of Ontario
- **B** Bata Shoe Museum
- **C** Casa Loma
- **D** Children's Own Museum
- **E** CN Tower
- **F** Hockey Hall of Fame
- **G** McMichael Canadian Art Collection
- **H** Metro Toronto Zoo
- **I** Ontario Science Centre
- **J** The Pier
- **K** Royal Ontario Museum
- **L** SkyDome
- **M** Toronto Islands
- **N** Wonderland

each other. If you get hungry, you can stop to buy a snack from one of the many the street vendors.

The city is laid out in a grid pattern, making it easy to orient yourself. Starting at the waterfront and moving north, the major east-west streets are Queen's Quay, Front Street (CN Tower and the SkyDome), King Street, Queen Street, and Dundas. Farther north, Bloor and Eglinton are big cross streets. The major north-south artery is Yonge Street (pronounced "young"), reputedly the world's longest street. It runs from the Toronto waterfront to Rainy River, Ontario, near James Bay, 1,900 kilometers (1,140 miles) away. Yonge also divides cross-street addresses into east and west. Bay Street (Canada's Wall Street), University, Spadina, and Bathurst are to the west of Yonge, while Jarvis and Parliament are to the east.

The main subway artery runs in an elongated U along Yonge Street and University Avenue, looping through Union Station at the base of the U. The other line runs east-west along Bloor Street. Up on the streets, streetcars and buses round out the efficient public transit system. Pick up a copy of the "Ride Guide" at subway entrances, or call the Toronto Transit Commission information line, 416/393-4636.

Pearson International Airport, the busiest in Canada, handles more than 35 airlines in three terminals. The Toronto Island Airport in Toronto Harbor handles short-haul commuter flights and is located minutes from downtown. Via Rail and Amtrak trains stop in Union Station downtown. (The magnificently cavernous Union Station is worth seeing even if you're not arriving by train.)

Year-round, the Metropolitan Toronto Convention and Visitors Association operates a Visitor Information Centre at the Metropolitan Toronto Convention Centre, 255 Front Street West. It's open from 8 a.m. to 8 p.m. daily. Or contact the association's main office in Toronto at 416/203-2600 or 800/363-1990. An Ontario Travel information outlet is located in the Eaton Centre.

SIGHTSEEING HIGHLIGHTS: DOWNTOWN TORONTO

★★★★ **CN TOWER**
301 Front Street West, 416/360-8500, www.cntower.ca
Toronto's most famous landmark, the tallest free-standing structure in the world, provides a bird's-eye view of the terrain for miles around. The revamped visitors center at the base of the tower has

shops, restaurants, and several interactive attractions, including a multimedia presentation about how the tower was built, an IMAX theater, and two motion-simulator rides (one recreating a gentle airplane flight across the country, the other replicating a wild roller coaster ride). The very tip of the tower is 533 meters (1,815 feet) high—the equivalent of 187 stories—and the Lookout Level is about three-quarters of the way up. The ride up or down to the Lookout Level takes 58 seconds. In addition to the panorama all around, you can sit, stand, or even lie down on the glass floor so that Toronto is literally at your feet. This attraction is definitely not for people who don't like heights. If you want, you can then go even higher in the tower to the Sky Pod, which, at 447 meters (1,465 feet), is billed as the highest observation gallery in the world.

Details: *Union Station subway stop. Open Apr–Dec daily 8–11; Jan–Apr Sun–Thu 9–10, Fri–Sat 9–11. Entrance to the Lookout Level: $15.99 adults, $13.99 seniors, $10.99 children 4–12. Extra for Sky Pod and the various attractions at the base of the tower; a variety of combo tickets available. (2–3 hours)*

★★★★ ROYAL ONTARIO MUSEUM
100 Queen's Park, 416/586-8000, www.rom.on.ca

This museum is one of the five most popular in North America and, as Canada's largest, it's home to an enormous variety of artistic, archeologic, and scientific treasures. The most-visited displays are the dinosaur hall and the bat cave, the latter being a dark eerie exhibit in which the bats seem creepily alive. A large gallery houses life-size animals, from musk ox and caribou to lions, tigers, and reptiles, plus a Chinese collection that's renowned for its range and quality. The museum's newest and largest permanent gallery, called Dynamic Earth, uses innovative, interactive features to showcase the forces that have shaped our planet, starting with an entryway made of more than two tons of quartz crystals. The minerals section of this gallery is breathtaking, featuring more than one thousand gemstones and gold specimens. At the museum's Discovery Centre, meant for kids, you can examine slides under microscopes, use ultraviolet lights to view rocks' mineral contents, inspect butterflies up close, and pursue other hands-on activities.

Details: *Museum subway stop. Mon and Wed–Sat 10–6, Tue 10–8, Sun 11–6. $10 adults; $5 seniors, students, and ages 5–14; $22 families. (3–4 hours)*

★★★ ART GALLERY OF ONTARIO
317 Dundas Street West, 416/979-6648, www.ago.on.ca

At any given time, about 10 percent of the gallery's 16,000 works of Canadian and international art is on exhibit. Highlights include a wealth of Canadian works by the Group of Seven and others, the Henry Moore Sculpture Centre, and a collection of Inuit art. The AGO, as it's commonly called, is the tenth-largest public art gallery in North America thanks to a massive renovation and expansion project completed a few years ago.

Details: St. Patrick subway stop. Tue–Fri 12–9, Sat–Sun 10–5:30. $5 per person donations suggested. Admission charged to special exhibits. (2 hours)

★★★ BATA SHOE MUSEUM
327 Bloor Street West, 416/979-7799
www.batashoemuseum.ca

Imelda Marcos's closets pale in comparison to this place! This unusual and fascinating museum boasts a collection of more than 10,000 shoes and related objects that provide remarkable insight into social history. Shoes, after all, are personal artifacts that reveal a lot about their owner's social status, habits, culture, and religion. Spanning 4,500 years, the display ranges from platform boots worn by Elton John and purple-sequined pumps that belonged to Madonna to space boots worn by astronauts, funereal shoes from the royal tombs of Egyptian pharaohs, and ancient sandals worn by Australian Aborigines. The four-story museum is the brainchild of Sonja Bata, wife of the owner of the Bata shoe manufacturing and retail empire. Since the 1940s she has been scouring the world for shoes, and they are all now in this museum, billed as unique in the Western Hemisphere. And yes, the collection does include a few of Imelda Marcos's pumps.

Details: St. George subway stop. Tue, Wed, Fri, Sat 10–5, Thu 10–8, Sun 12–5. $6 adults, $4 seniors and students, $2 children 5–14, $12 families. (2 hours)

★★★ CASA LOMA
1 Austin Terrace, 416/923-1171
www.digitalozone.com/casaloma

Toronto's spectacular "house on a hill" was constructed at great cost by a wealthy entrepreneur who later had to give it up because, curiously, he couldn't afford the taxes. Sir Henry Pellatt built it as his

TORONTO'S NEIGHBORHOODS

Toronto has particularly large Italian, Chinese, Greek, Korean, and Portuguese populations, and its colorful, diverse neighborhoods are well worth exploring.

Chinatown is a beehive of small streets around the intersection of Dundas and Spadina. **Little Italy**, on College Street between Ossington and Euclid, hums with trattorias, sidewalk cafés, and boutiques. **Greektown** on the Danforth features a wealth of restaurants and tavernas, most with a sidewalk patio. **Koreatown** is located in midtown along Bloor Street West between Christie and Palmerston. Somewhat off the beaten path is **Little India**, a crowded six blocks along Gerrard Street East between Highfield and Coxwell Avenue, featuring restaurants, grocers, and shops, including more than 20 boutiques that specialize in traditional saris and other brightly colored silk creations. The area is busiest on Sundays and can easily be reached from downtown by the College Street streetcar.

Other neighborhoods are not so much ethnic as they are trendy. In midtown, **Yorkville** is packed with exclusive designer boutiques and chic cafés. **Queen Street West** between University and Spadina is Toronto's answer to Greenwich Village; it's lined with funky shops, offbeat restaurants, and trendy bars. **Cabbagetown**, around Ontario and Berkeley south of Carleton Street from Gerrard to Queen Street, is a gentrified area replete with charming Victorian houses. Still farther east lies **The Beaches**, a former resort community whose summer cottages have been converted to permanent homes. Queen Street East in The Beaches has a lively nightlife and is a favorite area for brunch on the weekends. To get there, take the "red rocket" streetcar along Queen Street East and get off just past Woodbine.

dream home between 1911 and 1914. With the economic downturn after World War I, however, Sir Henry found himself in arrears on his city taxes and was forced to turn the 98-room castle over to the city of Toronto. The outstanding rooms are the conservatory on the main floor and, on the second floor, Lady Pellatt's Wedgwood-blue suite next door to Sir Henry's suite. When first built, Casa Loma was the only castle in the world to have an electrically operated elevator and an indoor swimming pool. The castle is connected by a 450-meter (1,470-foot) tunnel to the stables, where the stalls are made of mahogany, and the floors laid with Spanish tile. With dancing fountains, unusual sculptures, and the rainbow of colors of a traditional English garden, you may want to linger awhile on the grounds surrounding the mansion.

Details: *Dupont subway stop. Open daily 9:30–4, but you can wander around until 5:15. $9 adults, $5.50 seniors and ages 14–17, $5 children 4–13. Parking, $2.30/hour. Self-guided audio tours provided. (2 hours)*

★★ CHILDREN'S OWN MUSEUM
90 Queen's Park, 416/542-1492

This place is perfect if you're traveling with young kids. Created for kids ages one to six, it focuses on the joys of play. To ensure that they got it right, the team that created the museum received input on the design from children. The result is an innovative and popular museum with crawl spaces everywhere, a construction area. a pint-sized house with an attic full of treasures, and a pint-sized Main Street with, among other things, a veterinary clinic filled with stuffed animals that the kids can kiss and make all better. In the theater area, children can choose a costume, have their makeup applied by a staff member, and perform before their parents and an audience of other museum-goers. Young kids love this museum, even with no electronic gadgets in sight.

Details: *Next door to the Royal Ontario Museum. Museum subway stop. Tue 10–8, Wed–Sat 10–5, Sun 12–5. $3.75. (2 hours)*

★★ TORONTO ISLANDS
416/203-0405

A series of interconnected islands in Toronto Harbor, the Toronto Islands are accessible by ferry year-round. Centre Island, with its small amusement park, picnic grounds, and bicycle rentals, is the most popular destination among the three islands. The charming Ward's Island at the eastern end of the islands is one of the most delightful to visit because it remains relatively uncrowded even on summer weekends. About 300 people live in a small community of tiny old houses on Ward's Island. As you get off the ferry, to the left you'll see small houses nestled in a clump dissected by tiny streets. The streets are so minuscule that they actually look more like pathways, but they do have street names. The island has lots of park land and picnic tables, as well as a beach and boardwalk. It's like being in another world, yet just across the water is a magnificent view of the heart of Toronto.

Details: Frequent departures from the ferry terminal next to the Harbour Castle Hotel; 416/392-8193 for ferry information. (3 hours)

★ HOCKEY HALL OF FAME

30 Yonge Street, 416/360-7765, www.hhof.com/index.htm

This attraction is a hockey fan's heaven. It's billed as the world's most comprehensive collection of hockey artifacts, displays, and memorabilia. It covers everything from the history of hockey to a display on the Grand Old Houses of hockey (Boston Garden, Chicago Stadium, Detroit Olympia, Madison Square Garden, Montreal Forum, and Maple Leaf Gardens) and even contains a re-creation of the Montreal Canadiens' dressing room at the Forum in the 1990s, authentic right down to the piles of laundry.

Details: Entrance is in the concourse level of BCE Palace, at the corner of Yonge and Front Streets. June–Sept Mon–Sat 9:30–6, Sun 10–6; Sept–May Mon–Fri 10–5, Sat 9:30–6, Sun 10:30–5. $10 adults, $5.50 seniors and children under 14. (1 hour)

★ THE PIER

245 Queen's Quay West, 416/338-7437
torontohistory.on.ca/thepier

Similar to many great cities, Toronto began at the water's edge. This museum in an historic warehouse on the waterfront explores the maritime history of Toronto and the Great Lakes. Interactive exhibits let you learn the nautical rules of the road, explore a shipwreck, or move a Great Lakes ship through canal locks. You can also watch artisans building traditional wooden boats and even rent one of the boats to explore the harbor yourself.

Details: TTC streetcar #510 from Union Station or Spadina Station. May–Oct 10–6. $7 adults, $5 students and seniors, $4 children, $15 families. (2 hours)

★ SKYDOME

One Blue Jays Way, 416/341-3663

The SkyDome is the only stadium in the world with a fully retractable roof. The 32-story-high roof opens and closes in about 20 minutes, at a cost of $500 each way. The stadium is home to the Toronto Blue Jays baseball team. The SkyDome Hotel abuts the stadium, and some hotel rooms with big picture windows actually look out onto the playing field. Shortly after the complex opened in 1989, the hotel received more publicity than money can buy when a couple in one such two-level suite took time out from watching the game to play some games of their own on the bed upstairs. They neglected to draw the curtains, and the incident was front-page news the next day as far away as Los Angeles. A guided tour of the stadium, available when event schedules permit, includes a film about its construction and visits to a dressing room, the press box, and a skybox.

Details: Next door to the CN Tower. Events permitting, tours begin hourly starting at 10. (1 hour)

SIGHTSEEING HIGHLIGHTS: GREATER TORONTO

★★★ ONTARIO SCIENCE CENTRE
770 Don Mills Road, 416/696-3127, www.osc.on.ca
The hands-on displays here will captivate children and adults, science fans and neophytes alike. You can climb a rock wall, race an Olympic bobsled, go on a space expedition exploring Mars, test your memory, and get lost in a limestone cave. At once diverting and educational, this facility houses more than 800 high-tech interactive exhibits plus an Omnimax theater with a wraparound screen.

Details: 10 minutes from downtown; take Don Valley Parkway North to Don Mills Road North. From Highway 401, take Don Valley Parkway South and exit at Wynford Drive. Pape subway station and 25 Don Mills bus north. July–Aug daily 10–8; Sept–June Wed 10–8, Fri 10–9, otherwise 10–5. $10 adults, $7 seniors and children 5–16; combo tickets available that include Omnimax. (4 hours)

★ McMICHAEL CANADIAN ART COLLECTION
10365 Islington Avenue, Kleinburg, 905/893-1121
www.mcmichael.on.ca
Although it isn't in Toronto proper, this collection in nearby Kleinburg is worth the trip. The gallery features an impressive collection of works by the Group of Seven artists—the most famous landscape

painters in Canada—with works by other Canadian artists as well as Indian and Inuit artists. Outside, the woodland setting is dotted with sculptures, and on Sunday afternoons you can stop by a drop-in studio to watch artists at work.

Details: About 30 minutes north of downtown Toronto by car. From Highway 401, take Highway 400 north to Major Mackenzie Drive. Turn left (west) on Major Mackenzie Drive to Islington Avenue. Turn right (north) on Islington Avenue to Kleinburg. May–Oct 10–5; Nov–Apr Tue–Sat 10–4, Sun 10–5. $7 adults, $5 seniors, $15 families. (1 hour)

★ TORONTO ZOO
361A Old Finch Avenue, 416/392-5900
www.torontozoo.com

If you're traveling with children, a visit to this highly rated zoo should keep them enthralled. It has more than four thousand animals housed in six "zoogeographic" regions covering the Americas, Australasia, and so on. The African Savannah Project, one of the newest zones, is billed as an authentic re-creation of the African landscape, populated by rhinoceroses, hippopotamuses, giraffes, cheetahs, and lions, and offering an African market bazaar. At the other end of the temperature scale, the zoo also has polar bears.

Details: Highway 401 to the suburb of Scarborough (exit 389), then go north on Meadowvale Road and follow the signs. Mid-May to early Sept 9–7:30; early Sept to mid-Oct and mid-Mar to mid-May 9–6; mid-Oct to mid-Mar 9:30–4:30. $12 adults, $9 seniors and ages 12–17, $7 children 4–11. Parking is $5. (5 hours)

★ WONDERLAND
Highway 400, Vaughan, 905/832-7000
www.canadaswonderland.com

Another good daytrip option if you're with children, Paramount Canada's Wonderland, as it's officially called, lies just north of Toronto and features more than 50 rides (some terrifying, some for small children) and a waterslide theme area, as well as live shows and assorted other attractions. New thrills and chills are added every year; recent additions include the Fly coaster, which is designed to give every rider the feeling of sitting in the front car, and Drop Zone in which riders in buckled seats plummet 70 meters (230 feet) down the side of a tower.

Details: North of Toronto off Highway 400, 10 minutes north of

TORONTO

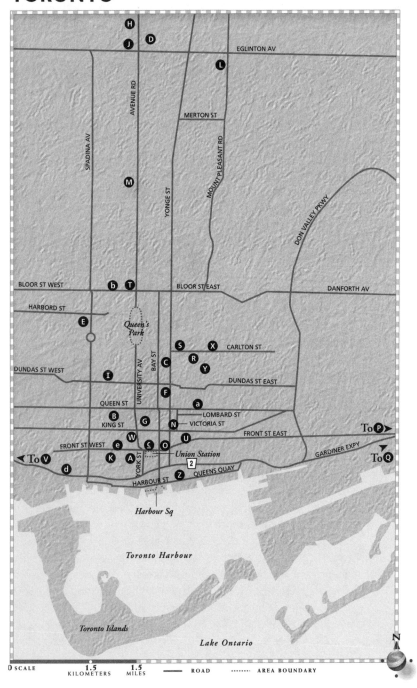

EGLINTON AV

AVENUE RD

SPADINA AV

MERTON ST

MOUNT PLEASANT RD

DON VALLEY PKWY

YONGE ST

BLOOR ST WEST   BLOOR ST EAST   DANFORTH AV

HARBORD ST

Queen's Park

DUNDAS ST WEST

Carlton St

DUNDAS ST EAST

QUEEN ST

LOMBARD ST

KING ST

VICTORIA ST   FRONT ST EAST   To P

FRONT ST WEST

GARDINER EXPY

To V   Union Station   To Q

HARBOUR ST   QUEENS QUAY

Harbour Sq

Toronto Harbour

Toronto Islands   Lake Ontario

N

0 SCALE   1.5 KILOMETERS   1.5 MILES   ROAD   .... AREA BOUNDARY

Highway 401. Exit Rutherford Road if heading north on Highway 400, or exit at Major MacKenzie if traveling south on Highway 400. By public transit, Wonderland Express "GO" buses run regularly from Yorkdale and York Mills subway stations. Mid-May to early Sept daily 10–11; early May and mid- to late-Sept weekends. $39.99 adults, $21.99 seniors and children under 7. (4–6 hours)

FITNESS AND RECREATION

The Leslie Street Spit, which reaches out into the east end of the harbor, is a popular spot for cyclists and walkers. The end of the spit affords a great view of the skyline. Toronto Islands Park, 416/203-0405, offers both bicycle rentals and bike paths. The boardwalk at The Beaches is a good place for jogging and in-line skating. You can rent in-line skates at Harbourfront, a shopping and entertainment complex on the waterfront, and on Centre Island in the Toronto Islands. Several outstanding golf courses are located outside Toronto, including Glen Abbey, 905/844-1800, www.glenabbey.com, a renowned public course in suburban Oakville that is also home to the Canadian Golf Hall of Fame.

FOOD

Unlike in Montreal, vendors hawk hot dogs, sausages, soft drinks, pretzels, and fruits from food carts on downtown Toronto sidewalks. Of course, when you

---

FOOD

- Ⓐ 360
- Ⓑ Bamboo
- Ⓒ Bangkok Garden
- Ⓓ Centro Grill & Wine Bar
- Ⓔ Kensington Kitchen
- Ⓕ Licks'
- Ⓖ Mövenpick
- Ⓗ North 44
- Ⓘ Ohh Kitchen
- Ⓙ Oliver's
- Ⓚ Pronto Ristorante
- Ⓛ Scaramouche
- Ⓜ Senator Steakhouse
- Ⓝ Shopsy's Deli & Restaurant
- Ⓞ Tejas
- Ⓟ Whitlock's

LODGING

- Ⓠ Ambassador Inn
- Ⓡ Days Inn Toronto Downtown
- Ⓢ Grand Bay Hotel
- Ⓣ King Edward Hotel
- Ⓤ Inn on the Lake
- Ⓥ Hotel Victoria
- Ⓦ Jarvis House
- Ⓧ Neill-Wycik College Hotel
- Ⓨ Novotel Toronto Centre
- Ⓩ Quality Hotel Downtown
- ⓐ Quality Hotel Midtown
- ⓑ Royal York Hotel
- ⓒ Seahorse Inn
- ⓓ SkyDome Hotel
- ⓔ Strathcona Hotel

want something more substantial, plenty of choices are available at the more than 5,000 restaurants that serve every variety of food imaginable from the four corners of the globe. Here are just a few recommendations, starting with downtown.

The view from **360,** CN Tower, 301 Front St. W., 416/362-5411, is unmatched. The world's highest revolving restaurant is the place to go for the ultimate, intimate romantic dinner, and the fresh market cuisine and outstanding wine selection (the "cellar in the sky") are pretty good, but it's expensive, of course. The **Bangkok Garden,** 18 Elm Street, 416/977-6748, serves a range of Thai dishes and is pretty swanky as well. For steak and seafood, try **Senator Steakhouse,** 253 Victoria Street, 416/364-7517, a venerable eatery featuring classic ambience, succulent beef and seafood alike, and, for especially romantic occasions, seven curtained booths. Some of the tastiest Chinese food in town can be found at **Ohh Kitchen,** 23 Baldwin, 416/977-1255, which uses entirely fresh ingredients, whether Szechwan snapper or melon shrimp. **Bamboo,** 312 Queen Street West, 416/593-5771, serves Caribbean dishes along with live entertainment in the evenings. For really casual fare, head for **Shopsy's Deli & Restaurant,** 33 Yonge Street, 416/365-3333, a Toronto institution for more than 70 years that continues to turn out popular fare like hearty corned beef on rye and cheesecake amid a 1930s decor. If you can't quite decide what you feel like, check out **Mövenpick,** 165 York Street, 416/366-5234, an outlet of the Switzerland-based chain that's proved tremendously popular since setting up shop in Toronto. Make that shops; it's actually several restaurants in one, serving a wide array of Swiss specialties, pastas, and seafood at moderate prices.

In the midtown area, you'll find the crowd-pleasing **Kensington Kitchen,** 124 Harbord Street, 416/961-3404, with a wide-ranging, moderately priced menu and a rooftop patio that draws a crowd in summer. For French cuisine that doesn't get much better—or much pricier—make a reservation at **Scaramouche,** 1 Benvenuto Place, 416/961-8011, an acclaimed establishment with impeccable service and haute, haute, haute cuisine.

North of Eglinton Avenue, in the so-called north-central section of town, **North 44,** 2537 Yonge Street, 416/487-4897, offers stylish decor and a wide selection of creative dishes described as "New World Italian with Californian-Asian undertones." The sleek and trendy **Centro Grill & Wine Bar,** 2472 Yonge Street, 416/483-2211, whips up Italian dishes with a California accent. The menu at **Oliver's,** 2433 Yonge Street, 416/485-8047, a Mediterranean-style bistro, is wide in scope and reasonably priced. The open kitchen at **Pronto Ristorante,** 692 Mount Pleasant, 416/486-1111, cooks an inventive selection of Italian-themed dishes, including homemade pasta and prosciutto-wrapped Cornish hen.

SIDE TRIP: GEORGIAN BAY AND THE BRUCE PENINSULA

A wonderful playground lies amid breathtaking scenery about 90 minutes north of Toronto. Georgian Bay, a mammoth Lake Huron inlet, is dotted with pine-studded islands and framed with rugged cliffs and sandy beaches. It's the perfect destination for outdoor activities or just relaxing in the sun. **Wasaga Beach,** for instance, is a fabulous 15-kilometer beach of fine white sand, with cottages to rent along its length. At the western edge of Georgian Bay, the resort town of Tobermory is the jumping-off point for **Fathom Five National Marine Park,** a national park encompassing 20 islands and 22 known shipwrecks—a renowned divers' destination. Also on the Bruce Peninsula is the upper section of the **Bruce Trail,** which, at 782 kilometers (470 miles), is Ontario's longest hiking trail

Other noteworthy regions in the area north of Toronto, which the provincial tourism people alternately refer to as "the Lakelands" and "Ontario's Playground," include the **Haliburton Highlands** (exceptional resort country noted for its beauty and wide variety of accommodations), **Muskoka** (another "cottage country" area), and the **Kawartha Lakes.** Or you might want to explore via houseboat **the Trent-Severn Waterway,** which begins at Georgian Bay and meanders southeast to Lake Ontario. If you want to bone up on your tennis or golf game amid pristine natural surroundings, you might book a stay at the Inn at Manitou, 705/389-2171 or 800/571-8818, a five-star spa, tennis, and golf resort alongside a lake in McKellar, two-and-a-half hours north of Toronto.

For detailed information on activities and lodging around Georgian Bay and the Lakelands, call 800/ONTARIO.

Over in the Beaches, a trendy area to the east of downtown, the dining is generally pretty casual and relaxed. **Whitlock's,** 1961 Queen Street East, 416/691-8784, serves a mix of Continental and Canadian dishes at moderate prices. **Tejas,** 2485 Queen Street East, 416/694-2643, is a Tex-Mex cantina offering tortillas, beans, and other goodies to be washed down with big bottles of U.S. beer. And **Licks',** 1960 Queen Street East, 416/362-5425, dishes out terrific hamburgers.

In Koreatown to the west of midtown you might try Korea House, 666 Bloor Street West, 416/536-8666, offering fiery dishes as well as milder fare. In Greektown to the east of midtown, numerous choices are located along Danforth, including Ouzeri, 500 Danforth Avenue, 416/778-0500.

LODGING

Toronto is a big city, so staying downtown makes particular sense. The trade-off is that it's generally more expensive, although even downtown you can find price ranges from budget to deluxe. Moreover, most hotels offer cheaper weekend rates, along with special theater packages and the like.

Expensive but noteworthy hotels downtown include the grand old **Royal York Hotel**, 100 Front Street, 416/368-2511 or 800/866-5577, which recently underwent a multimillion-dollar renovation and is looking better than ever. Located opposite Union Station, it's right in the heart of things. The **King Edward Hotel**, 37 King Street East, 416/863-9700 or 800/225-5843, is a smaller, luxurious European-style boutique hotel. Sports fans might want to check into the **SkyDome Hotel**, One Blue Jays Way, 416/341-7100 or 800/441-1414, where 70 of the 300-plus rooms, including 31 luxury suites, boast stadium views.

More moderately priced downtown hotels include the **Quality Hotel Downtown**, 111 Lombard Street, 416/367-5555 or 800/228-5151, a newly renovated establishment where the rooms now all have large, well-lit work tables and in-room coffeemakers. The **Strathcona Hotel**, 60 York Street, 416/363-3321 or 800/268-8304, is one block from the SkyDome and has recently revamped all guestrooms as well as the lobby, the lobby bar, and the restaurant. **Novotel Toronto Centre**, 45 The Esplanade, 416/367-8900, offers reasonable rates and is close to the St. Lawrence Market and the theater district. **Hotel Victoria**, 56 Yonge Street, 416/363-1666 or 800/363-8228, is a small boutique hotel in the heart of downtown that's comfortable and affordable. Among the least expensive options downtown is the student residence at **Neill-Wycik College Hotel**, 96 Gerrard Street East, 416/977-2320 or 800/268-4358, offering dorm, single, twin, double, and family rooms.

In midtown, where attractions include the Royal Ontario Museum and the Bata Shoe Museum, the posh **Grand Bay Hotel**, 4 Avenue Road, 416/924-5471, in fashionable Yorkville has recently undergone extensive renovations (and a name change; it used to be the Park Plaza) and now features ultra-luxurious rooms and a branch of the famed Golden Door Spa. **Quality Hotel Midtown**, 280 Bloor Street West, 416/968-0010 or 800/228-5151, is a laid-back place catering to both business and leisure travelers with moderately priced rates. Also in the moderate range is **Days Inn Toronto Downtown**, 30 Carleton Street, 416/977-6655 or 800/325-2525, which is next door to Maple Leaf Gardens, former home of the Toronto Maple Leafs, and naturally features a sports bar.

One way to shave costs, of course, is to stay in a B&B. **Jarvis House**, 344 Jarvis Street, 416/975-3838, is a Victorian mansion that has been renovated into a spotlessly clean B&B located near Yonge and Carleton in the downtown area. The **Ambassador Inn**, 280 Jarvis Street, 416/260-2608, is a renovated hundred-year-old "mini-castle" with skylights, fireplaces, bay windows, and other luxuries, with room rates slightly higher than at Jarvis House. For other B&B choices, contact the Bed and Breakfast Homes of Toronto registry, P.O. Box 46093, College Park Post Office, 444 Yonge Street, Toronto, Ontario M5B 2L8, 416/363-6362. If you're considering opting to stay in a B&B, one particularly attractive area is The Beaches, a mere 10 minutes east of downtown but seemingly a world away.

For a different experience, the **Inn on the Lake**, 1926 Lakeshore Boulevard West, 416/766-4392, has recently refurbished its rooms and bills itself as an elegant but comfortable resort hotel in the city. Not far away, the **Seahorse Inn**, 2905 Lakeshore Boulevard West, 416/255-4433 or 800/663-1123, also overlooks Lake Ontario and is about six kilometers (four miles) from downtown. It offers both standard rooms and "second honeymoon rooms," with either sunken tubs or whirlpools for two, mirrors, and mood lighting, all at very reasonable rates.

You can ask about Toronto lodging reservations if you're calling the province's tourist information line, 800/ONTARIO.

SIDE TRIP: ROYAL BOTANICAL GARDENS

The Royal Botanical Gardens in the city of Hamilton, 680 Plains Road West, 905/527-1158, www.rbg.ca, about one hour from downtown Toronto, houses the world's largest collection of lilacs, plus more than 100,000 spring bulbs, an acre of irises, and two acres of roses. To see the lilacs at their peak, it's best to go in May. But the gardens are glorious all summer long in a setting that artfully blends cultivated landscapes with the natural wilderness environment. Shuttle buses transport visitors around the sprawling site.

NIGHTLIFE

The first thing to know about the nightlife in Toronto is that the bars close at 1 a.m., which means last call is at 12:30. A tram ride away from the center of the city, The Beaches at the eastern end of Queen Street East is a favorite area for people-watching, and on weekend nights the bars are hopping. The Queen Street West area is for the younger crowd, whereas Yorkville's bars attract an older, wealthier crowd. The Hard Rock Cafe near the Eaton Centre was the first in North America; it was opened by two Torontonians back in 1978. The latest hot spot for the young crowd is The Docks, a massive complex located in the docklands south of the Gardiner Expressway. Not long ago the docklands were grimy, rundown, and cut with foul waterways—and the odor in the air is still pretty suspicious. Located on Polson Street just off Cherry Street, the complex, open only in summer, offers everything from nightclubs to a beach and an in-line skating rink. In the same area is a large new Irish Rover Pub.

In the last decade, Toronto has emerged as a world-class theater center, drawing more than 7 million theatergoers a year, half of them out-of-towners. Lately, several old theater buildings have been restored and a new venue has opened. The Pantages Theatre, which was previously divided into a multi-screen theater, was restored to its original opulence at a cost of $20 million. The Elgin and Winter Garden Complex, 416/314-2871, one of the few remaining "stacked" theaters (one theater on top of the other), has also been restored. The Elgin is a large velvet and gilt theater, whereas the show-stopping Winter Garden upstairs features a ceiling of thousands of real leaves, columns disguised as tree trunks, a glowing moon, and trellised and handpainted walls. The Royal Alexandra Theatre frequently offers blockbuster productions such as The Phantom of the Opera. A relatively new entry on the theater scene is the Princess of Wales Theater, a 2,000-seat venue where fans left thousands of bouquets in the days after Princess Diana's death in 1997.

Many other smaller theaters offer innovative performances of classical and contemporary plays. The city's theater district lies east of Union Station, girded by Front, Jarvis, King, and Parliament Streets. Top ticket prices are about $90. For discounts on same-day theater tickets, try the T.O. Tix booth on Yonge Street north of Queen, across from the Elgin. In winter, through a program called Stages, theater and performing arts productions offer either discounted tickets, preferred seating, or special gifts, and several dozen hotels offer special rates as part of the same program.

For concerts and musicals, Roy Thomson Hall is a circular building with state-of-the-art acoustics and a lobby that encircles the concert hall. The facility is home to the Toronto Symphony. The Canadian Opera Company is constructing a new opera house downtown that's slated to open in 2000.

SIDE TRIP: STRATFORD

Stratford, 90 minutes west of Toronto, is internationally acclaimed for its annual June to November **Shakespeare Theater Festival,** 519/271-4040 or 800/567-1600, www.stratford-festival.on.ca. The festival features a dozen plays—from Shakespeare to contemporary works—on three stages: the Festival Theatre, the Avon Theatre, and the Tom Patterson Theatre. Tickets run $35 and up. Reserve accommodations and theater tickets well ahead. The festival phone number can conveniently line up both for you.

Quite apart from the festival, Stratford itself is tranquil and extremely pretty, with charming heritage mansions and lots of green space alongside the winding Avon River, on which numerous swans float. Picnicking alongside the river is made ridiculously easy by local takeout places specializing in picnics-to-go. Pathways lead from the river's edge to the Victorian downtown area, where an abundance of small shops along York and neighboring streets offer everything from antiques and collectibles to souvenirs and books. Similarly, the area has restaurants to suit most tastes and budgets. For lodging, bed-and-breakfasts and inns are big in Stratford, although hotels and motels are also available. Again, most budgets can be accommodated, but note that Stratford is so popular that its room rates tend to be on the high side. During the festival, the population of 28,000 balloons by half a million visitors.

From Toronto, take Highway 40 west to Kitchener, then follow Highway 8 northeast to Stratford.

For those interested in professional sports, the Toronto Blue Jays baseball team plays at the Skydome, 416/341-1234, and the Toronto Maple Leafs hockey team and the Toronto Raptors basketball team play at the new Air Canada Centre, 416/214-2255. (Basketball was invented in 1881 by Canadian James Naismith, of Almonte, Ontario. Naismith was teaching in Springfield, Massachusetts, at the time.) Both the SkyDome and the Air Canada Centre also serve as venues for rock concerts by the Rolling Stones, Alanis Morrisette, Celine Dion, and so on.

For complete listings of what's going on, pick up one of Toronto's four daily newspapers (the *Toronto Star,* the *Globe and Mail,* the *National Post,* and the *Toronto Sun*), or grab a copy of *Now* or *Eye,* two free weekly alternative newspapers.

SHOPPING

Toronto is one of those cities where you really could shop 'til you drop. The Eaton Centre (which will likely be renamed now that Eaton's has declared bankruptcy) on Yonge Street between Queen and Dundas has more than 350 boutiques, services, and restaurants on five levels, anchored by two department stores, Eaton's and The Bay. The nearest subway stops are Dundas and Queen. Queen's Quay Terminal on the waterfront is a renovated landmark building with more than one hundred specialty boutiques and restaurants that are open seven days a week. For antiques, check out the Harbourfront Antique Market at 390 Queen's Quay West, where Goldie Hawn and Kurt Russell have been known to shop. The nearest subway stop is Union Station.

If money is no object, head for the Yorkville-Bloor area, arguably the city's most exclusive shopping district. In the 1960s, Yorkville was a rundown hippie haven, Toronto's equivalent to San Francisco's Haight-Ashbury at its peak. Now it's home to tony shopping centers such as Hazelton Lanes and the Holt Renfrew Centre (Holt Renfrew is a Canadian-owned chain of extremely upscale clothing stores). The nearest subway stop is Bay.

To soak up some atmosphere while shopping, visit the Kensington Market, a multi-ethnic bazaar of foodstuffs, clothes, and street vendors centered on Kensington just west of Spadina. The best time to go is Saturday morning. The nearest subway stops are St. Patrick and Queen's Park. The St. Lawrence Market, on Front Street at Jarvis, a few blocks east of Union Station, is a large, popular indoor market where you can pick up fresh meat, cheeses, and produce, along with gourmet specialties such as caviar. Queen Street West has funky, offbeat shops and restaurants. The subway stop nearest to this area is Queen. The Annex, west of Yorkville on Bloor Street, is populated with students, writers, and artists, and consequently features budget bookstores, specialty shops, and cafés. The World's Biggest Bookstore (now a Chapters outlet), a Toronto institution on Edward Street around the corner from the Eaton Centre, purportedly holds more than 180,000 titles.

You can keep shopping even when the weather turns foul, thanks to the city's extensive network of underground malls.

2
NIAGARA FALLS

Niagara Falls, one of the world's most famous tourist attractions, is truly breathtaking. You've probably seen a gazillion photos and video images of the falls, but you don't really get a sense of how incredible the falls are until you see them in person. They are worth the trip, at least once in a lifetime, and millions of people make that trip. Be prepared for crowds lured here by Canada's single most famous attraction. Niagara Falls, a city of 73,000, attracts somewhere between 10 and 12 million visitors annually.

Equally breathtaking, but in a different way, is the aggressive garishness of the city of Niagara Falls. It comes as a shock if you're not expecting it. Lined with kitschy attractions, Clifton Hill is like a somewhat downmarket Las Vegas, and Niagara Falls even has a casino—the biggest in Canada. Fortunately, the city's tackier aspects are fairly easy to avoid. Just concentrate on the falls and the wonderfully green, unspoiled area around them. In fact, the parklands alongside the falls run all the way south to Lake Erie and north to Lake Ontario, paralleling the Niagara River.

MORE NIAGARA FALLS FACTS

For the record, the Canadian Horseshoe Falls—the more spectacular of the two waterfalls—drops 52 meters (170 feet) into the Maid of the Mist pool. The waters at the American Falls plunge between 21 and 34 meters (70 to

NIAGARA FALLS

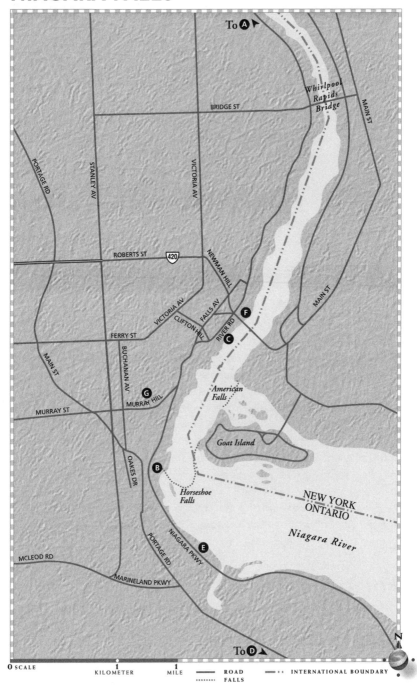

To **A**

Whirlpool
Rapids
Bridge

MAIN ST

BRIDGE ST

PORTAGE RD

STANLEY AV

VICTORIA AV

ROBERTS ST 420

NEWMAN HILL

MAIN ST

VICTORIA AV

FALLS AV

CLIFTON HILL

RIVER RD

F

C

FERRY ST

BUCHANAN AV

MAIN ST

G

MURRAY HILL

*American
Falls*

MURRAY ST

OAKES DR

Goat Island

B

*Horseshoe
Falls*

NEW YORK
ONTARIO

Niagara River

MCLEOD RD

PORTAGE RD

NIAGARA PKWY

E

MARINELAND PKWY

To **D**

N

0 SCALE

1
KILOMETER

1
MILE

ROAD

FALLS

INTERNATIONAL BOUNDARY

110 feet) onto a rocky slope at their base. More than 168,000 cubic meters (6 million cubic feet) of water go over the Horseshoe Falls crest every minute—that's about one million bathtubs full of water every second. The torrents of waters are eroding the rock underneath at the estimated rate of 36 centimeters (about 14 inches) every 10 years. Some 12,000 years ago, the falls were 11 kilometers (7 miles) downstream from where they are now. But the erosion rate has actually slowed since the early 1950s, thanks to major water diversions for a generating plant and construction of something called an International Control Works, which spreads the flow more evenly over the entire crest of Horseshoe Falls.

Niagara Falls does not shut down in winter. From late November until mid-January, the Winter Festival of Lights is a miles-long lighting extravaganza centered on a "motion light" display from 5:30 p.m. to 11:30 p.m. each evening in Queen Victoria Park adjacent to the falls. Trees and buildings along the Niagara Parkway and in the city itself are also festooned with lights during the festival, which organizers say is the largest holiday lighting display in the world. The seven-week festival has a full calendar of family-oriented activities—including alcohol-free festivities on New Year's Eve—plus theater, symphonies, and craft shows.

A PERFECT DAY AT NIAGARA FALLS

Work your way closer and closer to the falls as the day progresses. First, check out the IMAX show to bone up on the history of the falls. Then ride to the top of the Skylon Tower for a panoramic view, followed by lunch at the Table Rock Restaurant, right next to the falls. After touring the scenic tunnels, which bring you still closer to the torrent, proceed to the famous *Maid of the Mist* for an awesome close-up view. If you feel like splurging, hang around long enough to go back to the Skylon and have dinner in the restaurant atop it, where the prices are sky high but so is the nighttime vista.

SIGHTS

- **A** Butterfly Conservatory
- **B** Journey Behind the Falls
- **C** Maid of the Mist
- **D** Marineland
- **E** Niagara Falls IMAX Theater and Daredevil Adventure
- **F** Ride Niagara
- **G** Skylon Tower

ORIENTATION

Arriving by road from the United States, the access points are four bridges across the Niagara River. Starting south of Niagara Falls, the Peace Bridge links Buffalo, New York, and Fort Erie, Ontario. After crossing the bridge, drive north on the Niagara Parkway for the scenic route or, for the fastest route, travel north on the Queen Elizabeth Way highway (widely known as the QEW). Either way, the drive is only about 20 kilometers (12 miles). The Rainbow Bridge and the Whirlpool Rapids Bridge both link Niagara Falls, New York, with Niagara Falls, Ontario. North of Niagara Falls, travelers entering Ontario via the Queenston-Lewiston Bridge can drive south on the Niagara Parkway. Arriving from Toronto, the most direct route is via the QEW, which connects Toronto with Niagara Falls.

If you want to try something a little different, you can catch one of two ferry services linking Toronto and Niagara-on-the-Lake (with shuttle service to Niagara Falls): a high-speed catamaran, Waterways Transportation Services, 905/682-5555 or 888/581-2628; and a hydrofoil service, Shaker Cruise Lines, 905/934-2375 or 888/842-5253.

The major attractions are all within walking distance of each other. For instance, the scenic tunnels that take you behind the falls are about a 10-minute walk along the Niagara Parkway from the Skylon Tower. Because none of the attractions, except the IMAX show and Ride Niagara, involves sitting down a spell, you may want to get a pass for the Niagara Parks People Movers—buses that shuttle back and forth all day among various attractions along the parkway and operate between late April and October. The passes cost roughly $5 for adults and $2.50 for kids. The Niagara Falls Visitor and Convention Bureau is located at 5433 Victoria Avenue.

SIGHTSEEING HIGHLIGHTS

★★★★ JOURNEY BEHIND THE FALLS
Queen Victoria Park, 905/355-2241
www.niagaraparks.com/attract/journey-idx.html

This attraction is well worth seeing, particularly since entrance fees are relatively low. After entering, you're given a cheap plastic rain cape. Hold on to it because you'll need it! Then you board an elevator, descend about 38 meters (125 feet), and emerge into a long, damp tunnel filled with the dull roar of the falls. The tunnel leading away from the elevator ends on an open bluff jutting from the cliff next to Horseshoe Falls. Another tunnel to the right ends directly under the falls; all that's visible is a thundering torrent of white water. For a drenching, get close to the railing.

Details: Located at the brink of Horseshoe Falls. Mid-June to early Sept 9 a.m.–10:30 p.m.; shorter hours the rest of the year. $6 adults, $3 kids 6–12. (1 hour)

★★★★ MAID OF THE MIST
5920 River Road, 905/358-5781, www.maidofthemist.com

It's almost a cliché, but it's also a must: If you have time to do nothing else in Niagara Falls, take the *Maid of the Mist* boat ride. The *Maid of the Mist* building is at the foot of Clifton Hill. You walk down a winding ramp and ride an elevator down still farther to the base of the cliff. Passengers are handed oilskins (waterproof jackets) before going out on the dock. On board the *Maid of the Mist*—several of them operate from both the Canadian and American sides of the river—the best view is from the bow of the lower level. Otherwise, head for the front of the upper level. A recorded commentary is provided, but you probably won't be able to hear it over the roar of the falls. The boat pauses briefly opposite the American Falls, then heads up into the Horseshoe Falls basin and hovers there, its

A particularly dramatic way to see the falls and the surrounding area is by helicopter. It's expensive, but if you're game, call Niagara Helicopter Rides, 3731 Victoria Avenue, 905/357-5672, the day or evening before you want to go. Rates are $85 for adults and $35 for children, with a variety of other package options depending on the size of your group.

powerful engines fighting the raging current. This vantage point is the closest you can get, and from here the visuals are awesome—a wall of water soaring into the sky.

Details: Located in the Maid of the Mist Plaza at the bottom of Clifton Hill. Operates mid-Apr to Oct, weather permitting. Departures every 15 minutes. Trip lasts roughly half an hour. $10.65 adults, $6.55 children 6–12. (1 hour)

★★★★ NIAGARA FALLS IMAX THEATER AND DAREDEVIL ADVENTURE
6170 Buchanan Avenue, 905/358-3611

www.tourismniagara.com/imax

To learn about the falls and their history, stop first at the IMAX Theatre, a pyramid-shaped building on Buchanan Avenue behind the Skylon Tower, to see the 45-minute film on a screen so enormous—six stories high, they say—that it makes you feel like you're right there. The movie, *Niagara: Miracles, Myths and Magic,* wondrously conveys the power and beauty of the falls as well as their strange allure for assorted eccentric daredevils. The building also houses a display on the history of the falls, complete with some of the barrels and other contraptions in which people have gone over the edge.

The Niagara Peninsula also offers forts, scenic riverside drives, canals, and a host of other exciting things to explore if you have the time. For tourist information, call the Niagara and Mid-Western Ontario Travel Association, 800/267-3399.

Details: *Next to the Skylon Tower. July–Aug 10–9; slightly shorter hours the rest of the year. $7.50 adults, $7 seniors and ages 12–18, $5.50 children. Parking is free. Film shown regularly throughout the day; call for schedule. Allow approximately half an hour to see the exhibit before or after the film. (1–2 hours)*

★★★ **BUTTERFLY CONSERVATORY**
Niagara Parkway, 905/371-0254 or 800/877-642-7275
www.niagaraparks.com/attract/butterfly-idx.html
This nature attraction is home to one of North America's largest collections of free-flying butterflies. Visitors can walk through a lush rainforest setting and view more than 2,000 butterflies from around the world (the path is wheelchair accessible). The conservatory is located in the Niagara Parks Botanical Gardens, the site of one hundred acres of immaculately maintained gardens that are also a pleasure to explore.

Details: *9 kilometers (6 miles) north of town along the Niagara Parkway. Open daily dawn to dusk. $7.50 adults, $3.75 children 6–12. (1 hour)*

★★★ **SKYLON TOWER**
5200 Robinson Street, 905/356-2651, www.skylon.com
Head up to the observation deck for a panoramic view of the falls, the river, and the entire surrounding area. On a really clear day you can see Toronto across Lake Ontario. (Up the road apiece, the

Minolta Tower also offers panoramic views of the falls, but it isn't as tall as the Skylon.)
   Details: $7.95 adults, $6.95 seniors, $3.95 children, $21.50 families. The tower has souvenir shops aplenty, both on the ground level and at the observation-deck level. (30 minutes)

★★ MARINELAND
7657 Portage Road, 905/356-9565
www.marinelandcanada.com
This activity is a good bet for the kids. Marineland includes everything from performing killer whales and dolphins to wildlife exhibits, an aquarium, and theme-park rides.
   Details: 1.6 kilometers (1 mile) from Horseshoe Falls. From the QEW, take the McLeod Road exit and follow the Marineland signs. From the Rainbow Bridge, take Highway 420 to Stanley Avenue, turn left, continue to the end, turn left, and follow the signs. Mid-May–June 10–5; July–Aug 9–6; Sept–mid-Oct 10–4. Depending on the month, up to $26 adults, $20 children. (4–6 hours)

★★ RIDE NIAGARA
5755 River Road, 905/374-7433, www.rideniagara.com
This ride is for the kid in all of us. You've seen the falls, now how about going over them in a space-age capsule? Ride Niagara is a simulator ride in a "space-age shuttle" that propels you through a tunnel system to emerge above the falls. You're surging toward the brink, and then . . . Suffice it to say, this entertaining ride holds some surprises.
   Details: The Ride Niagara building is under the Rainbow Bridge. Open daily 10:15–7:30. Rides every half hour. $8.95 adults, $4.25 children 6–12. (½ hour)

FITNESS AND RECREATION
Protected Niagara Parks land stretches for 56 kilometers (35 miles) from Fort Erie to Niagara-on-the-Lake, along the length of the Niagara River. The Niagara River Recreation Trail, 905/984-3626, runs along the entire route, offering dazzling views, quaint bridges that span various creeks and ravines, and plenty of picnic areas. You can jog, walk, cycle or in-line skate along the paved trail. Niagara Falls sits halfway along the trail, so you can head south to Fort Erie or north to Niagara-on-the-Lake.
   Golfers can head for the Niagara Parks Whirlpool Public Golf Course,

NIAGARA FALLS

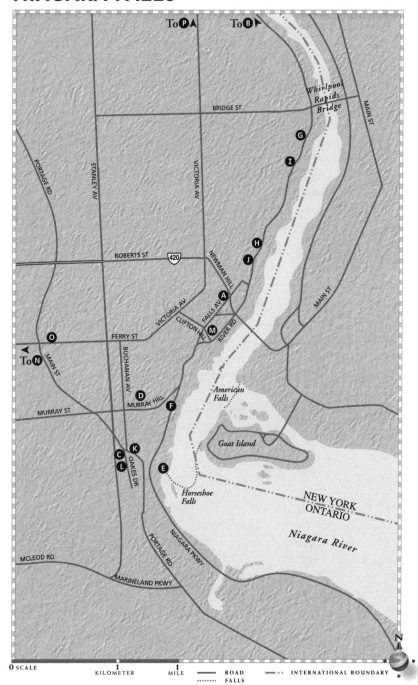

To P

To B

Whirlpool Rapids Bridge

BRIDGE ST

MAIN ST

PORTAGE RD

STANLEY AV

VICTORIA AV

G

I

ROBERTS ST

420

NEWMAN HILL

H

J

VICTORIA AV

FALLS AV

A

MAIN ST

CLIFTON HILL

M

RIVER RD

O

FERRY ST

To N

MAIN ST

BUCHANAN AV

American Falls

D

MURRAY HILL

F

MURRAY ST

Goat Island

C

K

OAKES DR

L

E

Horseshoe Falls

NEW YORK
ONTARIO

Niagara River

MCLEOD RD

PORTAGE RD

NIAGARA PKWY

MARINELAND PKWY

N

0 SCALE

1 KILOMETER

1 MILE

ROAD

FALLS

INTERNATIONAL BOUNDARY

905/356-1140, rated one of the best in Canada. It's seven kilometers (4.4 miles) north of the falls, near the Whirlpool rapids. Approximately 20 other courses are also located on the Niagara Peninsula; call 905/984-3626 to obtain a brochure titled "Golf Niagara."

FOOD

Niagara Falls has dozens of restaurants of every style. The ones that stand out are those with views of the falls, such as **Table Rock Restaurant**, Queen Victoria Park, 905/354-3631. A good choice for lunch, it's right next to Horseshoe Falls and has floor-to-ceiling windows. If you're traveling with kids, you might prefer to duck into Table Rock Fast Food downstairs, for burgers, pizza, or salads. Otherwise, try Table Rock's upstairs option for a more leisurely meal. You don't need reservations during the off-season, but even then you may have to wait about 20 minutes. Prices are reasonable, given the dramatic location, and the food is quite good. The restaurant opens at 11:30 a.m.

The Table Rock is operated by the Niagara Parks Commission, which also runs a couple of other scenically situated eateries in the area. **Victoria Park Restaurant**, 905/356-2217, Queen Victoria Park, faces the American Falls and is open for lunch and dinner. An affordable cafeteria is also housed in the same building. **Diner on the Green**, Niagara River Parkway North, 905/356-7221, a short drive north along the Niagara Parkway, is next to the Whirlpool golf course. You can watch golfers from your table.

If budget is irrelevant, try one of the restaurants in either the Skylon or Minolta towers. In the **Revolving Dining Room**, 905/356-2651, at the top of the Skylon (5200 Ribinson St.), for instance, luncheon main courses can

---

FOOD

- Ⓐ Casino Niagara
- Ⓑ Diner on the Green
- Ⓒ Pinnacle Restaurant
- Ⓓ Skylon Revolving Dining Room
- Ⓓ Skylon Summit Suite Dining Room
- Ⓔ Table Rock Restaurant
- Ⓕ Victoria Park Restaurant

LODGING

- Ⓖ Bedham Hall
- Ⓗ Cairngorm
- Ⓘ Chestnut Inn
- Ⓙ Glen Mhor Guesthouse
- Ⓚ Oakes Inn
- Ⓛ Sheraton Fallsview Hotel
- Ⓜ Skyline Foxhead Hotel

CAMPING

- Ⓝ Campark Resorts
- Ⓞ Niagara Falls KOA
- Ⓟ Niagara Glen-View

Note: Items with the same letter are located in the same area.

run around $20, and dinner main courses are twice that. A second Skylon restaurant, the **Summit Suite Dining Room**, 905/356-2651, offers buffet-style meals and is more casual and less pricey than the revolving restaurant. Reservations are a must for either establishment. The **Pinnacle Restaurant**, 67 Oakes Drive, 905/356-1501, in the Minolta Tower, overlooks Horseshoe Falls.

With three restaurants, including a Hard Rock Cafe, a coffee shop, and a 24-hour food court, **Casino Niagara**, 5705 Falls Avenue, 905/374-3598 or 888/946-3255, offers everything from fine dining to fast food at practically any hour of the day or night.

LODGING

Although Niagara Falls is often viewed as an expensive destination, accommodation costs vary depending on the season and even on the numbers of visitors, which in turn can depend on factors such as the weather. Most hotels and inns have honeymoon suites with Jacuzzis. On the other hand, scores of establishments also offer packages for families that allow kids under age 12 to stay and eat for free. Overall, you have a vast range of accommodations from which to choose. In June, July, and August, reserve ahead. The rest of the year, except for holiday weekends, just drive around and choose.

At the budget end of accommodations, the main motel strip is along Lundy's Lane. Generally, the farther you go from the center of town, the cheaper the rates. But it also heavily depends on the time of year; room rates can double over the summer compared to what they are in winter.

Numerous more expensive hotels are situated in the downtown tourist core. Hotels offering rooms with views of the falls include the **Oakes Inn**, 6546 Buchanan Avenue, 905/356-4514 or 800/263-7134, a full-service establishment with a range of rooms and rates, including honeymoon suites with various combinations of fireplaces, heart-shaped Jacuzzis, and so on. The **Sheraton Fallsview Hotel**, 6755 Oakes Drive, 905/374-1077 or 800/267-8439, is a luxury establishment that stands just 300 yards from the edge of the Horseshoe Falls and offers amenities such as an indoor pool, sauna, and children's activity

Reservations can be made for some properties by contacting the Niagara Falls visitors information line at 800/563-2557. You can also reserve accommodations at selected hotels and resorts through Ontario's tourist information line, 800/ONTARIO.

STAY AWHILE LONGER

Besides the attractions highlighted here, dozens of other sightseeing options are available in and around Niagara Falls. Most sites are geared toward families, such as the **Great Gorge Adventure,** 4330 River Road, 905/374-1221, a tunnel that leads to the edge of the lower Niagara Gorge Rapids.

One lesser-known attraction worth checking out is the lovely **Niagara Parks Commission Greenhouse,** River Road, 905/371-0254 or 877/642-7275, offering seasonal floral displays and free-flying tropical birds. Best of all, admission is free. The greenhouse is just south of Horseshoe Falls.

For those with Lady Luck on their side, **Casino Niagara,** 5705 Falls Avenue, 905/374-3598 or 888/946-3255, is open 24 hours every day of the year and is located across from the Rainbow Bridge on Falls Avenue.

For more information on these and other attractions in Niagara Falls, phone the Niagara Fall Visitor and Convention Bureau at 905/356-6061 or 800/563-2557.

center. Another hotel that overlooks the falls is the recently renovated and redecorated **Skyline Foxhead Hotel,** 5875 Falls Avenue, 905/374-4444 or 800/263-7135, where you can feel the fine mist from the falls when you stand on some of the room balconies.

A string of bed-and-breakfasts can be found in Victorian-era houses along River Road, part of the Niagara Parkway overlooking the Niagara River Gorge and within walking distance of the falls. **Glen Mhor Guesthouse,** 5381 River Road, 905/354-2600, is a cozy turn-of-the-century home with a sun porch and a restored verandah.

The Victorian **Bedham Hall,** 4835 River Road, 905/374-8515, is set amidst a lovely English garden on a quiet part of the street. Each of the bedrooms at the stately plantation-style **Cairngorm,** 5395 River Road, 905/354-4237, has an in-suite bathroom with Jacuzzi tub, and the three front rooms have their own private balconies. The colonial **Chestnut Inn,** 4983 River Road, 905/374-7623, offers large, antique-filled rooms, each with a private deck overlooking the Niagara River Gorge.

CAMPING

Several campgrounds can be found in the immediate area. **Campark Resorts**, 9387 Lundy's Lane, 800/323-8899 or 905/358-3873, provides spacious facilities, including a playground, a heated pool, and mini-golf. **Niagara Falls KOA**, 8625 Lundy's Lane, 905/354-6472, has an indoor pool, sauna, and spas, and it offers a shuttle bus to the falls. Campark has both serviced and unserviced sites, whereas the KOA has only serviced units. Or try **Niagara Glen-View**, 3950 Victoria Avenue, 800/263-2570 or 905/358-8689, with a shuttle to the falls and the casino, as well as access to a long bicycle trail.

Scenic Route: The Niagara Parkway

Winston Churchill once described the Niagara Parkway as the "prettiest Sunday-afternoon drive in the world." The parkway runs lazily along the Niagara River and ends at Niagara-on-the-Lake. The drive is only 22 kilometers (13 miles) from Niagara Falls to Niagara-on-the-Lake, but with the rolling, scenic parkland on either side, you'll probably want to take your time. After strolling through pretty little Niagara-on-the-Lake, tour one of the many wineries on the Niagara Peninsula.

A sleepy but historic village on the Canadian side of the Queenston-Lewiston Bridge, **Queenston**, the first community you'll come across after departing Niagara Falls, is a stop mainly for history buffs. Here, during the War of 1812, in which the Americans tried to conquer British North America, Sir Isaac Brock routed the enemy in the Battle of Queenston Heights. Queenston Heights Park now features a towering monument to Brock, who died in the battle as commander of the British forces in Upper Canada, as Ontario was then called. On Partition Street in Queenston, the Laura Secord Homestead honors a Canadian heroine who saved the British from American attack at one point in the same war. She walked 30 kilometers (18 miles), skirting the enemy, to warn the British of an impending American attack.

From 1791 to 1796, **Niagara-on-the-Lake**, then called Newark, was Upper

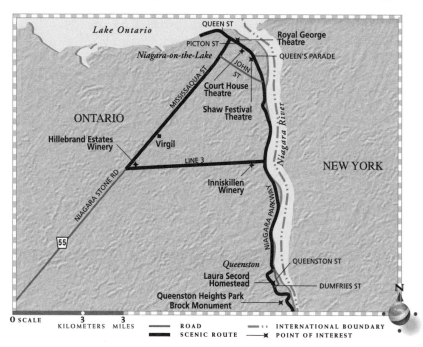

Canada's first capital. Nowadays it has a deliciously quaint nineteenth-century main street and back streets boasting 200-year-old mansions. The four-block stretch of Queen Street—the tourist hub of town—is chockablock with trendy country-style shops and restaurants. It's seriously crowded on most weekends except in winter. Prices are pretty high, but if the street's not too busy, it's a lovely place to browse and window-shop. Chocoholics should stop in at Renaissance, a shop and factory where workers make chocolate on vast marble slabs behind the counter. For reasonably priced food, get away from Queen Street. The tourist information office at 153 King Street can supply information and brochures. For lodging in the area, the Niagara-on-the-Lake Chamber of Commerce, 905/468-4263, offers a free reservation service covering more than 100 hotels, inns, and bed-and-breakfasts.

Note also that Niagara-on-the-Lake is home to the annual summer **Shaw Festival**, 905/468-2172 or 800/511-7429. Running from April to October every year, the renowned festival highlights the plays of George Bernard Shaw and his contemporaries with daily performances in three theaters—the Festival Theatre, the Royal George, and the Court House. Over the course of the 28-week season, 10 plays are usually presented. Tickets start around $25.

The Niagara Peninsula is a major wine-growing area, and winery tours are one of the most popular draws for visitors to the region. In international competitions, Ontario wines frequently take top honors in the Sweet Wine and Chardonnay categories; their other output isn't bad either. If you like ice wines, be sure to pick up a bottle while you're in the area. The **Inniskillin Winery**, 905/468-3554, provides 45-minute guided tours, offered twice daily in the summer, that conclude with free samplings of two wines. A nifty boutique with wine and wine paraphernalia is housed in an attractive old barn that also showcases original art by Canadian painters. Inniskillin is on the Niagara Parkway a few kilometers south of Niagara-on-the-Lake. Watch for the sign on the left-hand side of the road as you drive north.

Also recommended is **Hillebrand Estates Winery**, 905/468-7123 or 800/582-8412, on Highway 55 between Niagara-on-the-Lake and the QEW, the highway that leads to Toronto. It offers free tours and tastings seven days a week, all summer long. Altogether, 19 wineries make up the wine route on the Niagara Peninsula; the provincial tourism department has a "Wine Route" brochure, 800/ ONTARIO, that describes all of them.

Speaking of libations, if you're headed to Toronto from Niagara-on-the-Lake, you might want to take a small side trip en route to check out the **Ale Trail**, 800/334-4519, which links six craft brewers in the towns of Elora, Guelph, and Waterloo, clustered to the north of Highway 401.

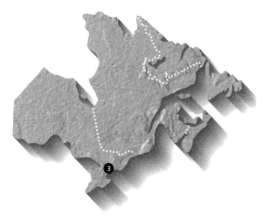

3
OTTAWA

Twenty-five years ago a federal cabinet minister was heard to declare that the best thing about Ottawa was the train to Montreal. Some people may still feel that way, but, in truth, the city has changed for the better, with improved dining, shopping, and nightlife. The ByWard Market, replete with restaurants, bars, and boutiques, is a downtown focal point for both visitors and locals. As the national capital, Ottawa is also home to more than two dozen museums that showcase the country's history, culture, and art.

With a vast network of bicycle paths, generous amounts of green space, and the Rideau Canal snaking lazily through its heart, this capital city is one of the prettiest you'll find anywhere. It reaches a picturesque peak during April and May, when millions of tulips burst into glorious blossom. During World War II, the Dutch royal family fled Holland and sought shelter in Ottawa. While there, Princess Juliana gave birth to Princess Margriet. A problem arose, however, because Dutch royalty must be born on Dutch soil—so the hospital room was declared to be part of the Netherlands. Every year since the end of the war, the grateful people of the Netherlands have shipped 10,000 tulip bulbs to Ottawa.

OTTAWA HISTORY
Ottawa was not always a government town. After the first Europeans arrived in 1613 behind the French explorer Samuel de Champlain, Ottawa became a

OTTAWA

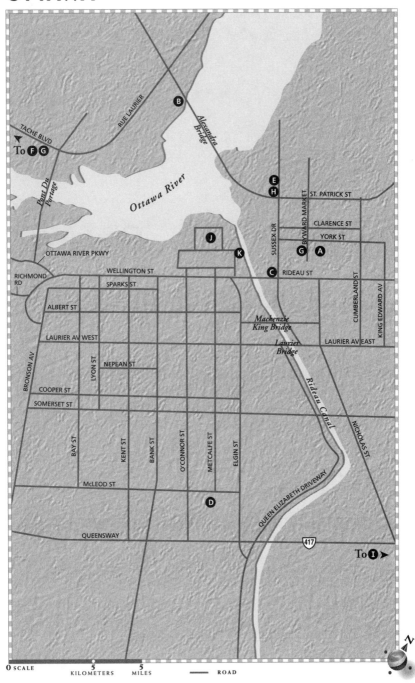

RUE LAURIER

TACHE BLVD

To **F** **G**

Pont Du Portage

Ottawa River

B

Alexandra Bridge

E
H

ST. PATRICK ST

BYWARD MARKET

SUSSEX DR

CLARENCE ST

YORK ST

G **A**

CUMBERLAND ST

KING EDWARD AV

OTTAWA RIVER PKWY

J

K

RICHMOND RD

WELLINGTON ST

C RIDEAU ST

SPARKS ST

ALBERT ST

LAURIER AV WEST

Mackenzie King Bridge

Laurier Bridge

LAURIER AV EAST

BRONSON AV

LYON ST

NEPEAN ST

COOPER ST

SOMERSET ST

Rideau Canal

BAY ST

KENT ST

BANK ST

O'CONNOR ST

METCALFE ST

ELGIN ST

NICHOLAS ST

McLEOD ST

D

Queen Elizabeth Driveway

QUEENSWAY

417

To **I** ▶

O SCALE

5
KILOMETERS

5
MILES

ROAD

N

trading center because of its location at the confluence of the Ottawa, Rideau, and Gatineau rivers. By the 1800s Ottawa and Hull, the settlement across the river, were brawling lumber towns. In 1857 Queen Victoria named Ottawa the capital of the United Provinces of Canada, chiefly because it was centrally located and politically acceptable to both Canada East and Canada West. Or, as Sir Edmund Head, then governor-general, put it, "I believe that the least objectionable place is the city of Ottawa. Every city is jealous of every other city except Ottawa."

A PERFECT DAY IN OTTAWA

A visit to Parliament Hill is de rigueur for first-time visitors, but if you've been there before, head for the always interesting photography museum, pausing outside to watch the boats going through the Rideau Canal locks. Then head down the slope to the ByWard Market area, where cafés, restaurants, bars, and shops provide hours of pleasurable wandering, snacking, and socializing. The area is admittedly touristy and almost too quaint, but you can't help but enjoy it. For culture, several best bets are the National Gallery of Canada, across Sussex Drive, and the fascinating Canadian Museum of Civilization, across the Ottawa River in Hull.

ORIENTATION

With a population of 310,000, Ottawa boasts the great advantage of a small city: The major hotels, noteworthy sights, and great shopping and dining are virtually all within walking distance of one another in the downtown area. Confederation Square, the heart of the city, is actually a triangular piece of land rimmed by Parliament Hill and the stately Château Laurier hotel, the National Arts Center (Ottawa's showcase for performing arts), and the Sparks Street Mall. The ByWard Market, a lively area of shops, bars, and restaurants,

---

SIGHTS

Ⓐ ByWard Market
Ⓑ Canadian Museum
  of Civilization
Ⓒ Canadian Museum
  of Contemporary
  Photography
Ⓓ Canadian Museum
  of Nature

Ⓔ Canadian War Museum
Ⓕ Ecomuseum of Hull
Ⓖ Laurier House
Ⓗ National Gallery of
  Canada
Ⓘ National Museum of
  Science and Technology

Ⓙ Parliament Hall
Ⓚ Rideau Canal
  Promenade

---

and the Rideau Centre, Ottawa's largest shopping mall (with more than 230 boutiques), lie below the Château Laurier. Down Sussex Drive and behind the hotel is the attractive National Gallery of Canada. Hull, the city across the Ottawa River, is the site of several worthwhile attractions, and it's only about a 10-minute drive or bus ride across either of two bridges. Generally speaking, it's best to leave your car at the hotel and get around on foot or on city transit. For information on fares, routes, and passes, contact the O.C. Transpo offices, 294 Albert Street, 613/741-4390.

SIGHTSEEING HIGHLIGHTS: DOWNTOWN OTTAWA

★★★★ BYWARD MARKET
George Street to Murray Street between Sussex Drive and Dalhousie Street

This formerly seedy section of town is now a quirky mix of pricey boutiques and secondhand stores, food markets, and yuppie bistros. The Market, as locals call it, is in the oldest part of Ottawa. The city's first houses and taverns went up here 150 years ago in what was then called Lower Town. Over the last 25 years, the six-square-block area has been fully restored. But part of the Market has remained

TAKE TO THE AIR

As a government town, Ottawa has a reputation for producing lots of hot air, so it seems apt that it considers itself a prominent hot air balloon destination. Scan the skies above the city at dawn or twilight on clear, quiet days, and you may well see a hot-air balloon or two drifting past. It's a unique way to see the city, both thrilling and peaceful (although not cheap). Trips are usually taken early in the morning or early in the evening because that's when the winds tend to be calmest. The light at those times of the day can be pretty amazing, too. **Skyview Ballooning,** 800/463-0897, offers balloon trips year-round, with each landing capped off with a celebratory drink of champagne.

unchanged, with meat, fish, poultry, cheese, and produce shops that boast the freshest food and best prices in town. In summer, farmers set up outdoor stalls selling fruit, vegetables, and flowers. Ottawans do their marketing here in droves on weekends. The Market also houses pubs, wine bars, live-music bars, French bistros, health-food cafés, and restaurants. A takeout stand called Hooker's, at the corner of William and York, serves a uniquely Ottawan pastry known as "beaver tails"— paddle-shaped yeasty dough, deep-fried. Sprinkle cinnamon and sugar on the puffy, soft confection and enjoy.

The countryside around Ottawa is dotted with small, quaint villages and picturesque backroads. A local company, Oakroads, 613/748-0114, offers day-trips to historic villages and other sights in the region, giving you plenty of time to explore on your own at each stop.

Details: *(2 hours)*

★★★★ NATIONAL GALLERY OF CANADA
380 Sussex Drive, 613/990-1985 or 800/319-2787
http://national.gallery.ca

A luminous structure of glass and granite, the National Gallery rises from a promontory downstream from the parliament buildings. Prominent Canadian architect Moshe Safdie divided the building by creating a series of smaller pavilions to house the various permanent collections and temporary exhibits, including what is billed as the world's most comprehensive collection of Canadian art. One stand-out permanent exhibit is the reconstructed interior of the Rideau Street Chapel with its neo-Gothic, fan-vaulted ceiling. The museum also offers a bookstore, a gift shop, and two restaurants.

Most summers, you can count on the National Gallery to host a blockbuster exhibition—and an exciting one is coming up in the summer of 2000. From June 2 to August 27, 2000, "Monet, Renoir, and the Impressionist Landscape" will be on view. Ottawa is the only Canadian stop for the show that features some of the world's most renowned painters, including Cézanne, Monet, Renoir, Gauguin, and van Gogh.

Details: *Facing the ByWard Market. Mid-May–mid-Sept Fri–Wed 10–6, Thu 10–8; mid-Sept–mid-May Wed–Sun 10–5, Thu to 8 p.m.*

Free admission to permanent collection, but charges apply to special exhibitions. (2 hours)

★★★★ **PARLIAMENT HILL**
Wellington Street
613/239-5000 or 800/465-1867
The Gothic-style parliament buildings rise regally from a cliff overlooking the Ottawa River. Free tours begin at the main entrance and last from 30 to 45 minutes. Even if the whole idea of government bores you, you can't help but be awed by the magnificent interior of the Centre Block, as it's known, and by the stunning circular library. After each tour, except for the final one of the day, visitors are free to take the elevator to the observation deck of the Peace Tower, the central tower that rises 92 meters (300 feet) over Parliament Hill. When parliament is in session, visitors may obtain tickets to sit in the public galleries of the senate and the House of Commons and listen to debates. If you're on Parliament Hill when the changing of the guard happens, fine; otherwise, don't sweat it.

Details: In July and August you should book same-day free tours through Info-Tent on Parliament Hill. The rest of the year, free tours are offered daily except on Christmas and New Year's. Changing of the Guard daily at 10 a.m., weather permitting, from late June to late Aug. (2 hours)

★★★★ **RIDEAU CANAL PROMENADE**
This walk is particularly scenic in a city filled with scenic walkways. The canal was designed and built after the War of 1812 to provide a protected military supply route from Montreal to the Great Lakes. It runs for 202 kilometers (121 miles) between the Ottawa River and Lake Ontario at Kingston. The Ottawa portion has a promenade running nearly 8 kilometers (5 miles) through downtown and beyond and is one of the city's most popular attractions for residents and visitors alike. One place to linger awhile is at the Rideau Canal locks, wedged between Parliament Hill and the Château Laurier, where eight locks drop from the Rideau Canal to the Ottawa River. On fine summer days, the locks are crammed with pleasure boats making their way between the canal and the river, with scores of people watching the slow process from the sidelines.

Details: Start your walk next to Confederation Square or take a boat ride. Paul's Boat Lines, 613/225-6781, offers tours departing from near the National Arts Centre. (2 hours)

FULL STEAM AHEAD

One of Canada's few remaining authentic steam-powered trains, the **Hull-Chelsea-Wakefield Railroad,** 819/778-7246 or 800/871-7246, offers a five-hour excursion from Hull, across the river from Ottawa, to Wakefield and back. The 58-kilometer (35-mile) trip runs through the picturesque, wooded Gatineau Valley, then makes the return trip after passengers have spent two hours exploring quaint Wakefield. En route, passengers are entertained with live fiddle music, Quebec folksongs, and tales from history told by guides dressed in old-fashioned railway coveralls.

★★★ **CANADIAN MUSEUM OF CONTEMPORARY PHOTOGRAPHY**
1 Rideau Canal, 613/990-8257, www.cmcp.gallery.ca
Canada's first photography museum houses an impressive collection of some 158,000 images (not all on display at one time!). This sister museum to the National Gallery of Canada is located in a reconstructed railway tunnel alongside the Rideau Canal locks. Its boutique, by the way, should delight photography buffs.
   Details: *Located between the parliament buildings and the Château Laurier. May–Sept Fri–Tue 11–5, Wed–Thu 11–8; Sept–May Wed and Fri–Sun 11–5, Thu 11–8, closed Mon and Tue. Free, but a donation of $2 per visitor is encouraged. (1 hour)*

★★★ **CANADIAN MUSEUM OF NATURE**
240 McLeod Street, 613/566-4700 or 800/263-4433
www.nature.ca
This venerable establishment displays educational exhibits on everything from insects to dinosaurs. It provides a good opportunity to entertain the kids for a couple of hours, thanks to its hands-on exhibits, live animals, mini-theater presentations, and a children's discovery area.
   Details: *At Metcalfe Street. May–mid-Oct daily 9:30–5, Thu 9:30–8; mid-Oct–Apr closed Mon. $5 adults, $4 seniors and students, $2 children, $12 family. (2 hours)*

★★ CANADIAN WAR MUSEUM
330 Sussex Drive, 613/776-8600 or 800/555-5621
www.civilization.ca
The Canadian War Museum houses the most comprehensive military collection in Canada, chronicling the country's military activities over the past three centuries. Of all the artifacts on display, the most popular—and macabre—may well be Adolf Hitler's 1940 Mercedes.
Details: *Next door to the National Gallery of Canada. Open daily 9:30–5, closed Mon in winter. Nominal admission fee. (2 hours)*

★★ LAURIER HOUSE
335 Laurier Avenue East, 613/992-8142
http://parkscanada.pch.gc.ca
This century-old mansion was the residence of Canada's longest-serving prime minister, William Lyon Mackenzie King. Another prime minister, Sir Wilfrid Laurier, also lived there, but King was in some ways more interesting, ranking among the most eccentric of Canada's prime ministers. He seemed rather a colorless man during his tenure in office, however, it has since been revealed that he believed in spirits and communed regularly with the dead, chief among

SIDE TRIP: CHÂTEAU MONTEBELLO

The Château Montebello, 819/423-6341 or 800/866-5577, is a wonderful hotel and reputedly the largest log-cabin structure in the world. This resort stands on the shores of the Ottawa River at the western edge of Quebec's Laurentian Mountains, which puts it at about one hour northeast of Ottawa (take Highway 417, the Trans Canada, east from Ottawa, then turn north up Highway 158 and then west again, briefly, on Highway 148). A destination unto itself, it has an 18-hole golf course and is surrounded by an unspoiled wilderness where you can hike, canoe, fish, bird-watch, or picnic. It's also a good winter destination, partly because of the cross-country skiing and dogsledding, but also because of the mammoth six-sided fireplace in the center of the hotel lobby, which has to be seen to be believed.

them his mother. Among the goodies at this national historic site are King's crystal ball and an eerie portrait of his dearly departed mother. *Details:* Apr–Sept Tue–Sat 9–5, Sun 2–5; Nov–Mar Tue–Sat 10–5, Sun 2–5. Nominal admission fee. (1 hour)

SIGHTSEEING HIGHLIGHTS: GREATER OTTAWA AND HULL

★★★★ CANADIAN MUSEUM OF CIVILIZATION
100 rue Laurier, Hull, 819/776-7000 or 800/555-5621
www.civilization.ca

Through its vast archaeologic, ethnologic, folkloric, and historic collections, this museum traces Canada's development from the arrival of the Vikings to the present day. The massive complex houses a world of wonders, including a History Hall featuring life-size buildings that represent historic Canadian scenes. For kids, the Children's Museum is reputedly one of the largest in the world, with lots of hands-on activities designed to impart information about other cultures. Interactive computer terminals are located throughout the museum, allowing visitors to learn more about each exhibit. A convertible IMAX-Omnimax theater, known as Cineplus, which surrounds viewers and imparts the sensation of flying and movement as few other theaters can is also located in the building. The museum is housed in a futuristic, undulating building overlooking the Ottawa River, across from Parliament Hill.

Details: May–Sept Fri–Sun 9–6, Thu 9–9; Sept–May Tues–Sun 9–5, Thu 9–9. $8 adults, $7 seniors, $6 ages 13–17, $3 children, $18 families. Free admission Sun 9–12. Admission to Cineplus is $5.50–$8, or you can get combined admission to both museum and theater. (3 hours)

★★★ NATIONAL MUSEUM OF SCIENCE AND TECHNOLOGY
1867 St. Laurent Blvd., 613/991-3044
www.science-tech.nmstc.ca

This museum is a great bet for kids, and indeed for grownups interested in gidgets and gadgets, of which the facility houses some captivating examples. You can explore a lighthouse, giant steam locomotives, and large-scale models of sailing ships, lose your balance in the Crazy

OTTAWA

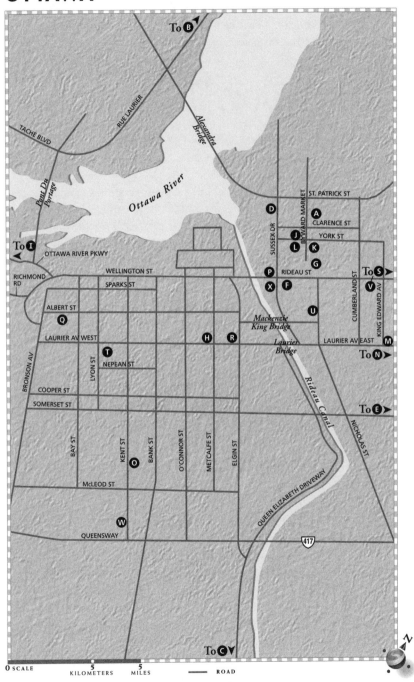

Kitchen, view hatching chicks, play with endless electronic gizmos, learn about space exploration, and much more.

Details: *Queensway to St. Laurent exit, St. Laurent south until you see a lighthouse on your left. May–Labor Day Sat–Thu 9–6, Fri 9–9; Sept–Apr Tue–Sun 9–5. $6 adults, $5 students and seniors, $2 children, $12 family. A ride on the virtual SimEx simulator costs an extra $5. (3 hours)*

★★ ECOMUSEUM OF HULL
170 Montcalm Street, Hull, 819/595-7790
www.ecomusee.ville.hull,qc.ca

The exhibits at Hull's newest museum trace the origins of life up to the arrival of humans. Although small, the museum displays more than five thousand insects from around the world, plus collections of rocks and crystals. Other exhibits deal with topics such as underground public utility services and the vanishing ozone layer. Two star attractions are a life-size replica of a dinosaur from Alberta and a high-tech simulator that reproduces the shocks of an earthquake.

Details: *Apr–Oct daily 10–6; Nov–Mar 10–4. $5 adults, $4 seniors, students, and children. (1 hour)*

FITNESS AND RECREATION

Long before cycling gained popularity as a healthy and environmentally correct activity, Ottawa was renowned for its bicycle paths. A network of more than 150 kilometers (90 miles) of recreational pathways winds along the

FOOD
- **A** Blue Cactus Bar and Grill
- **B** Café Henry Burger
- **C** Canal Ritz
- **D** Earl of Sussex Pub
- **E** Eclectic Noodle
- **F** Elephant & Castle
- **G** Haveli Restaurant
- **H** Japanese Village
- **I** Mill Restaurant
- **J** Fish Market Restaurant
- **K** Vineyards Wine Bar Bistro
- **L** Zak's Diner

LODGING
- **M** Auberge King Edward
- **N** Australis Guest House
- **O** Brighton House Bed & Breakfast
- **P** Château Laurier
- **Q** Doral Inn
- **R** Lord Elgin Hotel
- **S** McGee's Inn
- **T** Minto Place Suite Hotel
- **U** Ottawa International Hostel
- **V** Quality Hotel
- **W** Voyageur's Guest House
- **X** Westin Hotel Ottawa

picturesque Rideau Canal and throughout the Greenbelt, a vast, multipurpose green space surrounding the city. Bicycle rentals are available downtown; check at the tourist information center on Wellington Street (across from Parliament Hill) for details.

Hikers, meanwhile, can head for the hills—the hills of Gatineau Park, 819/827-2020, across the river on the far side of Hull in the province of Quebec, that is. Dotted with lakes, blanketed with forests, and laced with endless kilometers of nature trails, Gatineau Park is also a hugely popular camping and canoeing destination, and well worth the 20-minute drive from Ottawa. To get there, head for Hull and then follow Taché Boulevard west from Hull and turn north onto the Gatineau Parkway.

Golfers can choose from among approximately 20 courses within an hour or so of the city. Daredevils can challenge the white water on the Ottawa River. Reputedly, some of the best white-water rafting in North America is found about 90 minutes outside Ottawa, maybe because more water flows down the Ottawa River than in all the rivers of Britain combined! Esprit Rafting, 819/683-3241 or 800/596-7238, Owl Rafting, 613/646-2263 or 800/461-7238, River Run, 613/646-2501 or 800/267-8504, and Wilderness Tours, 613/646-2291 or 800/267-9166, all offer rafting trips on the Ottawa River.

FOOD

Stroll through the ByWard Market and you've got such a wide range of choices it's almost overwhelming. **Zak's Diner**, 16 ByWard, 613/241-2401, a retro establishment with Beatles music blasting from the jukeboxes and Formica tabletops, is a particularly good bet if you're with kids or teenagers, or are feeling nostalgic. The **Blue Cactus Bar and Grill**, 2 ByWard, 613/241-7061, serves a mix of Cajun, Southwestern, and Texan dishes, with specialties including dishes like Voodoo chicken—be aware, however, that it specializes in large-group reservations, so the place might be full of bus groups. A long-time fixture in the ByWard Market area is the **Fish Market Restaurant**, 54 York Street, 613/241-3474, which has been serving deliciously fresh seafood for more than 30 years now. The **Haveli Restaurant**, 87 George Street, 613/241-1700, also in the ByWard Market, specializes in exotic

Canada's Capital Infocentre, 613/239-5000 or 800/465-1867, www.capcan.ca, can provide information about hotels, or drop by the visitor information center at 90 Wellington Street, across from Parliament Hill.

VISITING IN WINTER?

It must be noted that Ottawa is the coldest national capital in the Western world (Ulan Bator, Mongolia, holds the world record). The pain of those snowy, subdued months is eased by Winterlude, an annual February fête that draws one million people a year. During Winterlude, locals and visitors alike throw themselves into winter sports, chief among them ice skating on the Rideau Canal. The canal is transformed each winter into the world's longest skating rink— 7.8 kilometers (almost five miles) long. (Summer, however, is deliciously warm, and autumn is a prime time to check out Gatineau Park, a vast natural reserve of lakes and forests behind Hull.)

tandoori dishes laced with delicate spices as opposed to the red-hot seasoning of some Indian cooking. The **Vineyards Wine Bar Bistro**, 54 York Street, 613/241-4270, offers a wide selection of imported beer, malt whiskies, and bistro foods at reasonable prices, all served in the intimate surroundings of a candlelit cellar. The **Earl of Sussex Pub**, 431 Sussex Drive, 613/562-5544, is a cozy place offering bangers and mash, fish and chips, and other English fare.

The rest of the city also holds pleasurable discoveries. For designer pasta dishes, try the **Eclectic Noodle**, 287B Somerset Street East, 613/234-2428, a pasta and wine bar, or the perennially popular **Canal Ritz**, 375 Queen Elizabeth Drive, 613/238-8998, which offers a pretty view of the Rideau Canal. For pub grub, the **Elephant & Castle**, 50 Rideau Street, 613/234-5544, lies diagonally across from the Château Laurier and couldn't be more centrally located. Cooks at the **Japanese Village**, 170 Laurier Avenue West, 613/236-9519, prepare sushi before your eyes. The **Mill Restaurant**, 555 Ottawa River Parkway, 613/237-1311, has long claimed to have the best roast beef in town, along with salmon, chicken, and more. One of the best, most expensive French restaurants in the region is the **Café Henry Burger**, 69 rue Laurier, in Hull, 819/777-5646.

LODGING

At the high end of Ottawa's accommodations' spectrum stands the magnificent **Château Laurier**, 1 Rideau Street, 613/241-1414 or 800/866-5577, down a slope from Parliament Hill and a landmark in itself. It manages to offer both old-world charm and modern conveniences, and it sits amidst all the city's best tourist attractions. Other centrally located and upscale hotels include the **Westin Hotel Ottawa**, 11 Colonel By Drive, 613/560-7000 or 800/228-3000, and the **Minto Place Suite Hotel**, 433 Laurier Avenue West, 613/232-2200 or 800/267-3377. All three establishments are wheelchair accessible and offer child-care services.

In the moderate range downtown, the **Quality Hotel**, 290 Rideau Street, 613/789-7511 or 800/228-5151, is within walking distance of most major attractions. The grand old **Lord Elgin Hotel**, 100 Elgin Street, 613/235-3333 or 800/267-4298, has recently been renovated and offers pleasant rooms at reasonable rates.

Rates at a number of attractive Ottawa inns are in the low-end to moderate range. **McGee's Inn**, 185 Daly Avenue, 613/237-6089 or 800/262-4337, is a downtown Victorian mansion with modern conveniences such as Jacuzzis and dataports in some of the rooms. The **Doral Inn**, 486 Albert Street, 613/230-8055 or 800/263-6725, is not right downtown but is central enough and offers weekly as well as nightly rates—a bonus for anyone thinking of staying a while. The turn-of-the-century **Auberge King Edward**, 525 King Edward Avenue, 613/565-6700, offers large rooms outfitted with period furniture, fireplaces, enormous bay windows, and other homey details.

If you'd prefer a B&B, consider the **Australis Guest House**, 35 Marlborough Avenue, 613/235-8461, a bed-and-breakfast in residential Sandy Hill off Rideau Street that comes highly recommended. **Brighton House Bed & Breakfast**, 308 First Avenue, 613/233-7777, is in the trendy Glebe neighborhood off Bank Street. **Voyageur's Guest House**, 95 Arlington Avenue, 613/238-6445, near the city's bus terminus and a 15-minute walk to Parliament Hill and other major tourist attractions, offers clean, comfortable accommodations for reasonable rates.

For a rather eerie experience, try the **Ottawa International Hostel**, 75 Nicholas Street, 613/235-2595. It served as the Nicholas Street Jail for more than a hundred years before being converted into a hostel in 1973, with accommodation provided in the refurbished cells.

NIGHTLIFE

For nightlife, try the ByWard Market area or the clump of bars along Elgin Street, which runs up to the parliament buildings. To find out what's playing at the National Arts Centre, call 613/996-5051.

For those so inclined, the Hull Casino, 1 Casino Boulevard, 819/772-2100

FORT HENRY DRILL SQUAD

or 800/665-2274, offers the usual range of games plus various restaurants and bars. Perched at the edge of an Ottawa River tributary, the casino also has docking facilities for boaters. To find out what's going on around town, check the listings in the *Ottawa Citizen,* the *Ottawa Sun,* or the weekly *Ottawa X-Press.*

FESTIVALS

Ottawa's most famous annual festival is probably Winterlude, held over three weekends in February and centered on the Rideau Canal, which at that time of year is said to be the longest outdoor skating rink in the world (some seven kilometers, or roughly five miles). The other big event is the Canadian Tulip Festival, 613/567-5757 or 800/668-8547, held in May and billed as the biggest in the world. Parliament Hill is the focal point of the city's and the nation's annual Canada Day Celebration every July 1. The latter is expected to be particularly splashy in 2000.

MORE MUSEUMS

The museums covered in Sightseeing Highlights barely scratch the surface of Ottawa's museums. As the national capital, the city is home to approximately 30 museums devoted to a dizzying array of subjects. You can learn how

Canada makes it money at the Royal Canadian Mint, 320 Sussex Drive, 613/993-8990, or drop by the Bank of Canada's Currency Museum, Sparks Street Mall, 613/782-8914. You can wander through a "Walkway of Time" at the National Aviation Museum, Rockcliffe Airport, 613/993-4243. In Gatineau Park, 20 minutes north of Ottawa, you can explore the gorgeous historical gardens at Kingsmere, 613/827-2020, which served as the summer home of Mackenzie King, Canada's tenth and longest-serving prime minister. You can, in short, museum-hop 'til you drop. As if there weren't enough museums in town already, the federal government has approved plans for a multimillion-dollar National Portrait Gallery that may open as early as 2000.

For the record, 24 Sussex Drive is the Canadian version of 1600 Pennsylvania Avenue or 10 Downing Street. The prime minister's residence is set back from the street behind walls and shrubbery, and you can't see much of the house. Nearby, however, is Rideau Hall, 613/998-7113 or 800/465-6890, the governor-general's residence, with lush grounds that are open to the public in summer and are ideal for strolling and picnicking.

Scenic Route: The Thousand Islands

The Thousand Islands, a necklace of islands scattered along the St. Lawrence River from Kingston to Brockville, provide one of the most scenic stretches in all of Ontario. A cruise of the Thousand Islands is a must, and the best ones depart from **Gananoque**. The Gananoque Boat Line, 613/382-2144 or 613/382-2146, offers regular three-hour cruises. The Canada-U.S. border cuts right through the Thousand Islands, so you'll be in the United States for part of the cruise. Canadian and U.S. citizens should carry proper identification; foreign citizens should carry passports and a U.S. visa.

Boldt Castle, 800/847-5263, is a massive monument to a monumental kind of love. In 1900 George Boldt, millionaire proprietor of the Waldorf-Astoria hotel in New York City, decided to build a full-sized replica of a Rhineland castle for his wife, Louise. He bought heart-shaped Hart Island and renamed it Heart Island. Work was well underway on 11 buildings, when Louise died suddenly in 1904. Grief-stricken, George ordered construction halted immediately—mid-hammer-strike—and for decades the castle was left open to the elements and to those who cared to stop at the island. Many of the castle's interior walls and even some of the ceilings are covered with graffiti.

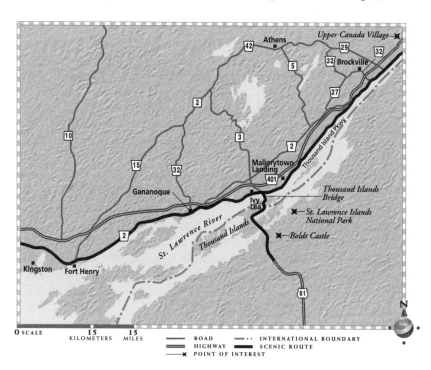

In 1977 the Thousand Island Bridge Authority assumed ownership of the castle and began charging visitors to see the place, using all net revenues for gradual restoration. The idea is not to make the castle what it would have been, but simply to bring it back to the way it looked when the construction workers laid down their tools. The exteriors of most of the buildings have been largely restored, and they look magnificent. Inside the castle is another story, and the contrast is compelling. One of the most remarkable buildings is the **Alster Tower**, or the Play House, as the Boldts called it. They actually lived in this whimsical mini-castle for a time.

Back on the mainland, head west along Highway 2, or the Thousands Islands Parkway, to **Kingston**, about a 20-minute drive. At the edge of the city you can stop at historic **Fort Henry**, 613/542-7388 or 800/437-2233, the so-called Citadel of Upper Canada. It was constructed during the War of 1812 on a point of land overlooking the confluence of Lake Ontario and the St. Lawrence. Nowadays the Fort Henry Guard re-creates drills and marches for the public, at least in summer.

Next head for the Kingston waterfront, park the car, and go exploring. One of the country's oldest settlements and once the capital of Canada, Kingston is filled with 150-year-old sandstone buildings and cobblestone lanes that lead to charming cafés and restaurants. For an overview of historic Kingston, take the 50-minute Confederation Tour Trolley, which departs from the tourist information center.

If you've more of a mind to enjoy nature, go east on the **Thousand Islands Parkway** from Gananoque. Riverside parks, beaches, playgrounds, bicycle paths, and walking trails dot the parkway, which runs the length of St. Lawrence Islands National Park. Canada's smallest national park, it consists of 21 islands and countless islets. To visit an island, you must take a private water taxi or rent a boat from a local marina. A mainland nature trail behind park headquarters at Mallorytown Landing makes for a pleasant half-hour walk.

St. Lawrence Islands National Park also operates **Upper Canada Village**, near Morrisburg, 613/543-3704 or 800/437-2233, one of Canada's best-known pioneer villages. The village re-creates life in 1866 via 40 period buildings and costumed staff members who work in the grist mill, bakery, general store, tinsmith shop, newspaper office, and other buildings.

For more information on the Thousand Islands, contact the Greater Kingston Tourist Information Office, 209 Ontario Street, Kingston, 613/548-4415 or 888/855-4555, or the Gananoque and Area Chamber of Commerce, 2 King Street East, Gananoque, 613/382-3250 or 800/561-1595.

4
MONTREAL

Ah, Montreal. The Paris of North America is known for its *joie de vivre*, cosmopolitan atmosphere, and European flavor. Montreal has much to offer—history, festivals, Old Montreal, drinking, and eating—all set against the background of a culture that's an odd hybrid of European and North American. You can be confused about which continent you're on, especially in Old Montreal. People in the tourism industry insist that visiting Montreal is like going to Europe without having to cross the Atlantic, and in this case they're not exaggerating.

Unlike many big cities, Montreal is eminently walkable. The downtown district is within easy distance of Old Montreal, as are the bars, shops, and cafés of the Saint-Denis Street area, otherwise known as the Latin Quarter. A few of the major attractions, such as the Olympic Stadium, are much farther east, but even they are only about 10 minutes by subway from downtown.

Be prepared to stuff yourself. Montreal is justly renowned for its dining. A friend tells the story of flying in from New York and discovering that her seatmate comes to Montreal twice a year on a sort of gourmet getaway. Coming from a New Yorker, that's quite a recommendation.

MONTREAL HISTORY

In 1535 French explorer Jacques Cartier, searching for a passage to India, became the first known white man to set foot on the island that would become

MONTREAL

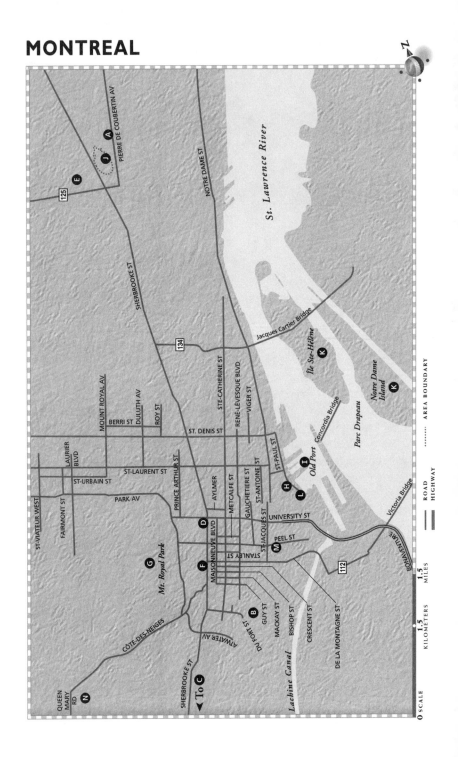

St. Lawrence River

Jacques Cartier Bridge

Île Ste-Hélène **K**

Notre Dame Island **K**

Concordia Bridge

Parc Drapeau

Victoria Bridge

Old Port **I**

H

L

PIERRE DE COUBERTIN AV

A

J

E

125

NOTRE DAME ST

SHERBROOKE ST

134

STE-CATHERINE ST

RENÉ-LÉVESQUE BLVD

VIGER ST

ST-PAUL ST

MOUNT ROYAL AV

BERRI ST

DULUTH AV

ROY ST

ST. DENIS ST

ST-ANTOINE ST

GAUCHETIÈRE ST

METCALFE ST

AYLMER

PRINCE ARTHUR ST

ST-LAURENT ST

LAURIER BLVD

ST-URBAIN ST

PARK AV

FAIRMONT ST

ST-VIATEUR WEST

Mt. Royal Park **G**

UNIVERSITY ST

ST-JACQUES ST

PEEL ST

STANLEY ST

MAISONNEUVE BLVD

D

F

M

DU FORT ST

GUY ST

MACKAY ST

BISHOP ST

CRESCENT ST

DE LA MONTAGNE ST

B

ATWATER AV

CÔTE-DES-NEIGES

SHERBROOKE ST

◄ To **C**

QUEEN MARY RD

N

Lachine Canal

BONAVENTURE

112

0 SCALE

1.5 KILOMETERS

1.5 MILES

——— ROAD

═══ HIGHWAY

········· AREA BOUNDARY

N

Montreal. It was then the site of Hochelaga, an Iroquois village. Cartier named the peak Mount Royal. In 1611 another French explorer, Samuel de Champlain, founder of New France, arrived and set up a fortified settlement that eventually grew into a busy trading center thanks to its location at the confluence of the St. Lawrence, Ottawa, and Richelieu rivers. In 1760 the British conquered New France, leaving behind British soldiers and a handful of British colonists to build a British Canada among a French population of approximately sixty thousand settlers. Gradually, Britain confirmed the right of French Canadians to retain their Roman Catholic faith, their language, and their legal code.

For more than two hundred years, the powerful English minority ran the province's economy. In the 1960s a separatist movement began to grow among French Quebecers, and in 1976 a political party, the Parti Québecois (PQ), whose main platform plank was independence, was voted into power. A provincial referendum on independence was narrowly defeated four years later. The PQ themselves lost the next election to the Liberals, then returned to power in 1994. Another referendum on October 30, 1995, was a squeaker—slightly more than one percentage point divided the two sides. That left Canada intact but the Quebec population deeply divided. The issue of separation has subsequently subsided somewhat, but you can be sure that another referendum looms inevitably in Quebec's future.

The debate over French versus English has continued for as long as many people can remember. It might never end, but meanwhile, life goes on much as usual. English-speaking Montrealers constitute about 14 percent of the city's 3.1 million residents, and many francophones are bilingual, so visitors get the best of both worlds—a distinct French flavor, but with plenty of English-speaking people around. However, most traffic and commercial signs are in French only. When driving, try to remember that est is east, ouest is west, sud is south, and nord is north. When shopping, keep an eye out for stickers in store

---

SIGHTS

Ⓐ Biodome
Ⓑ Canadian Centre for Architecture
Ⓒ Cosmodome
Ⓓ McCord Museum of Canadian History
Ⓔ Montreal Botanical Garden

Ⓕ Montreal Museum of Fine Arts
Ⓖ Mount Royal
Ⓗ Old Montreal
Ⓘ Old Port
Ⓙ Olympic Park
Ⓚ Parc des Îles (Biosphere, La Ronde, Montreal Casino)

Ⓛ Pointe-à-Callière Museum of Archaeology and History
Ⓜ Planetarium
Ⓝ Saint Joseph's Oratory

---

windows that say "F/E," which indicate merchants will serve you in French or English, whichever you prefer.

A PERFECT DAY IN MONTREAL

Start off with brunch in an outdoor café, probably on trendy Saint-Denis Street. Then set off to the east end of the city in search of nature at the Biodome and the Botanical Gardens. A stroll through Old Montreal and along the waterfront promenade at the Old Port, browsing the unique shops—maybe dropping into the Pointe-à-Callière archaeological museum and lingering over a drink at one of the outdoor terraces on Jacques Cartier Square—will cap off your afternoon. Deciding where to have dinner in this city known for its gastronomic delights will be the biggest problem of the day—the choices are overwhelming. Later, head to the pedestrian mall of Prince Arthur Street and settle in at one of the sidewalk cafés to do some serious people-watching long into the night.

ORIENTATION

Montreal has two international airports: Dorval, about 20 minutes from downtown, and Mirabel, an hour north of the city. Domestic, transborder, and international flights come into Dorval, whereas charter flights use Mirabel. Via Rail trains arrive at Central Station next to the Queen Elizabeth Hotel downtown, and intercity buses come into the Voyageur bus station on Berri Street east of downtown.

Sherbrooke Street is the major artery running east-west through Montreal. North of Sherbrooke Street, at least in the downtown area, the slopes of Mount Royal begin. Old Montreal is southeast of downtown, near the waterfront, spreading east from the corner of University and St. Jacques and south toward the river. Eight blocks east of University, St. Lawrence Street, alias Saint-Laurent, alias The Main, divides the city into east and west. The Olympic Stadium, the Biodome, and the Botanical Gardens are congregated in the east end, about 15 minutes by subway from downtown.

Downtown parking is hard to find, and driving in Montreal can be nerve-wracking for people who aren't accustomed to it. Just for starters, pedestrians jaywalk all the time, and few drivers seem to have any idea when to use a turn signal. It's advisable to drive—and walk—defensively.

Better yet, abandon your car at your lodging and use the public transit system: the clean, efficient, and relatively crime-free subway known as the métro. One of the subway lines runs right along St. Catherine and out past the

Olympic Stadium in the east end of the city; another passes through the edge of old Montreal. Single tickets for the bus or métro cost $1.90. A strip of 6 tickets is $8.25 and 12 tickets is $16. Or, the STCUM Tourist Card provides for unlimited public-transit access for an entire day for $5, or three days for $12. It's available at all downtown subways stations, the Infotourist Centre at 1010 St. Catherine Street West, and at the Old Montreal Tourist Information Office at 174 Notre-Dame Street East (corner Place Jacques-Cartier). For information on public transit routes, call 514/288-6287.

SIGHTSEEING HIGHLIGHTS: DOWNTOWN MONTREAL

★★★★ MONTREAL MUSEUM OF FINE ARTS
1380 Sherbrooke Street West, 514/285-2000
www.mmfa.qc.ca

Founded in 1860, the oldest art museum in Canada now consists of two buildings facing each other across Sherbrooke Street. The original is a magnificent neoclassical structure on the north side of the street; the new extension across from it was designed by Moshe Safdie, architect of the National Gallery of Canada in Ottawa. Permanent collections include prints, drawings, sculptures, and paintings by old masters and contemporary artists. The museum was recently the recipient of the entire collection of the Museum of Decorative Arts when the two facilities merged. The collection includes furniture, glass, ceramics, typewriters, and tableware, and is slowly being

Museum lovers should note that a Montreal Museum Pass is now available, providing entrance to 19 museums around the city. A one-day pass costs $15 for adults or $30 for families, and a three-day pass (which can be used over a three-week period) costs $28 for adults and $60 for families. The passes are sold at participating museums, Infotouriste, and numerous hotels.

integrated into the MMFA's collection. It's also worth noting that the museum usually brings a blockbuster show to Montreal each summer; in the summer of 2000, it's going to be an exhibit titled *From Renoir to Picasso* (see Tip on page 72.)

EXPRESSIONISTIC EXTRAVAGANZA

Exhibitions of Impressionist art are packing people in at art museums around the world these days, and the Montreal Museum of Fine Arts is no exception. From June 1 to October 15, 2000, the museum will be the venue for *From Renoir to Picasso: Masterpieces from the Musée de l'Orangerie*. The exhibition brings together 81 masterpieces from the museum in Paris, including 14 paintings by Cézanne, 10 Matisses, 5 Modiglianis, 1 Monet, 7 Picassos, and 16 Renoirs. Montreal and Fort Worth, Texas, will be the only North American stops on the show's international tour, so if you're going to be in Montreal during this period, this show is a definite must-see.

Details: Peel or Guy-Concordia subway stop. Tue–Sun 11–6. $12 adults, $6 seniors and students, $3 children under 13. (2 hours)

★★★★ **OLD MONTREAL**
From St. Antoine Street to de la Commune Street between McGill and Berri Streets
The city's premier tourist attraction is a picturesque enclave of narrow cobblestone streets lined with buildings dating as far back as the seventeenth century. You might want to drop in to Notre-Dame Basilica at 110 Notre-Dame Street on Place d'Armes. One of the largest and most beautiful churches in North America, the ornate basilica is home to a 7,000-pipe organ that must be seen to be believed. Another must-see is the Bonsecours Market, a striking heritage building capped by a silver dome that makes it easy to find. The nucleus of Old Montreal is Place Jacques Cartier, a cobblestoned square full of lively cafés, bars, and restaurants, and, on summer days, entertainment by buskers (street performers). The imposing white building across the street from the top of the square is City Hall, and the Old Port lies at the bottom of the square.
Details: Place d'Armes or Champ-de-Mars subway stop. A tourist information kiosk is located on Place Jacques Cartier. (3 hours)

★★★★ OLD PORT
514/496-7678 or 800/971-7678
www.oldportofmontreal.com
The waterfront area at the foot of Old Montreal is a popular year-round recreation site. Wander the 2.5-kilometer (1.5-mile) waterfront esplanade, which in summer is crowded with in-line skaters, cyclists, and strollers. You can rent in-line skates or bicycles at the site. Various attractions are housed in pier buildings, including an IMAX theater. (To find out what's playing, call 514/496-4629.) Old Port also features a variety of harbor cruises, including the entertaining Amphi-Bus, 514/849-5181, which takes you aboard an amphibious vehicle that rumbles along the streets and then heads serenely out into the river. The port also offers walking tours, picnic facilities, organized children's activities, live performances, a yacht harbor, and a ferry that crosses to Île Sainte-Hélène departing from Jacques Cartier Pier.

Details: Champ-de-Mars or Place d'Armes subway stop. From May–Sept an information booth provides bilingual assistance at the entrances to the King Edward and Jacques Cartier piers. You can park on the piers. (2 hours)

★★★★ POINTE-À-CALLIÈRE MUSEUM OF ARCHAEOLOGY AND HISTORY
350 Place Royale, 514/872-9150,
www.musee-pointe-a-calliere.qc.ca
Unique and entertaining, this museum stands on the same spot where the city was founded more than 350 years ago. It houses vestiges of Montreal's past discovered in archaeological digs begun in 1980 at Place Royale and Pointe-à-Callière—that is, under where the museum now stands. The complex has three sites: the Éperon building, with archaeological artifacts and the remains of Montreal's first cemetery; the eerie archaeological crypt beneath Place Royale, which contains old stone foundations and artifacts; and the Old Customs House. A multi-screen film shows the history of Montreal, and computer-activated holograms inform and entertain. The interactive nature of the displays keep even children enthralled. To visit this museum is to take a walk through the city's foundations, in all senses.

Details: Tue–Fri 10–5, Sat–Sun 11–5, closed Mon. $8.50 adults, $6 seniors, $5.50 students, $3 children 6–12. (2 hours)

★★★ CANADIAN CENTRE FOR ARCHITECTURE
1920 Baile Street, 514/939-7026, www.cca.qc.ca
The CCA, devoted to architecture and its history, incorporates the landmark 1874 Shaughnessy House into its striking modern structure. The center was funded almost entirely by Phyllis Lambert, an architect who also happens to be one of the millionaire Bronfmans. The unique collection includes thousands of drawings and prints, books, and photographs. The CCA offers free lectures and film screenings on Thursdays, guided tours of the facility on weekends, and other programs. Don't forget to visit the unique sculpture garden, which the CAA calls its outdoor museum of architecture.
Details: Atwater, Georges-Vanier, or Guy-Concordia subway stops. Wed–Fri 11–6, Sat–Sun 11–5. $6 adults, $4 seniors, $3 students, free children under 12. (1 hour)

★★★ McCORD MUSEUM OF CANADIAN HISTORY
690 Sherbrooke Street West, 514/398-7100
www.musee-mccord.qc.ca
The museum was founded by wealthy lawyer and amateur historian David Ross McCord, who was an avid collector of anything related to the history of Canada, Quebec, and Montreal. A remarkable collection of artifacts, some fifteen thousand of which came from McCord's private collection, is showcased. With items ranging from First Nations artifacts to splendid gowns, the permanent exhibition, *Simply Montréal,* offers a multifaceted glimpse into this unique and richly diverse city. The temporary exhibits, devoted to subjects as diverse as hockey and cartoons, are generally fascinating and often fun.
Details: McGill subway stop. Mon–Fri 10–6, Sat–Sun 10–5. $7 adults, $5 seniors, $4 students, $1.50 children. (2 hours)

★★★ MOUNT ROYAL
The lower slopes of Mount Royal are layered with mansions, many of which now belong to McGill University. When they were privately owned, the homes formed part of the Golden Square Mile between Sherbrooke, the mountain, Côte-des-Neiges, and Avenue du Parc. At the turn of the century, an estimated 70 percent of Canada's wealth was controlled by about one hundred people who lived in this region. Mount Royal Park on the upper part of the mountain has been preserved as a 200-hectare (494-acre) green space overlooking the city. This area is best reached by car. Two lookouts provide

sweeping views from the mountain. From the Chalet Lookout you can see the upscale Westmount neighborhood and downtown, the islands of Île Sainte-Hélène and Île Notre-Dame in the river, and beyond them the hills of the Eastern Townships. The other lookout, the Camilien-Houde Belvedere, is farther along the same road and provides a view of the Olympic Stadium and the east end.

Details: *Head north on Guy Street, which becomes Côte-des-Neiges, and follow it until you see signs for Mount Royal. Free. (1 hour)*

★★ PLANETARIUM
1000 Saint-Jacques Street West, 514/872-4530
www.planetarium.montreal.qc.ca
This science museum is a good bet if you're with children, and it's much more centrally located than the Cosmodome. In addition to themed and interactive exhibits, the planetarium puts on shows that initiate young and old alike into the wonders of space. The main attraction is the Theatre of the Stars, where a giant, high-tech projector reproduces the night sky as seen by the naked eye from anywhere on earth.

Note that the charming Magdalen Islands (described in the Prince Edward Island chapter) are accessible by air from many Quebec cities and by boat from Montreal (418/986-3278 or 888/986-3278 for reservations), a trip that takes two days.

Details: *Bonaventure subway stop. Shows are in either English or French, and the schedule can change, so it's best to call ahead to confirm times. $6 adults, $4.50 seniors and students, $3 children. (2 hours)*

SIGHTSEEING HIGHLIGHTS: GREATER MONTREAL

★★★★ BIODOME
4777 Pierre-de-Coubertin Avenue, 514/868-3000
www.ville.montreal.qc.ca/biodome/ebdm.htm
The Biodome, a strange combination of zoo, aquarium, botanical garden, and museum, is one of Montreal's most-visited tourist

attractions. The word biodome comes from the Greek words *bio* (life) and *domos* (house). This particular "life house" displays four different ecosystems in an effort to educate visitors about the planet's fragility. The environments, spread over 10,000 square meters, are a tropical rain forest, Quebec's Laurentian forestlands, the St. Lawrence River's marine world, and the polar climes of the Arctic and Antarctic. Re-created with both live and artificial flora and fauna, the rainforest area is filled with suffocating heat, screeching birds, and chattering monkeys. The Laurentian woodland surrounds a huge beaver dam, and the centerpiece of the St. Lawrence River exhibit is a massive tank filled with cod, halibut, striped bass, and even sharks, with northern gannets skimming the surface. The Antarctic section, of course, contains live penguins. Because of the distinct temperature changes as you move from ecosystem to ecosystem through laser-prompted glass doors, wear something lightweight but carry a sweater or coat.

Details: *Viau subway stop. Open daily 9–7 in summer; the rest of the year 9–5. $9.50 adults, $7 seniors and students, $4.75 children 6–17. Get an Eyeful pass for the Montreal Tower, Biodome, Montreal Botanical Garden, and Insectarium: $22.50 adults, $15.75 seniors and students, $12 children. (2–3 hours)*

★★★ MONTREAL BOTANICAL GARDEN
4101 Sherbrooke Street East, 514/872-1400
www.ville.montreal.qc.ca/jardin

One of the largest of its kind in the world, this garden contains approximately 10 greenhouses and 30 theme gardens, including Chinese and Japanese gardens and pavilions. The attraction is particularly known for its outstanding collection of bonsai trees, billed as the largest group of the tiny trees outside Asia. The newest area is called Courtyard of the Senses. It was designed for visually impaired visitors, but it offers everyone a completely different take on experiencing a garden. It would take all day and then some to take all this in on foot, so take advantage of the mini-train that runs regularly around the grounds. Note that the Botanical Garden may be a place to avoid on weekends, when wedding parties galore are having photographs taken. Located on the grounds of the Botanical Garden, the Insectarium showcases every kind of bug imaginable, from butterflies to beetles, some live and some mounted. Housed in a building that looks like a stylized bug, the Insectarium may well be unique in North America.

Details: *Pie-IX subway stop. Mon–Fri 9–5, Sat–Sun 9–7. Admission to the gardens, greenhouses, and Insectarium is $9.50 adults, $7 seniors and students, $4.75 for kids. Get an Eyeful pass for the Montreal Tower, Biodome, Montreal Botanical Garden, and Insectarium: $22.50 adults, $15.75 seniors and students, $12 children. (3–4 hours)*

★★★ OLYMPIC PARK
4141 Pierre-de-Coubertin Avenue
514/252-8687 or 877/997-0919
http://www.rio.gouv.qc.ca/pages/eng/index_e.htm
The $1.2 billion Olympic Stadium was built for the 1976 Summer Olympic Games at monstrous cost overruns—hence its nickname, "The Big Owe." Its landmark tower wasn't completed, nor was its retractable roof installed and made workable, until nearly 15 years later. Still, problems persist; not long ago, part of what was then a nearly brand-new retractable roof collapsed under the weight of snow (fortunately, no one was seriously injured). The good news is that the stadium finally now boasts the world's tallest inclined tower. It's called the Montreal Tower, and a ride on the cable car to the observatory at the top of it affords a terrific panorama of the city, the St. Lawrence River, and Mount Royal.

Details: *Viau subway stop. In summer a free shuttle runs from the Viau subway station to the stadium, Biodome, and the botanical gardens across Sherbrooke Street from the stadium. In summer open daily 10–9; the rest of the year 10–6. Trip up the tower $9 adults, $5.50 children. Guided tours of the Olympic Park complex twice daily $5.25 adults, $4.25 children. Get an Eyeful pass for the Montreal Tower, Biodome, Montreal Botanical Garden, and Insectarium: $22.50 adults, $15.75 seniors and students, $12 children. (1 hour)*

★★ COSMODOME
2150 Autoroute des Laurentides, 450/978-3615 or
800/565-2267, www.cosmodome.org/index.html
This spot is a good bet if you're traveling with kids. The Cosmodome, located in the northern Montreal suburb of Laval, includes the Space Camp, a kind of training program for youngsters, and the Space Science Centre, a more traditional tourist attraction bound to appeal to children and anyone interested in the mysteries of the universe. It's divided into themed areas of interactive displays devoted to topics such as space exploration, the moon (including a

rock brought back from there), the solar system, and the forces that shaped the Earth's evolution. A jazzy multimedia presentation titled "Reach for the Stars" is also informative and entertaining.

Details: Exit 9 on Autoroute 15 North (autoroute des Laurentides). Henri-Bourassa subway, then STL bus 60. Open daily 10–6; mid-Sept–late June, closed Mon. $8.75 adults, $6.50 seniors, $5.50 children under 13, $23 families. (2 hours)

★★ PARC DES ÎLES
514/872-4537 or 800/797-4537
www.parcdesiles.com/Anglais/Anglais.html
Île Sainte-Hélène and Île Notre-Dame are the one-time Expo islands in the St. Lawrence River between Montreal and the so-called south shore. Île Notre-Dame has a floral park (open from mid-June to September) as well as the city's only beach. Both islands have lots of green space and make for enjoyable strolling, cycling, or in-line skating.

The **Biosphere,** 160 Tour-de-l'Isle Road, Île Sainte-Hélène, 514/283-5000, is housed in the one-time U.S. pavilion at Expo '67, a dramatic geodesic dome designed by Buckminster Fuller. After Expo, the dome was given to the city of Montreal. In 1976 a stray spark from a welder's torch set fire to the transparent plastic skin covering the dome, and the skeleton of the building remained a scorched landmark until it was reborn as the Biosphere, an interactive ecomuseum, in 1995. The exhibits are about water and the St. Lawrence River basin, focusing on its origins, chemistry, usage, and climate. Throughout, computers serve as interactive fonts of information about water. The real St. Lawrence flows past less than 200 meters away. The museum is open daily 10–5 but closed Monday in winter. Admission costs $6.50 adults, $5 seniors and students, $4 kids, and $16 families.

La Ronde on Île Sainte-Hélène, 514/872-6222, is the largest amusement park in the province. It was built for Expo '67 but has changed a lot since then with the constant addition of state-of-the-art, scare-you-to-death rides. It still has some oldies but goodies, too, such as the gigantic wooden rollercoaster. La Ronde is also the focal point of the annual fireworks festival that lights up the skies over Montreal twice a week from mid-June through the end of July. The park is open June to September daily. Admission costs $25 adults, $13 children under 12.

SIDE TRIP: THE LAURENTIANS

The major attraction in the Laurentians, north of Montreal, is Tremblant, 800/567-6760 or 877/873-6252. In winter it's one of the top ski destinations in eastern North America. The rest of the year, the colorful resort village at the foot of the mountain is a popular base for enjoying all the outdoor activities the region has to offer. Dozens of other charming villages and ski resorts in the Laurentians are well worth checking out as well. Gourmands might want to head for L'Eau à la Bouche, 450/229-2991, in Sainte-Adèle, which was named Montreal's top restaurant (even though it's an hour from the city) in a recent *Gourmet* magazine readership survey. To get to the Laurentians from Montreal, take Autoroute 15 North.

Montreal Casino, 1 avenue du Casino, Île Notre-Dame, 514/392-2746 or 800/665-2274, www.casinos-quebec.com/montreal.htm, is open 24 hours a day. It offers all the usual games, plus four restaurants and a cabaret room. Children are not admitted; you must be 18 or over to enter. Dress is generally casual, but no T-shirts, jeans, or sneakers are allowed. Parking is free, but the lots fill up rapidly; better to take a taxi or subway and bus (Île Notre-Dame subway, Bus 167).

Details: Île Notre-Dame subway stop. You can access Île Notre-Dame via de la Concorde bridge and Île Sainte-Hélène via the Jacques-Cartier bridge. By bicycle or on in-line skates, follow the Lachine Canal bicycle path; by ferry from Jacques-Cartier pier in the Old Port. (3 hours)

★★ ST. JOSEPH'S ORATORY
3800 Queen Mary Road, 514/733-8211
www.saintjoseph.org

This massively imposing basilica on a Mount Royal slope above Queen Mary Road is a renowned pilgrimage site—in fact, you may see a few people making their way on their knees up the impossibly long flight of stairs outside. Brother André, one of Quebec's most popular religious figures, founded the oratory. Functionally illiterate, he never advanced beyond lowly positions within his religious order,

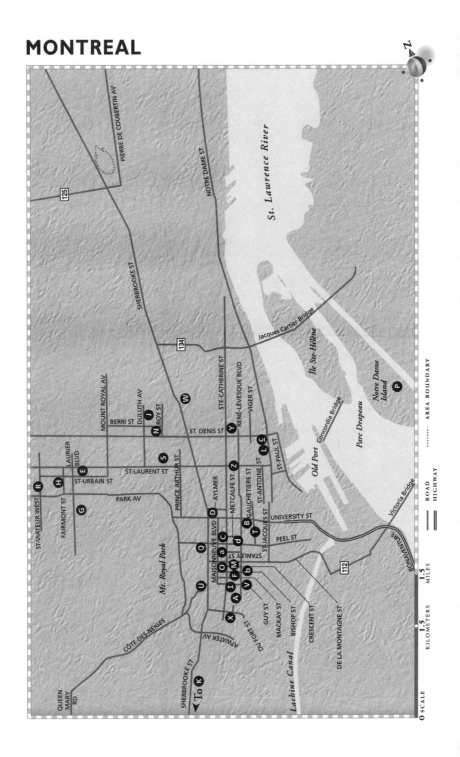

MONTREAL

St. Lawrence River

PIERRE DE COUBERTIN AV

125

NOTRE DAME ST

SHERBROOKE ST

134

Jacques Cartier Bridge

Île Ste-Hélène

Notre Dame
Island

P

MOUNT ROYAL AV

DULUTH AV

BERRI ST

ROY ST

J

N

STE-CATHERINE ST

RENÉ-LÉVESQUE BLVD

VIGER ST

ST. DENIS ST

W

Y

Concordia Bridge

Old Port

Parc Drapeau

LAURIER
BLVD

ST-LAURENT ST

S

ST-PAUL ST

L

C

Victoria Bridge

ST-URBAIN ST

E

PARK AV

PRINCE ARTHUR ST

AYLMER

METCALFE ST

GAUCHETIÈRE ST

ST-ANTOINE ST

Z

R

H

G

ST-VIATEUR WEST

FAIRMONT ST

Mt. Royal Park

MAISONNEUVE BLVD

STANLEY ST

ST-JACQUES ST

UNIVERSITY ST

PEEL ST

D

B

T

Q

a

c

d

O

F

M

A

I

b

V

U

X

GUY ST

MACKAY ST

BISHOP ST

CRESCENT ST

DE LA MONTAGNE ST

112

BONAVENTURE

CÔTE-DES-NEIGES

ATWATER AV

DU FORT ST

Lachine Canal

QUEEN
MARY
RD

SHERBROOKE ST

To K

K

0   SCALE

1.5
KILOMETERS

1.5
MILES

ROAD

HIGHWAY

AREA BOUNDARY

but he was also a faith healer with St. Joseph as his patron. Although his work scandalized much of the established church, thousands of people attributed their miraculous healings to him, and in 1904 some of his fans helped him build a small oratory in honor of Joseph on the slopes of Mount Royal. Eventually the church got involved, and a basilica was built on the site. The copper dome that caps it is reputedly the second largest in the world after the one atop St. Peter's in Rome. The oratory also provides a lookout over the city.

Details: *Daily 6–9. Côte-des Neiges subway stop. (1 hour)*

FITNESS AND RECREATION

Cycling and in-line skating seem to be the most popular sports in Montreal these days. You can rent bikes and skates at the Old Port, 514/496-7678, and then wheel along the Lachine Canal bike path or head out to the Parc des Îles, 514/872-4537 (see Sightseeing Highlights). Mount Royal is always a good place for a brisk walk. Adventure seekers can head for the Old Port to catch the jet boat ride through the Lachine Rapids, a wet and wild trip that's popular among tourists and Montrealers alike; contact Jet Boating, 514/284-9607.

If you happen to visit Montreal in the winter, more than 100 outdoor skating loops, ovals, and rinks inside a seven-kilometer (four-mile) radius of downtown await you. All of them are free and many offer rentals as well as heated changing areas. The city is also within about one hour or so of ski hills in two directions—the Laurentians to the north and the Eastern Townships to the southeast (see Side Trips).

One of the most popular activities in the Laurentians is white-water rafting on the thrilling Rouge River; contact New World River Expeditions,

FOOD
- Ⓐ Bar-B-Barn
- Ⓑ Beaver Club
- Ⓒ Ben's Delicatessen
- Ⓓ Biddles
- Ⓔ Chao Phraya
- Ⓕ Curry House
- Ⓖ Exotika
- Ⓗ Fairmount Bagel Bakery
- Ⓘ Faubourg Sainte-Catherine
- Ⓙ Jardin de Panos

FOOD *(continued)*
- Ⓚ La Louisiane
- Ⓛ Le Jardin Nelson
- Ⓜ Les Halles
- Ⓝ L'Express
- Ⓞ Nickels
- Ⓟ Nuances
- Ⓠ Ritz-Carlton Kempinski
- Ⓡ Saint-Viateur Bagel Shop
- Ⓢ Schwartz's

LODGING
- Ⓣ Bonaventure Hilton
- Ⓤ Château Versailles
- Ⓥ Days Inn Downtown
- Ⓦ Hotel de Paris
- Ⓧ Hotel du Fort
- Ⓨ Hotel Saint-Denis
- Ⓩ Hotel Travelodge
- ⓐ Loews Hotel Vogue
- ⓑ Novotel
- ⓒ Pierre du Calvert
- ⓓ Queen Elizabeth Hotel

800/361-5033, or Propulsion Inc., 800/461-3300. The Laurentians are also home to some of the best golf courses in the province: Lac Carling in Pine Hill, 450/533-9211, and the two courses at Tremblant Resort, 800/465-3700, Le Géant and Le Diable (the Giant and the Devil). For cyclists, a bicycle trail called Le Petit Train du Nord, a route that once carried tourists by train from Montreal into the Laurentians, runs for 200 kilometers (120 miles) from Saint-Jerôme to Mont-Laurier and is probably the best bicycle route in the province.

FOOD
On a summer night in Montreal, try any of the restaurants along Prince Arthur or Duluth Streets. Prince Arthur, a lively three-block pedestrian mall of bars, cafés, and restaurants (a few blocks north of Sherbrooke off Saint-Laurent), is a great place to eat, linger, people-watch, and party in the summer. Duluth, several blocks north of Prince Arthur, is not a pedestrian mall and is not as lively but does have some good restaurants. For example, the **Jardin de Panos,** 529 Duluth Street East, 514/521-4206, is a Greek restaurant that has a wonderful open-air terrace out back that seats 350 and is usually crowded.

The great thing about the restaurants on Prince Arthur and Duluth is that most are bring-your-own-wine establishments. As long as you remember to buy a bottle before getting there, this one small factor makes eating out signif-

SUGAR AND SYRUP
Canada produces almost 70 percent of the world's maple syrup supply, with Quebec accounting for 90 percent of that. If you're in Montreal in the spring, try to find time to attend that great Quebec tradition, a "sugaring off." From mid-March to mid-April, sugar shacks in the countryside around Montreal convert the sap from maple trees into Quebec's fabled maple syrup, and many establishments open to the public during this period. You can watch the process by which the sap becomes maple syrup and then sit down for a huge meal of Québecois fare such as baked beans, *tourtière* (meat pie), and pancakes, all smothered in maple syrup. Ask for the names of some *érablières* (sugar shacks) at Infotouriste.

icantly cheaper. Most of the restaurants on both streets are often crowded, and most don't take reservations, so you may have to line up.

You have nothing short of a zillion other restaurants to choose from in Montreal. Some of the best include **Biddles**, 2060 Aylmer, 514/842-8656, which serves live jazz along with its ribs; **L'Express**, 3927 Saint-Denis, 514/845-5333, a French bistro–style place with affordable prices that remains so steadfastly popular that reservations are essential; **La Louisiane**, 5850 Sherbrooke Street West, 514/369-3073, which specializes in Cajun and Creole cuisine and is a 10-minute cab ride from downtown; **Chao Phraya**, 4088 Saint-Denis, 514/843-4194, a fine Thai restaurant; and **Curry House**, 1433 Bishop Street, 514/845-0326, one of the best Indian restaurants in town and very reasonably priced. With three stories of art, music, palm trees, and whimsical decor, plus a restaurant that serves exotic and creative international fare, oh-so-trendy **Exotika**, 400 Laurier Avenue West, 514/273-5015, is an experience unto itself. At the high end is **Les Halles**, 1450 Crescent St., 514/844-2328, a French restaurant that's one of Montreal's most expensive establishments and well worth it.

Several places around town tend to attract lots of tourists. The **Bar-B-Barn**, 1201 Guy Street, 514/931-3811, features excellent ribs but serves you so quickly and hustles you out so fast that it becomes an eat-and-run experience. For a good deal in touristy Old Montreal, try **Le Jardin Nelson**, Place Jacques Cartier, 514/861-5731, for its crepes, sandwiches, and salads on a courtyard terrace. **Nickels**, 1384 St. Catherine Street West, 514/392-7771, is one of several family-style eateries owned by pop diva Celine Dion.

In the cheap-but-lots-of-atmosphere category are **Ben's Delicatessen**, 990 de Maisonneuve W., 514/844-1000, a landmark establishment nestled downtown at the corner of Mackay; and **Schwartz's**, 3895 Saint-Laurent, 514/842-4813, which is small and often has long lines. Both establishments are known for their smoked-meat sandwiches. St. Catherine Street is lined with inexpensive to moderately priced places, and the big shopping centers invariably feature fast-food halls. One of the best, with a wide range of tasty ethnic dishes and all the old North American standbys, is the shopping center at **Faubourg Sainte-Catherine** at the corner of Guy Street.

Many Montrealers claim that Montreal's bagels are better than New York's. Find out for yourself at either of two well-known bakeries where you can watch the bagels being cooked in huge wood-burning ovens—**Fairmount Bagel Bakery**, 74 Fairmount Street West, 514/272-0667, or **Saint-Viateur Bagel Shop**, 263 Saint-Viateur W., 514/528-6361.

Finally, afternoon tea is still a grand tradition at one place in Montreal: the **Ritz-Carleton Kempinski Hotel**, 1228 Sherbrooke Street West,

Montreal's Neighborhoods

When it comes to colorful ethnic neighborhoods, Montreal can't top Toronto. **Chinatown**, for instance, is only a few square blocks at the edge of Old Montreal; the corner of Saint-Laurent Boulevard and de La Gauchetière Street is the center of the community, and Place d'Armes is the nearest subway station.

Little Italy, in the north end of the city around the intersection of Saint-Laurent Boulevard and Jean Talon Street, is larger and livelier, probably because Italian Canadians make up the largest ethnic group in the city. The area abounds with imposing Roman Catholic churches, enticing shops, and lively trattorias and cafés. On the residential streets hereabouts, you'll see plenty of the exterior wrought-iron, winding staircases that are the city's most distinctive architectural feature. You might want to stop by the Madonna della Defesa church at 6810 Henri-Julien Street to see the extraordinary frescos in it; look closely enough and you'll see that one of the figures depicted amid all the saintly personages is Benito Mussolini. At the time the frescos were painted, in the years before World War II, the Italian-born artist was apparently a fan of Il Duce's. After stopping in at the church, head west along Dante Street to Saint-Laurent Boulevard for a latte. Another attraction in Little Italy is the Jean Talon market. The subway stop for all of these attractions is Jean Talon.

Home to one of the largest gay neighborhoods in the world, Montreal is a very gay-friendly destination. Bounded by Berri, Beaudry, and Papineau streets in the east end, **The Village**, as it's known, is renowned for its nightlife. Most of the action takes place along St. Catherine Street between Saint-Hubert and Papineau. The Montreal gay community also throws a dynamite gay pride parade in August called Divers Cité (Diverse City).

The Plateau, at the foot of Mount Royal, bounded by Sherbrooke Street, Van Horne, and Park Avenue, has become ultra-hip by the sheer force of being home to a kaleidoscope of people and cultures. Rich and poor, English and French, young and old, gay and straight, this multi-ethnic enclave is not only the trendiest address for Montrealers but also includes tourist-magnet streets such as Prince Arthur, Duluth, and St. Laurent.

514/842-4212. You can enjoy it inside the hotel or in the Jardin du Ritz, an exquisite garden café in the courtyard.

Montreal's position as gastronomic capital of Canada, by the way, was recently confirmed when the Mobil Travel Guide again named two Montreal restaurants as the only five-star establishments in the entire country. The top two are the **Beaver Club**, 514/861-3511, a restaurant at the Queen Elizabeth Hotel, 900 René Lévesque Boulevard West, and **Nuances**, 514/392-2708 or 800/665-2274, a restaurant at the Montreal Casino, 1 avenue du Casino, Île Notre-Dame.

LODGING

If money is no object, try the **Loews Hotel Vogue**, 1425 de la Montagne, 514/285-5555 or 800/866-5577, a relatively small European-style establishment that features a "designer floor" with futuristic, black-and-gray furnishings. At the venerable and recently renovated **Queen Elizabeth Hotel**, 900 René Lévesque Boulevard West, 514/861-3511 or 800/866-5577, people still sometimes leave flowers at the door of suite 1742, the site of John Lennon and Yoko Ono's 1969 "bed-in." Other central high-end establishments include **Bonaventure Hilton**, 1 Place Bonaventure, 514/878-2332 or 800/267-2575, with a heated outdoor pool on its rooftop; **Hotel du Fort**, 1390 du Fort Street, 514/938-8333 or 800/565-6333, another "boutique" hotel; and the **Château Versailles**, 1659 Sherbrooke Street West, 514/933-3611 or 800/361-7199, a beautiful, stately old building in the Museum Quarter.

More moderately priced accommodations can be found at the **Days Inn Downtown**, 1005 Guy Street, 514/938-4611 or 800/567-0880, which offers double rooms and fairly extensive amenities. The **Novotel**, 1180 rue de la Montagne, 514/861-6000 or 800/668-6835, is primarily tailored for business travelers but offers good weekend packages for leisure travelers. **Hotel Travelodge**, 50 René Lévesque Boulevard West, 514/874-8090 or 800/578-7878, offers the basics.

All of the above establishments are very centrally located. Farther east, in the trendy Saint-Denis Street area, budget-minded travelers can stay at the **Hotel de Paris**, 901 Sherbrooke Street East, 514/522-6861 or 800/567-7217, a 64-bed hostel that does not require membership, or at the **Hotel Saint-Denis**, 1254 Saint-Denis, 514/849-4526 or 800/363-3364. In Old Montreal, the **Pierre du Calvet**, 405 Bonsecours Street, 514/282-1725, is an historic mansion that has been converted into a very upscale inn with prices to match.

For B&Bs (gîtes, in French), contact the Bed & Breakfast Downtown Network, 514/289-9749, which offers rooms for two starting at $35 in the

SIDE TRIP: THE EASTERN TOWNSHIPS

Montreal lies within an hour or so of terrific outdoor playgrounds, including the Eastern Townships (Estrie) to the southeast. The townships, particularly the picturesque villages of Knowlton (also known as Lac Brome), Sutton, and North Hatley, still have substantial English populations and some charming country inns. You can follow a wine route around Dunham and soak in the atmosphere at the spa at the majestic Château Bromont, 450/534-3433. Lac Brome is known for its duck; there's a festival devoted to this food in October. The Granby Zoo, one of the most popular tourist attractions in the province, recently added a water park called Amazoo, themed on the Amazon. To get to the Eastern Townships from Montreal, take Autoroute 10 East.

downtown area, in Old Montreal, and in the Latin Quarter. Write to Bob Finkelstein, 3458 Laval Avenue, Montreal, Quebec H2X 3C8.

NIGHTLIFE

Montreal has lots to do after dark. Try the aforementioned Prince Arthur Street, Saint-Laurent (mainly north of Prince Arthur), Saint-Denis Street in the Latin Quarter, Crescent Street—still famous after all these years and still something of an English enclave—or neighboring Bishop Street.

English-language theaters include The Centaur, 453 Saint-Francois-Xavier Street, 514/288-3161, and the Saidye Bronfman Centre, 5170 Côte-Sainte-Catherine Road, 514/739-7944 or 514/739-2301. In summer, a professional theater company mounts Shakespeare-in-the-park performances at several parks around town. Take a blanket or folding chair if you attend one of these performances. Ballet, opera, and other stage shows can be found at Place des Arts, 514/842-2112. Big rock concerts are held either at the Molson Centre, 514/932-2582 (which doubles as the home base of the Montreal Canadiens National Hockey League team), or the Olympic Stadium, 514/252-8687 (home to the Montreal Expos).

Montreal is headquarters to the Cirque du Soleil, the magically theatrical circus troupe that started out in the 1980s as a ragtag band of street performers and eventually went on to far-reaching fame. The troupe is usually off touring the world, but they occasionally alight for a stint at home. If they're in town, get tickets—it's a must, no matter what your age.

If you want to catch a film, that's no problem either. The new Forum Entertainment Centre, housed in what used to be the home of the Montreal Canadiens hockey team at the corner of St. Catherine and Atwater streets, is billed as the biggest movie-theater complex in the world, with 30 screens.

For up-to-date entertainment listings, check the *Gazette,* the city's only English-language daily, or pick up copies of the *Mirror* or the *Hour,* weekly independent newspapers that are distributed free. You can go online to Montreal Online, an extensive arts and entertainment source at www. montrealonline.com.

SHOPPING

The city's main shopping strip runs along St. Catherine Street from Faubourg Sainte-Catherine, a trendy marketlike shopping center at the corner of Guy (nearest subway stop is Guy-Concordia), all the way east to Saint-Laurent. In between, the major emporia include the Place Montreal Trust shopping complex, Eaton Centre (which may soon be renamed), the Promenades de la Cathédrale, and The Bay department store. For trendier, funkier shops, check out Saint-Denis Street or Laurier Avenue. The local antique alley is on Notre-Dame Street West between Atwater Avenue and Guy Street. If money is no object, the south side of Sherbrooke Street between Drummond and Guy

The Infotouriste center at 1001 Dorchester Square, between Peel and Metcalfe Streets, can book hotels for you on the spot. It's open June through August daily from 8:30 to 7:30 and 9 to 6 the rest of the year. In addition to information and hotel reservations, it offers guided bus tours and currency exchange. Or, call 514/873-2015 or 800/363-7777 for more information on Montreal and the province.

If you're planning to camp, contact Camping Québec, 450/651-7396 or 800/363-0457, www.campingquebec.com, for a copy of its bilingual Campgrounds Guide, which covers the whole province.

Streets is filled with tony art galleries and clothing stores, including the very upscale Holt Renfrew at 1300 Sherbrooke Street West.

Montreal's vaunted underground city is made up of 29 kilometers (18 miles) of corridors lined with 1,000 boutiques, 200 restaurants, 30 movie theaters, and several universities. It sure makes life easier on blustery winter days: you can stay at downtown hotels that connect with the underground city and eat, shop, and party for days at a time—without ever stepping outside.

FESTIVALS

Summer in Montreal means almost wall-to-wall festivals. The season gets off to an explosive start in June with the International Fireworks Competition wherein countries show off their pyrotechnic prowess in the skies over La Ronde, the amusement park on Île Sainte-Hélène. Next up is the 10-day Montreal International Jazz Festival, with dozens of free concerts staged outdoors downtown. Around the end of the first week of July, the Just for Laughs international comedy festival begins. It started out as a tiny, French-only affair in the mid-1980s but is now big and bilingual with an English gala, a French gala, and dozens of shows in both languages by comedians from Quebec, the rest of Canada, and around the world. After that, the festivities pause until late August when the glamorous and gaudy Montreal World Film Festival begins.

5
QUEBEC CITY

With a population of 672,000, greater Quebec City sprawls over a sizable area. But the most interesting part for visitors is definitely Old Quebec *(Vieux-Québec)*, a truly enchanting section of the city perched atop soaring cliffs overlooking the St. Lawrence River. Entering Old Quebec through the Saint-Louis Gate is like stepping through a time warp into a world of twisting, narrow cobblestone streets lined with colorful, carefully preserved buildings.

In Lower Town at the foot of the cliffs, the charming Petit-Champlain district claims to be the oldest commercial quarter in North America. Its historic buildings are now home to boutiques and bistros. History buffs will find plenty to keep them occupied as well, including the Citadel, the star-shaped fortress atop the cliffs, and sprawling Battlefields Park, site of the Battle of the Plains of Abraham.

Founded as a fur-trading post in 1608 and billed as the cradle of French civilization in North America, Quebec City is the only remaining fortified city on the continent. Today it is a busy seaport and services center as well as the capital of the province. Mostly, though, it is one of the most picturesque cities in the entire country. Crank up your camera if you're going to visit.

MORE QUEBEC CITY HISTORY
The first known European in the area was French explorer Jacques Cartier, who arrived in the Algonquin village of Stadacona high on a cape above the

QUEBEC CITY

St. Lawrence River

DALHOUSIE RD

RUE ST-JACQUES

SAULT-AU-MATELOT

COTE DE LA MONTAGNE

RUE DU TRÉSOR

RUE MONT-CARMEL

TERRACE-DES-CARRIÈRES

I

C

L

UNIVERSITY ST

PORT-DAUPHIN

BUADE ST

A

RUE DES JARDINS

RUE STE-ANNE

ST-LOUIS ST

LAPORTE ST

ST-DENIS AV

DUFFERIN TERRACE

K

B

M

PROMENADE DES GOUVERNEURS

ST-PAUL ST

RUE DES REMPARTS

D'AUTEUIL ST

D

J

H

DUFFERIN AV

To E F G A

440

CHAREST BLVD

175

175

CHAMPLAIN BLVD

PLACE MONTCALM

GRAND ALLÉE

LAURIER BLVD

GEORGE VI AV

WOLFE-MONTCALM AV

ONTARIO AV

N

175

N

0 SCALE   MILE   KILOMETER   ROAD   HIGHWAY   RAMPARTS

river in 1534. Samuel de Champlain, founder of New France, settled in "Kebec" ("where the rivers meet" in the Algonquin language) in 1608. Because they considered it the gateway to the continent, the English kept trying to conquer the area. In 1759, as British armies marched on Montreal, General James Wolfe's army sailed up the St. Lawrence to Quebec. General Louis-Joseph de Montcalm and his men kept Wolfe from climbing the cliffs all summer long, but Wolfe's force finally ascended the cliff by scaling a narrow path under cover of darkness. Both generals were fatally wounded in the subsequent Battle of the Plains of Abraham from which the British emerged victorious.

In 1774 the Quebec Act allowed French Canadians to retain the right to practice their Roman Catholic religion (then banned in England) and to preserve their language and customs. The following year, American rebels, trying to get all of British North America to join their movement, stormed the city but were badly defeated. That was the last battle at Quebec City, although the British later completed the fortifications that make Old Quebec one of the few walled cities in the world.

A PERFECT DAY IN QUEBEC CITY

Exploring Quebec City on foot is tricky: you have to start at the Plains of Abraham and work your way down to the Petit-Champlain neighborhood. That way, you descend a lot of stairs and hills instead of climbing them. Begin by strolling through Battlefields Park on the Plains of Abraham, perhaps dropping by the Quebec Museum to see its latest art exhibit. Then walk along Promenade des Gouverneurs and Dufferin Terrace, drinking in the tremendous views. Take the dizzying funicular ride down the side of the cliff behind the Château Frontenac to the historic Petit-Champlain quarter to explore the curling cobblestone streets. Come nightfall, head for Grande Allée, the center of the nightlife, lined with pubs and bars offering outdoor seating.

SIGHTS

- Ⓐ Basilique-Cathédrale Notre-Dame-de-Québec
- Ⓑ Citadel
- Ⓒ Civilization Museum
- Ⓓ Fortifications of Quebec
- Ⓔ Grosse-Île and the Irish Memorial
- Ⓕ Île d'Orléans
- Ⓖ Montmorency Falls
- Ⓗ Observatoire de la Capitale
- Ⓘ Old Port
- Ⓙ Parliament building
- Ⓚ Petit-Champlain Quarter
- Ⓛ Place Royale
- Ⓜ Promenade des Gouverneurs and Dufferin Terrace
- Ⓝ Quebec Museum

ORIENTATION

Old Quebec consists of Lower Town (which runs along the riverfront and includes the Old Port and Quartier Petit-Champlain) and Upper Town atop Cape Diamond (Cap Diamant). Upper Town includes the Plains of Abraham (also known as Parc des Champs de Batailles or Battlefields Park), the provincial legislature, Grande Allée (lined with restaurants, bars, and cafés), and the ramparts. Grande Allée runs straight up to Porte Saint-Louis (Saint-Louis Gate), an entrance to the walled part of the city, after which it becomes Saint-Louis Street. Follow Saint-Louis a few blocks and you're at the Château Frontenac, set on a cliff above Lower Town and Quartier du Petit-Champlain, the oldest commercial quarter in North America. You can take the funicular (418/692-1132) from the Château down into Lower Town, or you can walk down the escalier Casse-Cou (which, literally translated, means "breakneck stairs," but they're not actually dangerous, just long and steep). Dufferin Terrace, behind the hotel, becomes Promenade des Gouverneurs and runs along the clifftop past the Citadel (Citadelle), providing a magnificent view of the

Tourism is big business in Quebec City, and you'll find that just about everyone who regularly deals with visitors speaks English.

harbor and the St. Lawrence River. For a different perspective, hop the ferry to the town of Lévis directly across the St. Lawrence; the ride takes only 10 minutes and departs every half-hour.

The city's tourist information bureau is at 835 Wilfrid-Laurier, 418/649-2608. The provincial tourism bureau is at 12 Sainte-Anne Street, 800/363-7777, across from the Château Frontenac. For information about city buses, call the municipal bus information line at 418/627-2511. Daily passes are available.

SIGHTSEEING HIGHLIGHTS: DOWNTOWN QUEBEC CITY

★★★★ CIVILIZATION MUSEUM
85 Dalhousie Road, 418/643-2158, www.mcq.org

This imaginative museum houses assorted interactive, multimedia, and other traditional exhibits focused on themes such as language, natural resources, society, and the human body. Anything from clothing to sculptures might be on display at any given time, along with two permanent exhibits: one on the history of Quebec, the

---

other showcasing the top artifacts in the museum's collection. English or French guided visits are available for many exhibitions, and plenty of workshops and interactive displays let you explore and learn. The building, located in the Old Port, is a blend of historic and new structures designed by the ubiquitous architect Moshe Safdie. **Details:** *Old Port. June 24–Sept 7 daily 10–7; Sept 8–June 23 Tue–Sun 10–5, closed Mon. $7 adults, $6 seniors, $4 students, $2 ages 12–16, free children under 12. (3 hours)*

★★★★ PETIT-CHAMPLAIN QUARTER
Du Petit Champlain Street to Dalhousie Street between des Traversiers and du Marché Champlain Street
The funicular takes you to the Petit-Champlain neighborhood (Quartier Petit-Champlain), the oldest commercial quarter in North America. Nestled at the foot of the cliff, Petit-Champlain's narrow sloped streets are lined with boutiques, art galleries, bistros, bars, and restaurants, housed in restored seventeenth- and eighteenth-century buildings. You can wander this area at will for as long as you please.
   Details: *Funicular entrance on Dufferin Terrace at the Château Frontenac. (3 hours)*

★★★★ PROMENADE DES GOUVERNEURS AND DUFFERIN TERRACE
Promenade des Gouverneurs (Governors' Walk) begins at a lookout atop Cap Diamant near the southwest corner of the Citadel and leads along the clifftops to Dufferin Terrace, behind the Château Frontenac. It's best to start at the Citadel end because the boardwalk has a total of 310 steps that lead down toward the Château Frontenac and up toward the Cap Diamant lookout. Whichever direction you go, however, a stroll here provides a magnificent panorama of Lower Town, the Old Port, and the St. Lawrence River.
   Details: *(1 hour)*

★★★ CITADEL
Côte de la Citadelle, 418/648-3563
http://parkscanada.pch.gc.ca
A star-shaped fortress with more than two dozen buildings perched atop the cliff at the eastern flank of the city's fortifications, this structure has inspired some writers to call Quebec "the Gibraltar of

America." It is the largest fortified group of buildings on the continent that is still occupied by troops—the Royal 22nd Regiment, or the "Van-Doos" as they are known in Quebec (from *vingt-deux*, or 22, in French). Buildings include the governor-general's summer residence, the officers' mess hall, and the Royal 22nd Regiment Museum. In summer, visitors can watch two ceremonies, the Changing of the Guard at 10:00 a.m. and the Beating of Retreat at 6:00 p.m. Guided tours last 55 minutes, but military history buffs could probably happily spend all day here.

Details: *Mid-June–early Sept 9–6; Apr–mid-May 10–4; mid-May–June 9–5. $5.50 adults, $4 seniors, $2.75 children 7–17, $13.75 families. (2 hours)*

★★★ **FORTIFICATIONS OF QUEBEC**
From the Citadel around Old Quebec to the Côte de la Sault-au-Matelot 418/648-7016, http://parkscanada.pch.gc.ca
Quebec is North America's only fortified city north of Mexico. To learn about the fortifications, and for a terrific view, walk the 4.6-kilometer (2.7-mile) network of walls, gates, and squares around the old city, some dating back to the seventeenth century. The path, a National Historic Site, features interpretative panels describing the defensive system. If you want more detail, guided walking tours (in English and French) are available.

Details: *Interpretation center at 100 rue Saint-Louis. Open mid-May–mid-Oct 10–5. Nominal admission fee. (2 hours)*

★★★ **OLD PORT**
100 rue Saint-André, 418/648-3300
http://parkscanada.pch.gc.ca
Quebec was one of the world's major ports in the nineteenth century, as well as a thriving center of the shipbuilding and lumber industries. The interpretive center for the Old Port of Quebec, operated by Heritage Canada, provides a glimpse into the lives of shipbuilders and information about the history of the oldest port in Canada.

Details: *Interpretive center open early May–Sept 10–5, Apr and Sept–Oct 12–4. Nominal admission fee. (1 hour)*

★★★ **PLACE ROYALE**
Cul-de-Sac Street, 418/643-6631

A charming cobblestone square near the waterfront, Place Royale is where the first French settlers landed. It includes an interpretive center detailing its development, an exhibition that traces the history of Place Royale and Lower Town, and an information center that's also the departure point for guided tours. In summer, Place Royale is the setting for an array of outdoor plays and shows.

Details: *Interpretive center and exhibit are free. (1 hour)*

★★★ QUEBEC MUSEUM
1 Wolfe-Montcalm Avenue, 418/644-6460, www.mdq.org

The Musée du Québec, the city's largest art gallery, is in the middle of the Plains of Abraham, an historic battlefield that is now 250 acres of woodlands and gardens known as Battlefields Park. The museum showcases a wide range of Quebec art, dating from earliest European life in the province to the present, and imports the occasional touring show (an amazing Rodin exhibit in the summer of 1998, for instance). One room of the museum is designed especially to entertain children.

Details: *Thu–Tue 10–5:45, Wed 10–9:45. $7 adults, $6 seniors, $2.75 students, $2 ages 12–16, free children under 12. A museum annex houses the National Battlefields Park Interpretation Center, an absorbing high-tech presentation about the history of the Plains of Abraham. Free. (2 hours)*

★★ BASILIQUE-CATHÉDRALE NOTRE-DAME-DE-QUÉBEC
16 Buade Street, 418/694-0665

First opened in 1650, this parish is the oldest on the continent north of Mexico. This richly ornate Roman Catholic basilica is replete with stained-glass windows, assorted artwork, a throned dais, a majestic organ, and a lamp that was a gift from Louis XIV. Numerous Québecois bishops and governors of New France are buried in the crypt. Guided tours are available in summer.

Details: *In summer a 45-minute multimedia production, Act of Faith, detailing the history of the city and the basilica, is presented four times a day at 20 Buade Street. $7.50. (1 hour)*

★★ OBSERVATOIRE DE LA CAPITALE
1037 rue de la Chevrotière Street, 418/644-9841

Arguably the most beautiful vista of Quebec City is the view from the Promenade des Gouverneurs. However, this observatory on the

31st floor of a government building provides a more sweeping view of the entire city, with the river to one side and the hills of the Laurentian Mountains to the other. As you walk around the observatory, an extensive exhibit explains the history of what you're looking at. The exhibit may be given in French only, however, at some times of the day.

Details: *De La Chevrotère Street runs between Grande Allée and René-Levesque Boulevard. Open June–Sept 10–7, Oct–May 10–5. Nominal admission fee. (½ hour)*

★★ PARLIAMENT BUILDING
Grande Allée East, 418/643-7239

Hôtel du Parlement is a Renaissance-style building off Grande Allée East that houses Quebec's legislature, known as the National Assembly. Its architecture is similar to the Louvre in Paris; in fact, some of the guides refer to it as "a baby Louvre." Outside you'll see bronze statues of various personages from Quebec's past, including a recently dedicated statue of René Lévesque, the founder and long-time leader of the Parti Québecois, the separatist provincial party that is currently in power. Opposite Hôtel du Parlement on Grande Allée, you'll notice a rather ugly concrete complex that houses the provincial premier's offices and is known semi-affectionately as "The Bunker."

Details: *30-minute guided tours are available in English and French. Free. (1 hour)*

SIGHTSEEING HIGHLIGHTS: GREATER QUEBEC CITY

★★★ ÎLE D'ORLÉANS
418/828-9411

A mere 15-minute drive from Old Quebec is the Pont de L'Île, which connects verdant Île d'Orléans to the mainland. When explorer Jacques Cartier came across the island in 1535, he named it Île Bacchus because of its abundant wild vines, but it was soon renamed after the Duke of Orléans. Dotted with heritage Norman mansions, traditional Québecois-style farmhouses, and the odd quaint village, the island is a sanctuary of historic homes depicting four centuries of history. The spot is also peacefully uncrowded, and its roads are relatively traffic-free and ideal for cycling or driving slowly along, taking in the bucolic scenery. If you're stopping for lunch, consider La Goeliche, an inn just off the main road in Sainte-Petronille parish. Dining on the inn's verandah offers wonderful views of Quebec City and the south shore of the St. Lawrence.

Details: 9 kilometers (5 miles) east of Quebec City along Highway 40, and across the Pont de L'Île. (3 hours)

★★★ **MONTMORENCY FALLS**
2490 Avenue Royale, 418/663-2877
www.chutemontmorency.qc.ca
Montmorency Falls have long been a tourist attraction, but until a few years ago they were hardly an exemplary one. A textile plant—one in a long line of industries to occupy the site—stood near the base of the falls. The land was recently cleared of all commercial traces, however, and new facilities were built, including a boardwalk, a cable car to get to the top of the falls, and panoramic stairs that zigzag for 487 steps up the cliff beside the falls. For the record, the falls are 83 meters high, which makes them 30 meters higher than Niagara Falls (they are not, however, anywhere near as wide). Manoir Montmorency, connected by a long, wide boardwalk to the suspension bridge at the top of the falls, features an attractive restaurant and a wraparound terrace that provides panoramic views of the falls, the river, and Île d'Orléans.

Details: 9 kilometers (5 miles) east of Quebec City along Highway 40, to suburban Beauport. Open mid-June–Aug 8:15–11; Sept–Nov and May–mid-June 8:15–7; Feb–Apr weekends only 8:15–4. $7 per car plus $6 for a one-way trip on the cable car or $8 for a return trip. (2 hours).

★★ **GROSSE-ÎLE AND THE IRISH MEMORIAL**
Grosse-Île, 418/248-8888, http://parkscanada.pch.gc.ca
This island in the middle of the St. Lawrence River to the east of Quebec City was used as a quarantine station for immigrants between 1832 and 1937. Many thousands of Irish immigrants were forced to stop on the island, and many of them died there, mainly during the typhoid epidemic of 1847. Their tragic story, one of the most moving in the history of Canada, is told throughout the many buildings (hospitals, nurses' residences, hotels, Anglican and Catholic chapels, and so forth), cemeteries, and monuments at this National Historic Site. The massive Celtic cross in particular

honors the memory of the Irish immigrants who perished from typhus in 1847 and 1848.

Details: *50 kilometers (30 miles) east of Quebec City via Highway 20 East. May–Oct 9–6. Guided tours $11.50 adults,$5.75 ages 6–16. (3 hours)*

FITNESS AND RECREATION

Battlefields Park, 418/649-6157, in Upper Town is ideal for jogging or walking; it's also used for cross-country skiing in winter. You can explore a 200-kilometer (124-mile) network of mountain biking trails at Station Mont-Sainte-Anne, 418/827-4561, in Beaupré, 40 kilometers (25 miles) east of the city. Rentals are available on-site. Île d'Orléans is laced with bicycle paths. The Cap Tourmente National Wildlife Area, 418/827-4591, 50 kilometers (31 miles) east of the city, boasts 14 hiking trails. Hiking, mountain biking, rock climbing, canoeing, kayaking, horseback riding, and white-water rafting are all available at Parc de la Jacques-Cartier, 418/848-3169, 30 minutes north of the city. Fishing enthusiasts should head for the Parc des Laurentides, northeast of the city, for its divine rainbow trout.

The Quebec City region, which enjoys exceptional natural snowfall, is home to several fine ski resorts that are within half an hour or so from Old Quebec. Particularly noteworthy are Mont-Sainte-Anne, 418/827-4561, with Canada's largest network of lit trails for night skiing; Stoneham, 418/848-2411 or 800/463-6888, which gets so much snow for so long each winter that it offers the region's longest ski season; and, a little farther along the coast, Le Massif de Petite-Rivière-Saint-François, 418/632-5876, a spectacular mountain overlooking the St. Lawrence River.

Also in winter, one of the most popular traditions in the city is to toboggan down the Dufferin Terrace slides to the foot of the Château Frontenac. An outdoor skating rink is available at the site as well.

For those willing to go a little farther afield, La Mauricie National Park, 819/538-3232, 190 kilometers (115 miles) west of Quebec City—midway between Quebec City and Montreal, in fact—is renowned for its forested Laurentian wilderness, dotted with lakes and rivers that are ideal for canoeing. Take Exit 55 (Saint-Jean-des-Piles) on Highway 55.

FOOD

Quebecers take their cuisine seriously; their capital city abounds with delights for all tastes. In addition, it's hard to beat the romantic atmosphere of restaurants that are tucked into former homes dating from the eighteenth and nineteenth centuries.

For memorable French dining within the walls in Upper Town, you can't go wrong at **Le Louis-Hébert**, 668 Grande Allée East, 418/525-7812. The food is wonderful, and you can eat it in the sun room abutting the main restaurant. The sun room is filled with natural light, wicker furniture, and plants, creating a summery setting even during Quebec City's severe winters. Many out-of-towners head for **Aux Anciens Canadiens**, 34 Saint-Louis Street, 418/692-1627, because it offers traditional French-Canadian dishes such as Lac-Saint-Jean meat pie, caribou with blueberry wine, and duck with maple syrup pie, all served in a heritage French-Canadian home. **Au Café Suisse**, 32 Sainte-Anne Street, 418/694-1320, is something of a local institution and specializes in fondues and raclettes, which always seem particularly scrumptious in winter. Or, if you can't decide what you want, head over to **La Maison Serge Bruyère**, 1200 rue Saint-Jean, 418/694-0618, where the Falstaff in the cellars serves German fare, the upscale La Grande Table on the upper floor offers exquisitely prepared gourmet dishes, and a café and a bistro are located in between.

You can choose from plenty of less expensive, more casual options as well in Quebec City. For a pub-style atmosphere, try **Le D'Orsay**, 65 Buade Street, 418/694-1582, or the **Pub Saint-Alexandre**, 1087 Saint-Jean, 418/694-0015, which whips up moderately priced salads, sandwiches, and steak and kidney pie accompanied by what the establishment claims is the city's largest selection of imported beers and single-malt scotches. If you're in the mood for crepes, check out the **Crêperie le Petit Château**, 5 rue Saint-Louis, 418/694-1616, next door to the Château Frontenac. The **Saint-James Resto-Bistro**, 1110 Saint-Jean, 418/692-1030, specializes in fresh pasta and sandwiches washed down with local and imported beer. **Sainte-Ursule Smoked Meat**, 7 Sainte-Ursule, 418/692-5315, boasts hearty smoked-meat sandwiches.

Bellissimo, 36 Côte de la Fabrique, 418/694-7979, is a terrific Mediterranean bistro, complete with deep, sunny colors and an open kitchen, on a steep hill that curls between Upper and Lower Town. In Lower Town, **L'Échaudé**, 73 Sault-au-Matelot, 418/692-1299, is a favorite French restaurant whose name, literally translated, means "scalded person." Located on a pedestrian-only street, it also offers open-air dining on its terrace. Also in the Petit-Champlain quarter is **Le Lapin Sauté**, 52 rue Petit-Champlain, 418/692-5325, a bistro-style place with lots of European élan, fairly reasonable prices, good brunches on weekends, and an attractive open-air terrace.

QUEBEC CITY

St. Lawrence River

N

DALHOUSIE RD

RUE ST-JACQUES
SAULT-AU-MATELOT
CÔTE DE LA MONTAGNE
RUE DU TRÉSOR
RUE MONT-CARMEL
TERRACE-DES-CARRIÈRES

UNIVERSITY ST
PORT-DAUPHIN
BUADE ST
RUE DES JARDINS
RUE STE-ANNE
ST-LOUIS ST
LAPORTE ST
ST-DENIS AV
DUFFERIN TERRACE
PROMENADE DES GOUVERNEURS

D'AUTEUIL ST
RUE DES REMPARTS
ST-PAUL ST
DUFFERIN AV

CHAMPLAIN BLVD

CHAREST BLVD

PLACE MONTCALM

GRAND ALLÉE
LAURIER BLVD
GEORGE VI AV
ONTARIO AV

WOLFE-MONTCALM AV

440
175
175
175

To R

SCALE
0
1 KILOMETER
1 MILE

RAMPARTS
HIGHWAY
ROAD

LODGING

In Old Quebec, the emphasis is on inns (or auberges), filled with antiques and suffused with history. The major exception is the magnificent **Château Frontenac**, 1 rue des Carriéres, 418/692-3861 or 800/866-5577, which sits atop a cliff in the heart of Old Quebec, overlooking the old town below and the river beyond. One of the most photographed buildings in Canada, it's a tourist attraction unto itself. Even if you don't stay there, it's the place to start a walking tour, take the funicular down the cliff, or wander along Dufferin Terrace. It's more expensive than most other establishments in the area; however, special packages are often available.

Another upscale place within the walls is **Hôtel Manoir Victoria**, 44 Côte du Palais, 418/692-1030, a European-style establishment with spacious rooms that carry a hint of Victorian decor. Numerous more moderately priced establishments are situated within the walls as well. **L'Hôtel du Vieux Québec**, 1190 Saint-Jean Street, 418/692-1850 or 800/361-7787, is an elegant place with a heritage exterior but modern furnishings inside. **Hôtel Manoir d'Auteuil**, 49 rue d'Auteuil, 418/694-1173, is housed in what used to be a private mansion and now has an art deco flavor.

Outside the walls in Upper Town, plenty of attractive, moderately priced options are available, particularly along Grande Allée. **Auberge Louis-Hébert**, 668 Grande Allée East, 418/525-7812, is a small, pleasant heritage inn with a terrific restaurant (see previous Food recommendation). Another establishment on the same street, **Mon Calme B&B**, 549 Grande Allée East, 418/523-2714, has spacious rooms and two large terraces where guests eat breakfast on sunny days. A block from Grand Allée, one of the biggest hotels

---

FOOD

- **A** Au Café Suisse
- **B** Aux Anciens Canadiens
- **C** Bellissimo
- **D** Crêperie le Petit Château
- **E** La Maison Serge Bruyère
- **F** L'Échaudé
- **G** Le D'Orsay
- **H** Le Lapin Sauté
- **I** Le Louis-Hébert
- **J** Pub Saint-Alexandre
- **K** Sainte-Ursule Smoked Meat
- **L** Saint-James Resto-Bistro

LODGING

- **M** Auberge Louis-Hébert
- **N** Auberge Saint-Antoine
- **D** Château Frontenac
- **O** Hôtel Manoir d'Auteuil
- **P** Hôtel Manoir Victoria
- **Q** L'Hôtel du Vieux Québec
- **R** Mon Calme B&B
- **S** Quebec Hilton

Note: Items with the same letter are located in the same area.

---

outside the walls is the 23-story **Quebec Hilton**, 1100 René Lévesque Boulevard, 418/647/2411 or 800/447-2411, which offers sweeping views of the city and a variety of packages throughout the summer, including one for families.

Down in the Petit-Champlain quarter, you might want to treat yourself to a stay at the **Auberge Saint-Antoine**, 10 rue Saint-Antoine, 418/692-2211 or 888/692-2211. A member of the Distinctive Inns, Small Hotels & Resorts organization, it's housed in a former nineteenth-century maritime warehouse that has been transformed into an exquisite inn with flawless furnishings and a refined ambience. A motel strip is located along Laurier Boulevard just after you come off Pierre Laporte Bridge into the city, but rooms here generally aren't much cheaper than in Old Quebec.

If you're planning to camp, the best bet is to contact Camping Québec, 450/651-7396 or 800/363-0457, www.campingquebec.com, for a copy of its bilingual Campgrounds Guide, which covers the whole province. The Quebec City Tourism and Convention Bureau publishes a comprehensive annual accommodation guide, available by calling 418/649-2608 or 800/363-7777.

NIGHTLIFE

Quebec's nightlife is chiefly along Grande Allée East, between the Loews Le Concorde Hotel and Place George V. In summer, this area is jammed with people because most of the restaurants and bars have streetside terraces. The tourism promoters like to refer to Grande Allée as "the Champs Elysée of Quebec City," although it's nowhere near as long or wide as the real thing. Saint-Jean Street is also very lively at night.

Most of the theater is French-language, but one highly recommended show is performed in English and has universal appeal. Quebecers are big-time Elvis fans, and *The Elvis Story*, 418/694-4444 or 800/261-9903, packs them in every summer at the beautiful, historic Capitole Theater. The show is terrific, and the impersonator is so good that you walk out of the theater feeling like you've just been to a concert by the King himself.

Quebec Experience, 8 rue du Trésor, 418/694-4000, is an entertaining half-hour film journey through Quebec City's past, worth seeing for the 3-D experience as well as the history lesson. Showings are given in English and in French.

SHOPPING

Rue Saint-Jean, the Côte de la Fabrique, and rue Cartier, all located in Upper Town, are popular shopping streets. Rue du Trésor near City Hall (Hôtel de

Ville in French) is a touristy outdoor art gallery where local artists sell their wares. The Petit-Champlain quarter, below the Château Frontenac, is crammed with more than 50 shops and boutiques in historic houses selling crafts, artwork, and stylish clothing. Nearby, in the Old Port, a two-block section at the eastern end of Saint-Paul Street is home to virtually all the city's antique shops and makes for a fine area in which to browse. The Petit-Champlain quarter is crammed with shops selling crafts, artwork, and stylish clothing.

FESTIVALS

The annual Quebec International Summer Festival, usually running the second and third weeks of July, offers a vast assortment of entertainment in the streets and parks of the city, especially Old Quebec. With more than 1,000 performers participating from around the world, it's billed as the biggest French-language cultural festival in North America.

In winter—Quebec City winters are brutally cold—locals and visitors warm up with a winter carnival called Carnaval, billed as the largest in the world. The 10-day blowout in early Fevruary is centered around a massive ice palace that's a glittering wonder to behold. The ice and snow sculptures—a big competition is held every year—are also remarkable, as is the big night parade that wraps up the carnival. Another star attraction is Bonhomme Carnaval, the jolly, snowmanlike festival mascot. During Carnaval, tradition calls for drinking a strong alcoholic concoction called Caribou out of hollow plastic canes.

Scenic Route:
Charlevoix and the Saguenay Fjord

Charlevoix County's starkly arresting scenery has been attracting tourists since holiday making began in Canada in the late eighteenth century. The region, which lies along the St. Lawrence River east of Quebec City, is filled with gently sloping hills strewn with countless lakes, rivers, and ponds. At the end of the route lies Tadoussac, a prime whale-watching area.

*Highway 138 skirts the north shore of the river between Quebec City and Tadoussac. The 206-kilometer (123-mile) drive can be done in a few hours if your time is limited. Ideally, however, take at least a day to slowly explore and savor the beauty of this region. Departing Quebec City, the first highlight is **Montmorency Falls** (see Sightseeing Highlights). Next is the town of **Sainte-Anne-de-Beaupré**, whose famous Catholic shrine draws more than 1.5 million pilgrims a year. Legend has it that St. Anne, the mother of the Virgin Mary, saved shipwrecked sailors off Cape Tourmante after they prayed to her. Similarly, modern pilgrims hope for miracles by coming here. A museum in town tells St. Anne's story. The scenic **Canyon Sainte-Anne** is a few kilometers farther along Highway 138, complete with a tumbling river at the bottom of the gorge. A one-kilometer trail leads around the rim of the canyon*

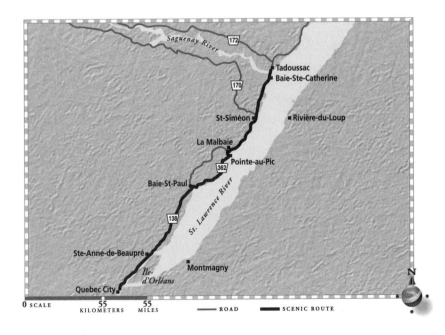

and is dotted with lookouts. You can also take a footbridge to the bottom of the canyon.

Nestled in a picturesque valley, the town of **Baie-Saint-Paul** is an artists' colony that draws performers as well as painters. Back in the 1970s, street performers in Baie-Saint-Paul formed a loose group that later became the acclaimed Cirque du Soleil. The town's narrow streets are lined with boutiques, outdoor cafés, and, naturally, art galleries. Baie-Saint-Paul is also the jumping-off point for Parc des Grands-Jardins, a mountainous, wooded park in the Charlevoix backcountry where mosses, lichens, and alpine plants flourish and caribou and gray wolves roam. The park is laced with 60 kilometers (36 miles) of hiking trails, and guided tours provide access to protected areas.

Farther along Highway 138, the summer resort town of **Pointe-au-Pic** is also worth a stop. The tourism people claim this village was the birthplace of tourism in Canada, drawing the affluent from Montreal, Quebec, and even New York City. These days it is more democratic, although if you want a taste of how the other half lived, spend a night at the breathtaking **Manoir Richelieu**, 418/665-3703 or 800/866-5577, a palatial old hotel on a bluff overlooking the river.

At Baie-Sainte-Catherine you can catch a car ferry across the Saguenay River to **Tadoussac**, a small but busy summer resort. The ferries run every 20 minutes in summer; call 418/235-4395 for exact schedules and reservations. Tadoussac draws scores of visitors to see the whales that congregate in summer at the confluence of the Saguenay and the St. Lawrence. If you're planning to stay overnight, book ahead. The historic and expensive **Hotel Tadoussac** is at 418/235-4421 or 800/463-5250, but lots of other possibilities are available, too.

Lined with soaring cliffs averaging 300 meters (980 feet) in height, accentuated by coves and bays, the glacier-carved **Saguenay River** is wildly beautiful. Walking trails in the heart of Tadoussac lead to clifftops that offer great views of Tadoussac, its bay, and the mouth of the Saguenay. The water in the Saguenay runs deep and swift and never really warms up, even at the height of summer. But at the confluence of the freshwater Saguenay and the saltwater St. Lawrence, the waters are shallow, containing an abundance of aquatic flora and fauna—and hence, a rich feeding ground for whales. Beluga whales, an endangered variety of white arctic porpoise, come here to feed, as do blue whales, humpbacks, finbacks, and assorted other species. **The Saguenay–St. Lawrence Marine Park**, 418/235-4703, the first marine conservation area in the province, protects the entire area.

Whale-watching cruises aplenty are available from both Tadoussac and Baie

Sainte-Catherine. It's advisable to make reservations ahead of time; possibilities include Croisière Navimex, 418/237-4274, Compagnie de la Baie de Tadoussac, 418/235-4548, and Croisière Express, 418/235-4770.

For further information on Charlevoix, call 418/665-4454 or 800/667-2275, or pick up a copy of Tourisme Quebec's Charlevoix guide. For information on Tadoussac, look into Tourisme Quebec's Côte-Nord guide. For copies of both, call 800/363-7777.

6
THE GASPÉ

The Gaspé Peninsula is one of the most scenic regions in the province of Quebec. The coast road is a panoply of rolling hills, craggy cliffs, and picturesque villages with whimsical names. Cap-Chat? Cape Cat was reportedly so named because of a rock near the lighthouse that resembles a crouching cat. Anse-Pleureuse? The winds in Crying Cove sound like people wailing. Cap-aux-Os? Cape Bones was named after the whale bones people used to find there.

The Gaspé Peninsula, one of the oldest land masses on earth, is sparsely populated (235,000 residents on the whole peninsula, the vast majority living along the coast). Thankfully, its wild beauty remains largely unspoiled despite its popularity as a tourist destination. One of its highlights is Forillon National Park, a dramatic product of erosion. Others include the famous Percé Rock, one of the most popular tourist draws in Quebec, and Île Bonaventure, a sanctuary a few kilometers offshore from Percé that attracts thousands of birds. As a bonus, you may spot blue, humpback, minke, and other whale species in the waters off Percé, Île Bonaventure, and the national park.

MORE GASPÉ FACTS
The Mi'kmaq, or "Indians of the Sea," have lived in the Gaspé for more than 2,500 years. In fact, the name *Gaspé* probably comes from a Mi'kmaq word

THE GASPÉ

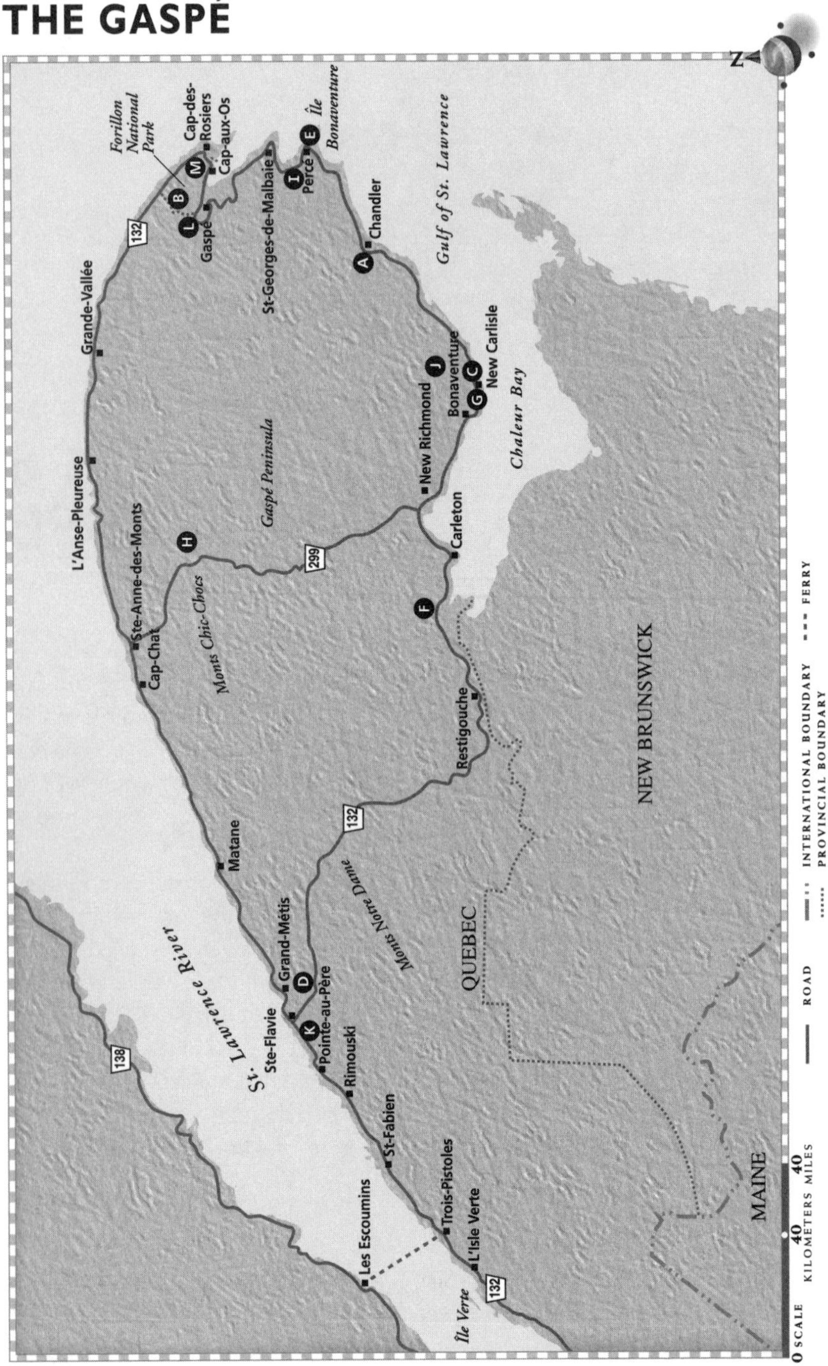

Forillon National Park
Cap-des-Rosiers
Cap-aux-Os
Gaspé
Île Bonaventure
Percé
St-Georges-de-Malbaie
Chandler
Gulf of St. Lawrence
Grande-Vallée
New Carlisle
Bonaventure
New Richmond
Chaleur Bay
Gaspé Peninsula
L'Anse-Pleureuse
Ste-Anne-des-Monts
Cap-Chat
Monts Chic-Chocs
Carleton
Restigouche
NEW BRUNSWICK
Matane
Grand-Métis
Ste-Flavie
Pointe-au-Père
Rimouski
St-Fabien
Trois-Pistoles
L'Isle Verte
Les Escoumins
Île Verte
St. Lawrence River
Monts Notre Dame
QUEBEC
MAINE
132
299
138
N
0 SCALE 40 KILOMETERS 40 MILES
ROAD
INTERNATIONAL BOUNDARY
PROVINCIAL BOUNDARY
FERRY

meaning "land's end." Over the years, myriad European ethnic groups and Loyalists (refugees from the American Revolution) also settled on the peninsula, making for a multicultural mix that continues to this day. The major industries in the Gaspé are fishing, forestry, and increasingly, tourism. You will not only see superb scenery here, but you'll also be providing a badly needed shot in the arm to the local economy.

A PERFECT DAY IN THE GASPÉ

It's difficult to pin down the best sites of the Gaspé, but several things stand out. All of them, come to think of it, are rather eerie. For starters, visit the *Grand Rassemblement,* or the "Great Gathering," a powerful work of art along the shore of Sainte-Flavie, wherein ghostly figures rise from the swirling gray water. It's the work of a local artist who spent several years on the project, and it's an amazing sight. Then look for the famous Percé Rock, another rather strange offshore spectacle. Finally, stop in Anse-Pleureuse to listen to the haunting sound of the winds.

ORIENTATION

Car ferries cross the St. Lawrence from Saint-Siméon, 33 kilometers (20 miles) southwest of Baie-Sainte-Catherine on Highway 138, to Rivière-du-Loup. Find out exact crossing times and make a reservation by calling 418/862-5094. From Rivière-du-Loup, take Highway 20 East, which soon becomes Highway

---

SIGHTS

- Ⓐ Chandler
- Ⓑ Forillon National Park
- Ⓒ Gaspé British Heritage Centre
- Ⓓ Les Jardins de Métis
- Ⓔ Île Bonaventure
- Ⓕ Miguasha Park
- Ⓖ New Carlisle
- Ⓗ Parc de la Gapésie
- Ⓘ Percé Rock
- Ⓙ Saint-Elzéar Cave
- Ⓚ Sainte-Flavie

FOOD

- Ⓛ Aux Quatre Temps
- Ⓛ Bistro-Bar Brise Bize
- Ⓚ Capitaine Homard
- Ⓓ Jardins de Métis
- Ⓘ La Maison du Pêcheur
- Ⓘ Le Matelot Resto-Bar
- Ⓚ Les Portes de la Mer

LODGING

- Ⓚ Le Gaspésiana
- Ⓘ Manoir de Percé
- Ⓘ Hôtel La Normandie

LODGING (continued)

- Ⓜ Le Pharillon Hotel-Motel
- Ⓞ Les Trois Soeurs Motel

CAMPING

- Ⓑ Cap Bon-Ami
- Ⓑ Petit-Gaspé
- Ⓑ Des Rosiers Campground

Note: Items with the same letter are located in the same area.

---

132. The 132, also known as Route de la Mer, loops all the way around the peninsula. You'll need at least two days to tour the Gaspé. For more information on the places along the route, use Tourisme Quebec's *Gaspésie* booklet; phone 800/363-7777.

SIGHTSEEING HIGHLIGHTS

★★★★ FORILLON NATIONAL PARK
418/368-5505, http://parkscanada.pch.gc.ca

A dramatic product of millennia of erosion, Forillon National Park boasts rugged, hilly inland forests that are framed by a coast of soaring limestone cliffs, pebble beaches, small sandy coves, and rocks sculpted by the pounding sea. Located on a small peninsula at the easternmost tip of the Gaspé Peninsula, the park has the strangest appearance from offshore—like a huge, jagged-edged block emerging at an angle from the sea, with one side sloping gently down to the water and the cliff side dropping precipitously. In summer, thousands of birds nest on the cliffs. Wildlife includes deer, moose, lynx, black bear, and red fox, and you might see whales and seals from coastal cliffs. The park is also home to an unusually wide cross-section of plant life given its relatively small size. You can explore on foot, or you can take a privately operated cruise from Des Rosiers. A whale-watching cruise is also available from Grand-Grave in the south of the park.

Details: The park has two reception centers: one is in Penouille, the other in L'Anse-au-Griffon. Nominal admission fee. (3 hours)

★★★★ PARC DE LA GASPÉSIE
Sainte-Anne-des-Monts, 418/763-3301
www.sepaq.com/En/Park/gaspesie/gaspesie.htm

Mountainous Gaspé Provincial Park is the only place in the province where moose, wood caribou, and Virginia deer all live in the same territory. It's also, quite simply, one of the most beautiful provincial parks in Quebec. A star feature is the Chic-Chocs, among eastern Canada's highest mountains. Mont Jacques-Cartier is the loftiest at 1,268 meters (4,145 feet). The summit of another, Mont Albert, is an immense plateau boasting mosses, lichens, and shrubs that are normally found only in the far north. More than 120 kilometers (72 miles) of hiking trails await you in the park, making this an outstanding hiking destination.

RIDING THE RAILS

Via Rail offers an overnight train, the *Chaleur*, between Montreal and the town of Gaspé. The train runs along the south shore from Montreal to Lévis, Rivière du Loup, Rimouski, and Mont Joli, then down the Matapedia Valley to Matapedia, east along the south Gaspé coast through New Carlisle and Percé, and finally to Gaspé. The trip takes 17 hours, and in both directions the sector between Matapedia and Gaspé takes place during daylight (at least in summer), allowing passengers to take in the spectacular scenery along the south Gaspé coast. In fact, some people believe this route is one of the most scenic train trips in Canada, second only to a trip through the Rockies. The *Chaleur* has comfortable coach cars, a dining car complete with a bar lounge, and sleeper cars with showers. Reserve well ahead for summer travel. For information, contact Via at 888/842-0123, or see a travel agent.

Details: *At Sainte-Anne-des-Monts, turn south on Highway 299; the park entrance is 15 kilometers (9 miles) down the highway. Several lodging facilities are available in the park. The reception center is open from early June until Labor Day. (4 hours)*

★★★★ **PERCÉ ROCK**
Percé, 418/782-2721
www.sepaq.com/En/Park/perce/perce.htm
An enigmatic, arresting presence, this monolith sits just offshore, brooding over the town of Percé. It was once attached to the shoreline, and at low tide you can still reach it on foot (be sure to check the tide schedules first). At 510 meters long, 100 meters wide, and 70 meters high (roughly 1,670 by 330 by 230 feet), it is named Percé because the sea has "pierced" holes in it to form archways. Way back in the mists of time, the rock reputedly boasted four such arches, but now only one large opening some 30 meters (98 feet) wide remains. Together, Percé Rock and Île Bonaventure make up the Parc de l'Île-Bonaventure-et-du-Rocher-Percé.
Details: *The interpretation center is on Rang de l'Irelande in Percé. Center open June–mid-Oct. (1 hour)*

★★★★ SAINTE-FLAVIE

418/775-2223 or 800/463-0323 (Visitor's Center)

The town of Sainte-Flavie is called "the gateway to the Gaspé," but the reason you should stop here has nothing to do with that. Sainte-Flavie is home to an outdoor art exhibit known as *le Grand Rassemblement*, or "Great Gathering." It's made up of more than 80 life-size figures created from firewood and bark by local artist Marcel Gagnon. Dozens of the sculpted human forms seem to file solemnly toward the shore, whereas other figures stand as if waiting. Still more human forms bob on seven rafts offshore. It is a strange and compelling sight. Some visitors have compared the work to the sculptures of Easter Island, others to the standing stones of Brittany and Ireland. You can also visit the artist's gallery at 564 Highway 132, 418/775-2829.

Details: *Visitor's Center at 357 route de la Mer (Highway 132).* (1 hour)

★★★ ÎLE BONAVENTURE

Percé, 418/782-2240

www.sepaq.com/En/Park/perce/perce.htm

An estimated 250,000 birds nest every year on windswept Bonaventure Island, a conservation park a few kilometers offshore from the town of Percé. The colony of gannets alone is 50,000 strong. The island is also rife with wildflowers, mosses, and mushrooms. You can take a boat excursion to Île Bonaventure from rue du Quai in Percé; charges vary depending on the operator. Admission to the island, however, is free.

Details: *Interpretation center at 4 rue du Quai in Percé. (2 hours)*

★★★ LES JARDINS DE MÉTIS

200 Highway 132, Grand-Métis 418/775-2222

www.versicolores.ca/jardins-du-quebec/en/html/metis_gardens.html

Stop in Grand-Métis to see the enchanting Jardins de Métis (Métis Gardens), featuring six different ornamental gardens that surround a luxurious villa, as well as experimental gardens for herbs and medicinal and aromatic plants. The most famous public gardens in the province, Métis Gardens is particularly known for the exotic blue poppy that blooms in July. Now owned by the Quebec government, the estate once belonged to the niece of Lord Mount Stephen, the first president of the Canadian Pacific Railroad. His niece, Elsie Reford, was an avid gardener who designed and created all this splendor. The mansion houses a museum, a restaurant, and a crafts shop.

Details: *Open June–Aug 8:30–6:30; Sept–Oct 8:30–5. $8 adults, $6 seniors, $3 ages 6–13. (2 hours)*

★★★ **MIGUASHA PARK**
231 Miguasha Road, Nouvelle, 418/794-2475
www.sepaq.com/En/Park/miguasha/miguasha.htm
The fish and plant fossils found in the cliffs at this provincial park make this one of the largest fossil sites in Canada. The cliffs were at the bottom of a lagoon 370 million years ago, which made them a rich source of exceptionally well-preserved fossils. You can examine some of the fossils under a microscope at the interpretation center at the site. In a happy mix of science and nature, you can also take a guided walk along the cliffs overlooking the Baie des Chaleur and still see the embedded fossils that attract researchers from around the world.

Details: *Access from Highway 132 in the towns of Nouvelle and d'Escuminac. June–Sept 9–6; shorter hours the rest of the year. Free. (2 hours)*

★★★ **SAINT-ELZÉAR CAVE**
198 Église, Saint-Elzéar, 418/534-4335
Stop in Saint-Elzéar for a guided tour of an enormous cave that's believed to be a half-million years old, making it the oldest in Quebec. This fascinating tour through a natural wonderland of stalactites and stalagmites takes about four hours, involves a lot of walking, and calls for warm clothing (the temperature is decidedly chilly deep inside the earth). You can also visit a museum about the cave for a nominal entrance fee. The official French name of this attraction is La Grotte de Saint-Elzéar.

Details: *Tour departures June–Oct every two hours starting at 8 a.m. $37 adults, $27 children; includes a snack, plus transportation to and from the cave and safety equipment. Reservations required. (4 hours)*

★★ **CHANDLER**
418/689-4912 (Visitor's Center)

FORILLON NATIONAL PARK, QUEBEC

Gene Ahrens

The wreck of the Peruvian freighter *Unisol* lies off Chandler and is visible from shore. The ship didn't sink when it hit some rocks there in 1983; it got wedged between the rocks, and half of it sticks out of the water at an angle, so that it looks eerily as if it is in the process of going down.

Details: *(1 hour)*

★★ **NEW CARLISLE**

This village is largely English-speaking, populated mainly by descendants of Loyalist families—American colonists who supported the British cause during the American Revolution and came to Canada in great waves in 1783 and 1784. For a taste of life in New Carlisle in the last century, you can tour **Hamilton House**, 115 Principale Street, 418/752-6498, an historic house museum (open in summer only) that was built nearly 150 years ago. New Carlisle was also the birthplace of the late René Lévesque, founder and leader of the Parti Québecois, champion of the separatist movement, and premier of the province in the late 1970s and early 1980s. Just recently, the white frame house where he grew up was recognized as an historic site by the Quebec government.

Details: *(1 hour)*

★★ GASPÉ BRITISH HERITAGE CENTRE

351 Perron Boulevard West, New Richmond, 418/392-4487

Founded by the Loyalists, New Richmond has a living-history museum, the Centre de l'Heritage Britannique de la Gaspésie (Gaspé British Heritage Center), that re-creates the Loyalist era, complete with houses, period furniture, store, restaurant, playground, and bilingual guided tours.

Details: *Open June–Sept daily 9–6. $6 adults, $5 seniors, $4.50 students, $14 families. (2 hours)*

FITNESS AND RECREATION

If you'd like to explore the area's waters, check out the diving shops in Percé. Horseback riding is available in several towns, including Bonaventure. For hiking enthusiasts, two parks—Gaspésie in the center of the peninsula, and Forillon at the eastern tip—provide ample opportunities. The Sainte-Anne River is known for its excellent salmon fishing, as is the river that runs through the town of Bonaventure. In winter, when tons of snow gets dumped on the Gaspé, you can cross-country ski all over the place. For a different thrill, try dogsledding; tour operators in Matane, Gaspé, and several other towns can take you on expeditions for an afternoon or an entire week.

FOOD

Any restaurant serving seafood should be fine; the seafood will be as fresh as the catch of the day. In Sainte-Flavie, **Capitaine Homard**, 180 Highway 132, 418/775-9308, specializes in fresh lobster (*homard* being French for lobster) and features an adjacent fish market. Also in Sainte-Flavie, you can indulge in steak as well as seafood at **Les Portes de la Mer**, 490 Highway 132, 418/775-8046. A little farther along Highway 132, in Grand-Métis, you might want to treat yourself to a meal at the restaurant in the Reford Villa at the **Jardins de Métis**, 418/775-3165.

In Percé, **La Maison du Pêcheur**, on the waterfront at 155 Place du Quai, 418/782-5331, serves seafood, French cuisine, and snacks, and **Le Matelot Resto-Bar**, 7 rue de l'Église, 418/782-2569, is a lively place (*matelot* means sailor) that dishes up fresh lobster, crab, scallops, and shrimp.

In Gaspé, try the **Bistro-Bar Brise Bize**, 2 Côte Charter, 418/368-1456, for moderately priced fare. Also in Gaspé, the food is fancier and the prices higher at **Aux Quatre Temps**, 135 rue de la Reine, 418/368-1455.

LODGING

Motels and inns abound around the Gaspé coast, and almost all of them are in the low-end to moderate range. Sainte-Flavie's **Le Gaspésiana**, 460 Highway 132, 418/775-7233 or 800/404-8233, is a three-star facility with spacious rooms and a dining room with a view of the St. Lawrence River.

In Percé, **Hôtel La Normandie**, 221 Highway 132, 418/782-2112 or 800/463-0820, is one of the pricier places in town, with luxurious rooms and a lovely restaurant right on the beach facing Percé Rock. Rates are more moderate at the hotel-motel **Manoir de Percé**, 212 Highway 132, 418/782-2022 or 800/463-0858, which also features panoramic views of Percé Rock and Bonaventure Island. Or try **Les Trois Soeurs Motel**, 77 Highway 132, 418/782-2183 or 800/463-9700, a nautically themed establishment at the water's edge with a wide range of reasonably priced rooms, including some with kitchenettes.

In Cap-des-Rosiers, the gateway to Forillon National Park, **Le Pharillon Hotel-Motel**, 1293 Cap-des-Rosier Boulevard, 418/892-5200, offers motel rooms with kitchenettes at moderate prices.

If you prefer bed-and-breakfasts, the entire coastline is dotted with establishments of every variety, most charging moderate rates. You'll find complete listings in Tourisme Quebec's Gaspésie guide.

CAMPING

Gaspé has a campground in practically every village along the coast, but some of the most scenic are located in Forillon National Park where the rates run around $17 for unserviced sites and $20 for serviced sites. **Petit-Gaspé** is in a lovely wooded area in the southern part of the park; **Des Rosiers Campground** overlooks the sea at the park's northern edge; and **Cap Bon-Ami**, for tenters only, is small and quiet, located in a semi-wooded area in the north of the park with a lookout nearby. Call 418/368-6050 to make reservations at any of the three parks at least 48 hours prior to your arrival.

7
THE BAY OF FUNDY

New Brunswick, which lies east of Maine and south of Quebec, covers some 73,000 square kilometers (28,000 square miles, making it slightly smaller than Maine) and is bordered on the north by the Baie des Chaleurs, on the east by the Northumberland Strait, and on the south by the Bay of Fundy. The entire province has a population of 724,000—a mix of French- and English-speaking people of varying ethnic backgrounds. For its size, New Brunswick's geography is diverse, with cliffs and rocky shores on some parts of the coast and sandy beaches and salt dunes on others. Inland, the terrain is a mixture of lush river valleys, farmland, forests, and wilderness.

Its most famous attraction is the Bay of Fundy, one of the top natural destinations in Canada. Its coast is a panorama of serene inlets, rugged cliffs, and picturesque Victorian villages. The bay is also home to the highest tides in the world and, throughout the summer months, some of the ocean's rarest, largest, and most endangered whales. At the western end of the bay, Franklin D. Roosevelt spent childhood summers on his beloved Campobello Island, one of the Fundy islands, in a humble "cottage" with 34 rooms. Another of the islands, Grand Manan, is a piece of paradise for nature lovers. What's the story on the tides? One hundred billion tons of seawater rushing into the bay twice a day, that's what.

A PERFECT DAY ON THE FUNDY SHORE

Take the coastal drive, which is scenic to be sure. You can drive almost any part of it and find something to marvel at. The plankton-rich open waters around Grand Manan and Campobello Islands attract more whales than any other place on the east coast, so chances are you'll spot whales of one variety or another, not to mention seals and porpoises. Next, visit Grand Manan, which is etched with trails that lead through bird-filled forests and across the tops of soaring cliffs. This scenic natural oasis is not yet overrun with tourists; generally, you'll have most of the place to yourself.

ORIENTATION

The Fundy Coastal Drive scenic route begins in St. Stephen and snakes along the north shore of the Bay of Fundy to Saint John. From there it loops up through Sussex and back down into Fundy National Park, then along to Hopewell Cape and up to Moncton. Stop anywhere you like along the way, whether to catch a ferry to one of the Fundy Isles or to watch some of the whales in the bay.

SIGHTSEEING HIGHLIGHTS: SAINT JOHN

With a population of 125,000, Saint John is New Brunswick's largest city. Known as the "Loyalist City," it was the first Canadian town to be incorporated, by British Loyalists who emigrated from the United States during the American Revolution. The city, particularly the downtown area with its lovely old buildings, is steeped in history, and the waterfront district has been beautifully restored in recent years. Saint John is also the New Brunswick terminal for the ferry to Digby, Nova Scotia, so the city has plentiful facilities for visitors as well as some interesting sights. For extensive tourist information on the city, contact the Saint John Visitor and Convention Bureau at 506/658-2990 or 888/364-4444.

★★★ MARKET SQUARE
Union and St. Patrick Streets
Market Square, part of the extensive restoration of Saint John's riverfront, is lined with boutiques, restaurants, and outdoor cafés. Market Slip, where the Loyalists landed in 1783, adjoins Market Square. A tourist information center is in a red nineteenth-century schoolhouse next door to Market Slip. Pick up a pamphlet that de-

SAINT JOHN

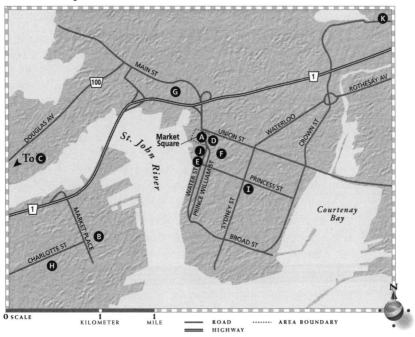

O SCALE | 1 KILOMETER | 1 MILE ━━━ ROAD ━━━ HIGHWAY ········ AREA BOUNDARY

SIGHTS

- **A** Market Square
- **A** New Brunswick Museum
- **B** Old City Market
- **C** Reversing Falls

FOOD

- **A** Food Hall at Market Square
- **D** Grannan's Seafood Restaurant and Oyster Bar
- **E** Incredible Edibles
- **F** Mexicali Rosa's

LODGING

- **G** Colonial Inn
- **H** Five Chimneys Bed and Breakfast
- **I** Parkerhouse Inn
- **J** Saint John Hilton

CAMPING

- **K** Rockwood Park

Note: Items with the same letter are located in the same area.

scribes the Loyalist Trail, a walking tour of central Saint John that includes the Loyalist Burial Ground, the nineteenth-century emporium known as Barbour's General Store (also on Market Square), the Old Loyalist House containing authentic period furniture and eight fireplaces, and other Loyalist-related sites in the downtown area.

Details: *(2 hours)*

★★★ NEW BRUNSWICK MUSEUM
277 Douglas Avenue, 506/643-2300

Stop in at this museum on Market Square for a tour of 350 million years of natural history, including life-size dinosaurs and whales. The museum also houses an eclectic collection of artifacts from elsewhere in the world, ranging from Tang Dynasty figures to silver and enamel works by Fabergé. The Tidal Tower, 40 feet tall and transparent, stretching up from the museum's central stairway, is hard to miss. An air tube connected to the Bay of Fundy causes the water in the tower to rise and fall in sequence with the tides, giving visitors a graphic illustration of the amazing height to which the water rises.

New Brunswick (along with Nova Scotia and Prince Edward Island) is on Atlantic time, which means that it's one hour ahead of eastern standard time.

Details: *On Market Square. Open Mon–Fri 9–9, shorter hours on weekends. $6 adults, $4.75 seniors, $3.75 students, $13 families. (2 hours)*

★★ OLD CITY MARKET
47 Charlotte Street, 506/658-2820

This site is reputedly the oldest continuing farmers' market in Canada, and it offers a mind-boggling array of seafood, vegetables, antiques, and myriad other goods. The block-long building, constructed in 1876, was one of the few public buildings to survive an 1877 fire that razed more than half the city. Its interior was modeled after the inverted hull of a ship.

Details: *Situated diagonally across from King Square. Closed Sun. (1 hour)*

★★ REVERSING FALLS
Highway 100, 506/658-2990

If you get the timing right in Saint John, you can see the Reversing Falls in action. Twice daily, the tides of the Bay of Fundy reach such heights that they actually force the St. John River to flow upriver in a raging torrent of foam and whirlpools, creating this unique phenomenon. You can watch from a lookout over the falls, or you can take a jet boat ride (506/648-1981 or 800/268-1133) right through the churning water.

Details: *Route 1, Exit 107, Catherwood St. (north), Friarvaile Blvd.*

(east), to Bridge St. The Reversing Falls Information Center is at the western end of Falls Bridge where there is also a lookout over the falls. Open year-round. Free. (15 minutes)

SIGHTSEEING HIGHLIGHTS: BAY OF FUNDY REGION

★★★★ CAMPOBELLO ISLAND
506/752-2922

Campobello contains a 2,800-acre international park, a joint Canada–U.S. venture intended to symbolize the friendship between the two countries. The centerpiece of the park is U.S. President Franklin D. Roosevelt's summer "cottage," a red mansion with a green roof and 34 rooms, where Roosevelt spent most of the summers of his youth; he also came to Campobello three times during his presidency (1933 to 1945). The house is surrounded by attractive gardens. The island also features walking trails, lighthouses, and a stretch of pebbly beach to explore, plus a golf course and plenty of accommodations and restaurants.

Details: *From Deer Island, a small private car ferry makes regular 45-minute crossings to Campobello from late June–mid-September. Rates are $13 for car and driver, $2 per passenger. Confirm departure times at local information centers because weather conditions can affect the ferry's operations. International Park is open late May–early Oct 10–6. (3 hours)*

★★★★ FUNDY NATIONAL PARK
506/887-6000, http://parkscanada.pch.gc.ca

This wilderness park on the shores of the Bay of Fundy is a sanctuary of sloping cliffs, tide-washed beaches, clear streams, and hiking and nature trails. During summer, two information centers are open. In the off-season, information panels, at Wolfe Lake and at the park administration building, provide basic orientation. In summer, an interpretive program features bilingual guides who take you walking on the bottom of the sea at low tide or on a nature trail. The activities are virtually limitless, from a spectacular nine-hole golf course to swimming, playing tennis, canoeing, and biking. The hiking is among the best in eastern Canada, with 104 kilometers (62 miles) of trails throughout the park.

Details: *Located next to the fishing village of Alma. Driving through* *the park takes from one to three hours, depending on how often you stop. One-day pass: $3.50 adults, $2.75 seniors, $1.75 children, $7 families. Four-day pass: $10.50 adults, $8.25 seniors, $5.25 kids, $21 families. (1 hour to full day)*

★★★★ HOPEWELL ROCKS
Hopewell Cape, 506/734-3429 or 877/734-3429
www.hopewellrocks.com

Sculpted by the mighty Fundy tides, these curious rock formations are known as the world's largest flower pots because that's sort of what they look like when the tide is out. Some are 15 meters (50 feet) tall. You can see them at any time, but only at low tide can you go down and explore the rock columns and caves. When the tide is in, the Hopewell Rocks become islands with tufts of greenery on them, and you can kayak past them if you wish. The Hopewell Rocks visitor facilities have recently been vastly improved with the addition of a full-service, state-of-the-art interpretive center, a new children's play area, expanded nature interpretation programs, and new trails leading to previously inaccessible lookouts.

Details: Off Route 114 at Hopewell Cape. Open mid-May–mid-Oct. $4.25 adults, $3.25 seniors, $2.25 ages 18 and under, $10 families. (2 hours)

★★★ MAGNETIC HILL
Moncton, 506/853-3519 or 800/217-8111

Magnetic Hill is a little dirt road outside Moncton that "defies gravity" by pulling your car backward up what seems to be an uphill slope. You drive into Magnetic Hill Park—a tourist trap if there ever was one—complete with a waterslide park. You can spend the day there or ignore it and just take in Magnetic Hill itself. Staff members direct you to the top of a gentle slope, although if cars are lined up waiting—and this attraction is hugely popular—it'll take awhile to get there. Once at the front of the line, you're instructed to drive slowly down the slope and swing over to the left side of the road when you get to the bottom. Then you put the car in neutral and, sure enough, the car starts coasting backward up the slope. It's probably just an optical illusion, but that doesn't spoil the fun.

Details: Exit 488 off TransCanada Highway; follow Route 126 to park entrance. Magnetic Hill $2 a car. Adjacent Magic Mountain Water Park open mid-June–early Sept. $59 a family. (15 minutes–full day)

TIDES

Twice a day, 100 billion tons of seawater pulse into shore in the Bay of Fundy. This tidal surge is estimated to nearly equal the 24-hour flow of all the rivers in the world combined. At the bay's eastern extremity, the tide has been measured at 14.8 meters (48.4 feet). That's the height of a four-story building. Mind you, it doesn't happen in a dramatic moment or two, but gradually over approximately six hours.

As happens everywhere else, the tides are powered by the gravitational pulls of the moon and the sun. Here, however, the ocean sweeps around the Atlantic coastline and surges into what is essentially a giant scoop—wide and deep at one end, narrow and shallow at the other.

Over the millennia, the tides have created rock formations of monumental proportions at Hopewell, along with all sorts of natural phenomena from sea caves to whirlpools. The flow is so powerful, in fact, that it actually causes the St. John River to reverse direction (see Reversing Falls in Sightseeing Highlights). The province's tourist literature refers constantly to the Bay of Fundy as "one of the marine wonders of the world," and in this case it's not hyperbole.

★★★ **ST. ANDREWS**
506/529-3555 or 800/563-7397 (St. Andrews Chamber of Commerce)

One of the oldest towns in the province, St. Andrews-by-the-Sea (actually, it's by Passamaquoddy Bay, a small inlet near the mouth of the Bay of Fundy) was founded in 1783 by United Empire Loyalists. Canada's first prefabricated houses are located here because many of the Loyalists dismantled their homes in Castine, Maine, brought them over in barges, and reassembled them in St. Andrews. More than half the town's buildings are over 100 years old, making for a quaint, picturesque little place that's fairly drenched in history. Walking-tour brochures are available at the St. Andrews Tourist Bureau where Highway 1 crosses Highway 127; a tourist information outlet is located on Harriet Street in town. The center of town, crowded with restaurants and shops, runs for four blocks along Water Street, anchored by the Market Wharf and the town square at the end of King Street. For decades, wealthy New Englanders flocked to St. Andrews in the summer, many of them staying at the famous turret-topped Algonquin Hotel that broods over the town from a nearby hill.

Kingsbrae Garden, 220 King Street, 506/529-3335, on the grounds of several fine St. Andrews estates, is a sprawling 27-acre enclave of rare and exotic flowers. It also features demonstration gardens that are constantly changing examples of design, construction, maintenance, and a variety of other horticultural marvels. The Therapy Garden, with its easily accessible raised herb and flower beds, is dedicated to the benefits of self-therapy through gardening. The Bird and Butterfly Gardens feature some of the most delicate and exotic creatures of eastern North America. The garden grounds also contain a maze, a white garden, an elegant café, and a

WILDLIFE VIEWING
A variety of whales feed in the Bay of Fundy from about mid-June to mid-October, which of course coincides with peak tourist season. Although whales are found in many parts of the world—indeed, in several other parts of Canada—the Bay of Fundy is a particularly good place to view them because it is a confined space, rather like an immense natural swimming pool.

Species include the finback, the humpback, the minke, the sei, and even the rare right whale (whose numbers worldwide now stand at fewer than 350). You may also spot white-sided dolphins and grey seals in summer. Harbor porpoises and harbor seals hang out in the bay year-round.

The entire bay, especially Grand Manan Island, is also known for its birding. From Atlantic puffins (June to July) to sandpipers and plovers (August) to northern gannets (August to September) to bald eagles (year-round), the skies above the bay teem with birdlife. So don't forget to bring binoculars.

gift shop in a stately mansion. The garden is on Frederick Street off Prince of Wales Street.

Details: St. Andrews is a 30-minute drive along Route 1 and Route 127 from the border crossing between Calais, Maine, and St. Stephen. Garden open 9–dusk daily. $6 adults, $4 seniors and children (2 hours–full day)

★★ DEER ISLAND
902/747-2027
http://new-brunswick.net/new-brunswick/deer

Catch the government-operated ferry from Letete to Deer Island, home to the world's three largest lobster pounds in Northern Harbour on the island's west shore. Old Sow, one of the world's largest whirlpools, can be seen off Deer Island, which also offers five beaches. Unspoiled and uncrowded, the island is ideal for walkers and cyclists, who can follow paths that lead to points overlooking the shore and several tiny communities.

Details: The ferry slip on the mainland is at the end of Highway 772. Crossing takes about 20 minutes. Free. From Deer Island, you can also catch a ferry to Campobello Island. (2 hours)

★★ SAINT GEORGE
http://st-george.new-brunswick.net

This fishing village is tattooed with granite outcrops that make for some dramatic scenes. Magaguadavic Falls ranks among the most picturesque. In summer, salmon on their way upriver to spawn struggle up the man-made fish ladder that was built so they could circumnavigate the falls. For some reason, Saint George is reputed to have the best drinking water in all of Canada.

Details: (1 hour)

★★ ST. STEPHEN
506/466-5416 (Visitor's Center)

St. Stephen is home to the Ganong chocolate factory, where Arthur Ganong invented the chocolate bar in 1906 by wrapping blocks of chocolate in paper as snacks to eat on fishing trips. The factory is on Chocolate Drive (what else?) on the outskirts of town. Tours are available only during the annual Chocolate Fest, usually in early August. The Chocolatier shop on Milltown Boulevard has historic candymaking equipment, chocolate-dipping demonstrations, and the

THE BAY OF FUNDY

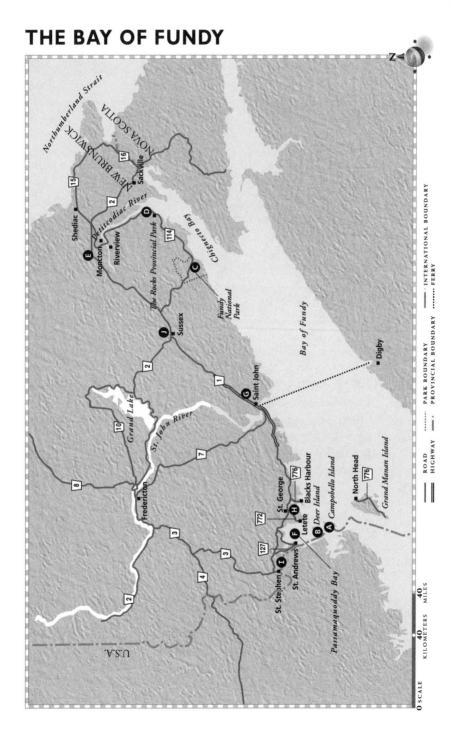

world's tallest jellybean display. St. Stephen is also a major entry point for visitors from the United States.

Details: *Visitor's Center at 101 King St. (1 hour)*

★ COVERED BRIDGES

Seventeen covered bridges, many on bucolic country roads, are located in Sussex and the surrounding Kings County. During the third week of August, Sussex hosts Country Living Days, a week of family-oriented events such as horse and livestock shows, auctions, woodsmen's competitions, a parade, and a farmers' market.

Details: *Stop in at the Kings County Tourist Center in Sussex, or call 506/433-3764, for a bridge-locator map. (1 hour)*

FITNESS AND RECREATION

New Brunswick's Day Adventures and Multi-Day Adventures make it ridiculously easy to sample any of the province's many activities, from sea kayaking to expeditions in Mi'kmaq birch-bark canoes to mountain climbing in the Appalachians, by packaging them. All a visitor really has to do is choose a particular outing. Transportation, equipment, guides, and so forth, are all arranged for you. All operators involved in the massive program are trained and certified and offer activities that contain an element of learning, a light lunch, and interpretation. The concept also carries over into winter with packages devoted to snowmobiling (a hugely popular activity in this province), cross-country skiing,

SIGHTS

- Ⓐ Campobello Island
- Ⓑ Deer Island
- Ⓒ Fundy National Park
- Ⓓ Hopewell Rocks
- Ⓔ Magnetic Hill
- Ⓕ St. Andrews (Kingsbrae Garden)
- Ⓖ Saint John
- Ⓗ Saint George
- Ⓘ St. Stephen
- Ⓙ Sussex Covered Bridges

FOOD

- Ⓑ Mabel's Table
- Ⓑ Windsor House

LODGING

- Ⓑ Algonquin Resort
- Ⓘ Amsterdam Inn
- Ⓘ Blue Bird Motel at Four Corners
- Ⓐ Friar's Bay Motor Lodge
- Ⓑ Kingsbrae Arms
- Ⓐ Owen House B&B
- Ⓑ Windsor House

CAMPING

- Ⓐ Herring Cove Provincial Park
- Ⓑ Passamaquoddy Park Campground

Note: Items with the same letter are located in the same area.

SIDE TRIP: FREDERICTON

Fredericton, a small, attractive city of 45,000 in south-central New Brunswick, is known as "the city of stately elms." Although it is the capital of the province, it has a small-town, laid-back feel because of its size and perhaps the character of its residents. One of the best features of Fredericton is its many beautiful old Victorian houses. On a summer day, strolling the streets lined with these houses is the ticket to an enjoyable afternoon. Fredericton's Tourist Information Center, at city hall on the corner of Queen and York Streets, offers a "Fredericton Visitor Guide" that includes a helpful five-block walking tour.

*An absolute must for art lovers is the **Beaverbrook Art Gallery**, 703 Queen Street, 506/458-8545, which houses a remarkable collection of British paintings spanning the sixteenth to twentieth centuries, including works by Thomas Gainsborough, Sir Joshua Reynolds, and John Constable, among others. The first painting you see on entering the building is Salvador Dali's massive masterpiece Santiago el Grande. A bench faces the painting; sit and contemplate it for awhile. Then stop in at **Old Government House**, a national historic site that reopened in the summer of 1999 after extensive restorations and was once, more than a century ago, the official residence for the province's Lieutenant-Governors.*

***Kings Landing**, Exit 259 off the TransCanada west of Fredericton, 506/363-4999, a re-created Loyalist village in a lovely setting on the St. John River not far outside town, is another must-see attraction. This town is one of the province's major tourist draws (rivaled perhaps by the Acadian Historical Village outside Caraquet). More than 70 buildings are situated on the sprawling site, ranging from a sawmill and a country inn to a one-room schoolhouse and an assortment of furnished houses, each reflecting the occupant's wealth and status in 1800s village life; the newest addition is a hotel called the Chateau Albert, built to the exact specifications of a period hotel, where you can dine on authentic Acadian cuisine and sleep in traditional Acadian style. Costumed staff members and volunteers work in and around the buildings and can answer just about any question you throw at them.*

dogsledding, skijoring (essentially cross-country skiing with sled dogs pulling you along), and the like. Day Adventures centers are scattered around the province, or you can call the tourist information line at 800/561-0123. In fact, even the province's travel planner, Tourism New Brunswick's main publication for tourists, is titled *The New Tide of Adventure* and features many pages of Day Adventures.

A wide variety of activities await you along the Fundy Shore. Whale-watching cruises are available from Campobello Island, Deer Island, Grand Manan, and, on the mainland, St. Andrews. Kayak trips are also enormously popular in the Bay of Fundy, with kayaking operators in Cape Enrage, St. Andrews, St. George, and St. Stephen offering outings for beginners and experts alike. You can go horseback riding on the trails around Hopewell Hill. In Sussex, several local tour operators offer organized cycling tours of the covered bridges. Indeed, cyclists can travel the whole Fundy Shore on two wheels.

Hikers along the Fundy shore are rewarded with stony beaches, clear cold brooks, forested promontories, and pristine shores. Check out the new Fundy Trail Parkway, featuring an 11-kilometer (seven-mile) low-speed roadway offering scenic lookouts and access areas to a 16-kilometer (10-mile) network of walking, hiking, and biking trails, many of which lead past electrifying vistas of the bay as well as such highlights as the sea caves of St. Martins and the steep cliffs of Black Point. Seventeen picnic shelters are situated along the roadway and trails, so you can easily make a day of it. Located about 10 kilometers (six miles) east of St. Martins, the Fundy Trail Parkway can be reached via Routes 1 and 2. The sandstone caves of St. Martins are popular among rock hounders and spelunkers.

Visitors to Saint John can get back to nature in Rockwood Park; located in the heart of the city, it's one of the largest municipal parks in Canada, complete with a zoo, an 18-hole public golf course, and endless hiking trails. Just outside Saint John is the Irving Nature Park (506/653-7367 or 506/632-7777), a winding coast road off Sand Cove Road on the city's west side that features several walking trails from which you're likely to see seals, porpoises and tons of birds. In Moncton, Cape Enrage, 506/887-2273, is the place to go for hiking, kayaking, canoeing, rock climbing, and rappelling.

FOOD

Plenty of lobster can be had in the restaurants hereabouts, of course, but you might also want to try a more unusual local specialty—dulce. It's a purple, salty sea vegetable from the Bay of Fundy that's sold as a snack. For a sweet treat, the town of Alma, near Fundy National Park, is known for its sticky buns.

The Best of the Rest of New Brunswick

New Brunswick has many more sights to offer than just the Bay of Fundy. **Kouchibouguac National Park**, 506/876-2443, located on the Acadian coast on New Brunswick's central eastern shore, is the province's largest park with kilometers of coastal beaches and board-walks leading over fragile sand dunes. The waters off this coast are sur-prisingly warm; the lagoon at Kouchibouguac is said to have the warmest saltwater north of the Carolinas.

Another option is **Parlee Beach Provincial Park**, 506/533-3363, on Shediac Bay, where the temperate waters reach 28 degrees Celsius (85 degrees Fahrenheit) in summer. Parlee's beauty and popularity have turned the nearest town, **Shediac,** into a favorite summer tourist re-sort. Calling itself "the Lobster Capital of the World," Shediac hosts an annual lobster festival, usually during the second week of July.

Farther north, the **Acadian Historical Village**, Route 11 west of Caraquet, 506/726-2600, a re-created settlement, tells the story of the Acadians from 1780 to the early 1900s. The village features costumed "residents" and special events. Another Acadian-flavored sight, **Le Pays de la Sagouine**, Acadie Street, Bouctouche, 506/235-0793, is based on the fictional world of Acadian writer Antonine Maillet. You'll walk over a boardwalk into a mythical turn-of-the-century community, where color-ful storytelling, dinner theater, and traditional Acadian cuisine compete for your attention.

Active, outdoorsy types will find plenty to do in New Brunswick as

The restaurants in Saint John's Market Square area range from fast food to elegant, from Chinese to pizza by way of fish and chips. Of course, the seafood is hard to beat; **Grannan's Seafood Restaurant and Oyster Bar**, 1 Market Square, 506/634-1555, offers the catch of the day, oysters, or seafood platters at prices ranging from $11 to $25. The **Food Hall at Market Square** provides an assortment of fast foods. **Mexicali Rosa's**, 88 Prince William Street, 506/652-5252, specializes in "Cali-Mex" food and is moderately priced. **Incredible Edibles**, 42 Princess Street, 506/633-7554, offers rich cheesecake and other desserts as well as salads, pasta dishes, and sandwiches. The cost is moderate—usually less than $15 for a meal.

well. **Mount Carleton Provincial Park**, 506/235-0793, home to the highest peak in the Maritimes, is ideal for hiking. **Sugarloaf Provincial Park**, 506/789-2366, on the Acadian coast outside Campbellton, offers good hiking and skiing opportunities. The **Petit Témis Interprovincial Linear Park** on the Madawaska River boasts 130 kilometers (81 miles) of biking and hiking trails. Fishing enthusiasts come to New Brunswick especially to fish the Miramichi River, legendary for its salmon. At the new **Irving Eco-Centre**, La Dune de Bouctouche, 506/743-2600, an enormously long boardwalk protects the great white sand dunes of Bouctouche on New Brunswick's northeast coast.

Finally, several scenic routes run through different parts of the province. In addition to the requisite **Fundy Route** (280 miles from St. Stephen to Aulac), the various drives take in the French-flavored Acadian coast (296 miles from Aulac to Campbellton), the Miramichi River (113 miles from Miramichi to Fredericton), and the northernmost tier of the Appalachian Mountains (137 miles from Campbellton to Perth-Andover). One of the best routes is the bucolic **St. John River Valley** drive (426 miles from St. Jacques to St. John). Its gentle curves offer panoramic vistas galore. Highlights include the Grand Falls Gorge, where the river plunges down a ravine more than one kilometer long, and the New Brunswick Botanical Gardens, north of Edmundston. You'll also cross the longest covered bridge in the world, measuring 385 meters (1,263 feet), at Hartland.

In St. Andrews, Water Street is lined with establishments catering to every taste; several offer fresh seafood. **Mabel's Table**, 182 Water Street, 506/529-4552, and the upscale **Windsor House**, 132 Water Street, 506/529-3330, are just a couple of the terrific options.

LODGING

Saint John offers a wide array of accommodations, from motels to heritage inns and B&Bs. The luxurious **Saint John Hilton**, 1 Market Square, 506/693-8484 or 800/561-8282, is right in the middle of things with moderately expensive rates. A block away, a beautiful old Victorian house, the **Parkerhouse Inn**, 71 Sydney Street, 506/652-5054, has moderate rates for room, breakfast, and parking. Other options in the moderate range include **Five Chimneys Bed and Breakfast**, 238 Charlotte Street West, 506/635-1888, midway between the Digby ferry slip and the city center; and **Colonial Inn**, 175 City Road, 506/652-3000 or 800/561-4667. Motels along Manawagonish Road and Rothesay Avenue offer basic budget accommodations.

If you feel the urge to stay overnight on Campobello Island, double rooms at the **Friar's Bay Motor Lodge**, Welshpool, 506/752-2056, are fairly inexpensive, and the **Owen House B&B**, Welshpool, 506/752-2977, is in the moderate range. Both establishments are open seasonally.

The one place everybody knows about in St. Andrews is the famous **Algonquin Resort**, 184 Adolphus Street, 506/529-8823 or 800/866-5577. Surrounded by beautiful gardens, this luxury landmark Canadian Pacific property is also known as the Castle by the Sea. The best way to absorb the atmosphere of this historic seaside resort is to stay in one of its charming heritage inns, which are expensive but a real treat. The ultra-upscale **Kingsbrae Arms**, 219 King Street, 506/529-1897, an idyllic five-star establishment, boasts fireplaces, marble baths, and sweeping water views. **Windsor House**, 132 Water Street, 506/529-3330 or 888/890-WIND, is the "newest" heritage inn in town; it is a 200-year-old former family home that was recently refurbished and converted into an elegant inn furnished with antiques and an extensive art collection.

Accommodations in Sussex on average are quite reasonable, with options including the **Amsterdam Inn**, 143 Main Street, 506/432-5050 or 800/468-2828, and the **Blue Bird Motel at Four Corners**, Exit 416, Route 2, 506/433-2557 or 888/583-9111.

CAMPING

The huge **Rockwood Park** campground, off Rothesay Avenue in Saint John, 506/652-4050, lies just north of the downtown area. It has small lakes, attractive sites, and a view of the city. Close to the center of things, it's open from May through October. The rate for tenters is $17 and for fully serviced sites, $18. On Campobello Island, a campground is located in **Herring Cove Provincial Park**, 506/752-7010; open from May through October, its unserviced sites cost $21.50 a night and its serviced ones are $24 a night. In St. Andrews, **Passamaquoddy Park Campground**, 506/529-3439, is also open May through October and charges $17 for unserviced sites, $21 for semi-serviced sites, and $25 for fully serviced ones.

Scenic Route: Grand Manan Island

The largest of the three Fundy Isles, Grand Manan is at once tranquil and exotically beautiful with its mix of forests, towering cliffs, and long beaches. You can whale-watch, bird-watch, or just take in the sun on the beach. In spring and summer, huge numbers of birds nest on the island's cliffs. Awed when he visited in the 1800s, John James Audubon did many of his sketches at Grand Manan. Indeed, the island is a wonderful place to sketch, paint, or take photos. The **Hole-in-the-Wall**, a massive shoreline rock formation that has a huge hole right through its middle, may be the most-photographed scene on the island; it's in the North Head area, along a trail that begins near the Marathon Hotel.

The island requires at least a full day to explore properly. (Just to get there and back by ferry takes nearly four hours.) About 25 kilometers long and 12 kilometers wide (roughly 15 by 7 miles), it can also be "done" in a week or a month; it all depends on your inclination. With Deer Island and Campobello, Grand Manan makes up the so-called West Isles Archipelago.

To visit Grand Manan, turn south off Highway 1 about 5 kilometers (3 miles)

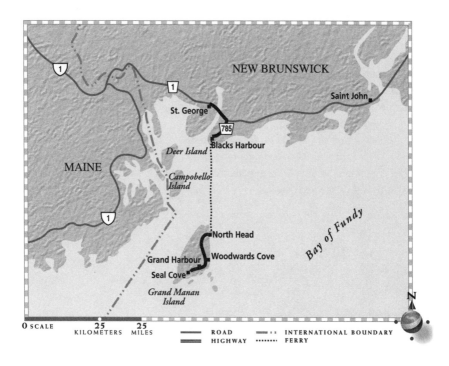

east of St. George onto Highway 785. It leads to **Blacks Harbour** where car ferries to Grand Manan can be found. The ferries run year-round, three times a day from Labor Day until late June, and six times a day from late June to Labor Day. Round-trip rates are $8.75 for adults and $4.40 for children ages 5 to 12, plus $26.20 per vehicle. Call Coastal Transport in St. John at 506/636-3922 for schedule information. The crossing to North Head on Grand Manan takes between one and one-half and two hours.

With scenic walking trails all over the island, a full day on Grand Manan passes quickly. Plus, you may want to take a whale-watching excursion on the bay, to view the behemoths from up-close. You can also watch and try to identify some of the more than 240 species of birds that visit here regularly. If you want to stay overnight in one of the island's several small communities, bear in mind that it is wise to book ahead because relatively few accommodations are available on the island.

North Head offers a couple of interesting places to stay. The Compass Rose (506/662-8570), a heritage inn, is actually two old houses with antique-furnished rooms looking out toward the sea. Breakfast, lunch, afternoon tea, and dinner are all available in the dining room. Double rooms run from $69 to $89, including breakfast. The century-old Marathon Inn (506/662-8144) is relatively luxurious, complete with a heated swimming pool. Rates run from $65 to $90 for doubles. Both are open from May to October. The Manan Island Inn (506/662-8624), also in North Head, offers double rooms for between $59 and $100. Several inns or B&Bs can be found in **Seal Cove**, including Rosalie's Guest House (506/662-3344) at $45 for a double. Campgrounds are found in Anchorage Provincial Park, 506/662-7022, and Hole-in-the-Wall Park, 506/662-3152.

When it's time to eat, go for seafood since fishing is the major occupation in this region. Restaurants on Grand Manan tend to be casual and include the Griff-Inn in North Head and, in Seal Cove, the Water's Edge, which serves homemade Italian dishes as well as seafood dinners.

8
PRINCE EDWARD
ISLAND

In 1543 French explorer Jacques Cartier described Prince Edward Island as "the fairest land that may possibly be seen." Indeed, its tranquil, bucolic beauty helped provide Lucy Maud Montgomery with inspiration for her perennial bestseller, *Anne of Green Gables*. The coastline is indented with tidal inlets, steep sandstone bluffs, and long sandy beaches. Inland, gently rolling hills and the distinctive rust-red soil caused by heavy concentrations of iron oxide provide a study in color contrast. In summer, visitors swell the population of 135,000 sixfold, and Charlottetown, Cavendish, and Summerside in particular can be pretty busy. Even so, long stretches of pristine coastline are virtually deserted, picturesque villages all over the island seem to doze in the sunshine, and red-earth roads snake away toward the sea.

Separated from Nova Scotia and New Brunswick by the Northumberland Strait, crescent-shaped Prince Edward Island is a mere 224 kilometers (135 miles) long and 60 kilometers (36 miles) wide at its widest point. Island life is based chiefly on the treasures of the sea and on farming the fertile red soil for, most notably, potatoes. Tourism also ranks highly. Canadians in other provinces refer to Prince Edward Island as PEI, whereas residents call it simply the Island and refer to nonresidents as being "from away." The island has other names that reflect its history and character: the Garden of the Gulf, the Million-Acre Farm, the Cradle of Confederation, or, less lyrically, Spud Island.

PRINCE EDWARD ISLAND

Gulf of St. Lawrence

Northumberland Strait

East Point
South Lake
North Lake
Elmira
Souris
Brundenall Provincial Park
Fantasyland Provincial Park
Wood Islands
Montague
Orwell
Point Prim
Hillsborough Bay
Charlottetown
Fort Amherst National Historic Park
Charlottetown Harbour
Mount Steward
Confederation Trail
Bonshaw
Cornwall
Strathgartney Provincial Park
Victoria
Borden
Brackley Beach
Prince Edward Island National Park
Cavendish
New London
Kensington
Summerside
Lennox Island
Park Corner
Malpeque
Burlington
Malpeque Bay
Miscouche
Mont-Carmel
Cap-Egmont
Mill River Provincial Park
Green Park Provincial Park
Lennox Island
Tignish
North Cape
Egmont Bay
West Point
Cedar Dunes Provincial Park

16A
2
2
4
3
2
2
209
2
2
6
2
8
20
101
1A
1
12
163
12
17
2
14

0 SCALE

25 KILOMETERS
25 MILES

——— ROAD
········· BOUNDARY

✦ PLACE OF INTEREST

MORE PRINCE EDWARD ISLAND FACTS

Around 8,000 to 10,000 years ago, ancestors of the Mi'kmaq Indians were the first humans to live on PEI. They spent summers along the shore feasting on the abundant shellfish. Eventually they stayed year-round, naming the island *Abegweit,* or "land cradled on the waves." The first Europeans to arrive were the French, but eventually the British took over and the island was settled mainly by English, Scottish, and Irish immigrants. Today, PEI's population remains overwhelmingly British in origin; in fact, it is arguably the most Celtic place in North America, although the Acadian culture still thrives on one part of the island.

PEI's major claim to international fame, of course, is *Anne of Green Gables.* Rescued from an orphanage, Anne wins the hearts of Matthew and Marilla Cuthbert and the community of Avonlea. But how could she not? She is articulate, plucky, sensitive, caring, and fiery all at once. Mark Twain described her as the "dearest and most moving and most delightful child in fiction since the immortal Alice." First published in 1908, Lucy Maud Montgomery's novel went on to win worldwide acclaim, and now some 350,000 visitors descend each year on Green Gables House, the re-creation of the Cuthbert home in Cavendish (see Sightseeing Highlights). That's almost half of the 800,000 visitors who come to the island every year. In addition to Green Gables House, visitors can tour several other Montgomery-related sites, including the author's birthplace. Needless to say, Anne dolls, Anne T-shirts, Anne books, Anne potato chips, and Anne souvenir license plates are available.

SIGHTS

- Ⓐ Acadian Pioneer Village
- Ⓑ Bottle Houses
- Ⓒ Charlottetown
- Ⓓ Confederation Trail
- Ⓔ Green Gables House
- Ⓕ Lennox Island
- Ⓖ Lucy Maud Montgomery Birthplace
- Ⓗ Orwell Corner Historic Village

SIGHTS (continued)

- Ⓘ Prince Edward Island National Park
- Ⓙ Victoria-by-the-Sea
- Ⓚ Woodleigh

FOOD

- Ⓐ Étoile de Mer
- Ⓛ Inn at Bay Fortune
- Ⓜ Mémé Jane's Restaurant
- Ⓙ Mrs. Profitt's Tea Shop
- Ⓝ Seasons in Thyme

LODGING

- Ⓞ Dalvay-by-the-Sea Country Inn
- Ⓟ Doctor's Inn
- Ⓛ Inn at Bay Fortune
- Ⓠ West Point Lighthouse
- Ⓡ Windsong Farm

CAMPING

- Ⓢ Cabot Beach Provincial Park
- Ⓣ Canvendish Campground
- Ⓤ Vacationland Travel Park

Note: Items with the same letter are located in the same area.

A PERFECT DAY ON PRINCE EDWARD ISLAND

Start off in Prince Edward Island National Park, where you can easily while away some lazy hours on the beach. Then rent a bike and travel some of the Confederation Trail to take in scenery that you can't see from the road. Stop in at the pretty little village of Victoria-by-the-Sea and browse through the quaint shops. Heading back to Charlottetown, stroll its tree-lined Victorian streets and enjoy a drink in historic Old Charlottetown on the waterfront. Then find an all-you-can-eat lobster supper and round out the day by going to a *ceilidh*, an evening of informal traditional maritime and Gaelic music.

ORIENTATION

You can't go wrong as a visitor to PEI; it's geared toward looking after tourists. The *Prince Edward Island Visitors Guide,* a 200-page publication updated annually by the provincial tourist board, divides the island into six scenic regions. "North by Northwest" takes in the western wing of the island, an area of contorted coastlines and red sandstone cliffs. The "Ship to Shore" region is home to Summerside, a popular tourist town and cradle of the island's Acadian culture. "Anne's Land" includes Cavendish, Green Gables House, Prince Edward Island National Park, and other popular attractions. "Charlotte's Shore" includes Charlottetown and the central south shore. "Bays and Dunes" in the northeast offers endless coastline and white-sand beaches. "Hills and Harbors" is the hilly, scenic region east of Charlottetown. Or you can opt to follow three scenic routes that together cover the whole island—Lady Slipper Drive in the west, Blue Heron Drive in the center, and Kings Byway Drive in the east.

Even if you get lost, the worst thing that can happen is you discover a side road that leads to red sandstone cliffs overlooking a deserted beach or emerald hills rolling gently away toward the coastline. PEI is so small that the sea is visible from almost anywhere on the island. "If only in a tiny blue gap between distant hills," Lucy Maud Montgomery wrote, "or a turquoise gleam through the dark boughs of spruce fringing an estuary."

SIGHTSEEING HIGHLIGHTS: CHARLOTTETOWN

In 1864, representatives of Canada (Ontario and Quebec), Nova Scotia, New Brunswick, and PEI met in Charlottetown to discuss federal union of the British North American colonies. It was the first of a series of meetings that eventually led to the Confederation of Canada. Charlottetown, capital of PEI, proudly calls itself "the Birthplace of Canada," although other colonies joined the new federation in 1867, but PEI did not do so until 1873. With its beautiful Victorian houses, Old Charlottetown is particularly lovely; go for a stroll on your own or book a walking tour led by a guide in period costume. For more information, call 800/955-1864.

★★★★ PEAKE'S WHARF
Waterfront, 800/955-1864
Charlottetown's recently renovated waterfront area is a magnet for visitors. A picturesque historic enclave and the focal point of Old Charlottetown, it offers restaurants and craft shops housed in refurbished heritage marine buildings, plus a landscaped boardwalk along the waterfront. Many of the eateries have outdoor seating overlooking the water. From Peake's Wharf you can stroll up Great George Street, a National Historic Area, or into Confederation Landing Park, also on the waterfront.
Details: (2 hours)

★★★ CONFEDERATION CENTRE ART GALLERY
145 Richmond Street, 902/628-1864 or 800/565-0278
www.confederationcentre.com
Housed in the Confederation Centre of the Arts adjacent to Province House in Charlottetown, the gallery's extensive permanent collection of works by Canadian artists makes it one of the country's major art galleries.
Details: Open summer 10–5; shorter hours in winter. Nominal admission fee. (2 hours)

★★★ PROVINCE HOUSE
2 Palmers Lane, 902/566-7626
http://parkscanada.pch.gc.ca
This house was the site of the historic 1864 Charlottetown Conference. Today it is a National Historic Site. The Confederation Chamber, where the meeting was held, has been restored to appear as it did in the 1800s, complete with dark red, floor-length curtains, and a long table where the delegates met. The building also houses the provincial legislature. Regular guided tours are available.
Details: Corner of Great George and Richmond streets. Open July–Aug 9–6; Sept–June 9–5. Free. (1 hour)

SIGHTSEEING HIGHLIGHTS: PRINCE EDWARD ISLAND

★★★★ **CONFEDERATION TRAIL**
888/734-7529

Prince Edward Island is custom-made for cyclists. It's not flat, exactly, but the slopes are gentle and it rarely gets really hot thanks to the ocean breezes. Best of all, miles of abandoned rail lines have been converted into a network of off-road trails for walkers and cyclists (and, in winter, snowmobilers). With more than 225 kilometers (135 miles) of excellent rolled stonedust surface completed, the island is well on its way to boasting a tip-to-tip network of trails that will ultimately run for 350 kilometers (210 miles) from Tignish in the west to Elmira in the east. (The portion of the trail that will run through the central part of the province will be the last to be completed.) Meanwhile, it's the perfect way to visit previously unseen areas, get close to nature, and yet still be just minutes from services like B&Bs and cafés.

Details: The trail has signage, rest stops, shelters every three miles or so, and easy-to-find entry points. Local companies are joining in the trail spirit, and many rentals, packages, and tours are available. (3 hours)

★★★★ **GREEN GABLES HOUSE**
Prince Edward Island National Park
902/672-6350 http://parkscanada.pch.gc.ca

If you loved *Anne of Green Gables*, you naturally must visit Green Gables House where author Montgomery's cousins lived and on which she based her heroine's home. It is now a museum that re-creates the house as described in the novel. You can also view an exhibit about the author and her works (she wrote eight books about Anne). On the grounds outside, visitors can explore the Haunted Wood, Lover's Lane, and other familiar settings from the novel, not to mention the graves of Montgomery and her husband. Expect to encounter hordes of visitors, including busloads of Japanese tourists; they adore the novel and visit PEI in great numbers to see Green Gables.

Details: The house is at the western end of Prince Edward Island National Park. May–Sept 9–5 but June 21–Aug 27 9–8. Nominal admission fee. (1 hour)

★★★★ PRINCE EDWARD ISLAND NATIONAL PARK
902/672-6350 or 800/213-7275
http:parkscanada.pch.gc.ca

This park of lovely beaches, sand dunes, and sandstone cliffs runs in a narrow strip along 40 kilometers (24 miles) of the island's north shore, facing the Gulf of St. Lawrence. Unfortunately, the incursion of tourists has done its share of damage here, and parts of the beach are closed to the public in summer to protect the piping plover, a small shorebird that has been declared an endangered species. Drive the Gulf Shore Parkway, which skirts the sand, and stop to take one of the boardwalks and paths that lead to the water's edge (the boardwalks were built to protect the dunes from foot traffic). In 1998, Parks Canada acquired the Greenwich Sand Dune System, an ecologically unique region of migrating dunes that separates St. Peter's Bay

"Passport to Prince Edward Island Heritage" is a booklet of maps, descriptions, and admission details for 31 museums; you can pick up a copy at visitor information centers and museums.

from the Gulf of St. Lawrence, as an extension to the national park. As of the year 2000, a full interpretive program will explain the unusual parabolic dunes and the archeological history of the site, and visitors will also have access to some of the amazon white-sand beaches surrounding the dunes system.

Details: *The Cavendish Visitor Centre contains an interpretive center at the western extremity of the park. Nominal admission fee. (3 hours)*

★★★★ VICTORIA-BY-THE-SEA
902/658-2649 (Visitor's Center)

Victoria is a delightfully quaint town nestled between hills and overlooking a harbor. The operating lighthouse has a museum that relates Victoria's history, but mostly this village is just nice to stroll around and an ideal place to stop for a break in one of the many tearooms. The shopping in Victoria is pretty good, too. Stop in at Island Chocolates if you're a chocoholic, and at the Studio Gallery for a sampling of photographs, batiks, etchings, and watercolors by local artists.

TRAVELING WITH KIDS

PEI's tourism industry is geared in many ways toward families with young kids, and you'll find all manner of amusement parks and the like designed to appeal to the young 'uns. One of the best, and one of the best-kept tourist secrets on the island, is **King's Castle Provincial Park,** Route 348 near Murray River, 902/962-7422, featuring lots of play equipment and statues of favorite storybook characters, like Goldilocks, Peter Rabbit, and Little Red Riding Hood. **Encounter Creek,** TransCanada Highway, New Haven, 902/675-2871, is a water and theme park near Charlottetown that's ideal for families. The **Mill River Fun Park,** Route 2 West, Woodstock, 902/859-2071, has activities for all ages, including toddlers. These options are just a few of the many activities available for families.

Details: Half an hour west of Charlottetown on the south coast (Charlotte's Shore region). (2 hours)

★★★ ORWELL CORNER HISTORIC VILLAGE
902/651-8510

A restored 1800s crossroads farming village, Orwell Corner is now an historic site featuring farms, a school, a church, and various other buildings. One of the most interesting structures is a farmhouse that also serves as a store and post office and has a dressmaker's shop upstairs. All the buildings have been restored on their original sites. In summer, *ceilidhs* are held every Wednesday, and Thursdays are kid's days.

Details: Off the TransCanada 30 kilometers east of Charlottetown; follow the signs. Open mid-May–mid-Oct 9–5. Nominal admission fee, free for children under 12. (2 hours)

★★ ACADIAN PIONEER VILLAGE
Route 11, Mont-Carmel, 902/854-2227 or 800/567-3228

This re-creation of the 1820s Acadian settlement of Mont-Carmel comes complete with church, school, blacksmith shop, store, and houses. They're all log structures—even the church's altar is made from logs. Visitors can also sample some authentic Acadian cuisine. **Details:** *Route 11, Mont-Carmel (Ship to Shore region). June–Sept 9–7. Nominal admission fee. (1 hour)*

★★ BOTTLE HOUSES
Route 11, Cap Egmont, 902/854-2987

These structures are so bizarre that you simply must see them: a chapel, a house, and a tavern all made entirely of bottles cemented together. Talk about recycling! They are the work of the late Edouard Arsenault, a retired fisherman who began the project in the mid-1970s and used more than 25,000 bottles by the time he was through. You can go inside each structure. **Details:** *Route 11 in Cap Egmont (Ship to Shore region). Open July–Aug 9–8; June and Sept 10–6. Nominal admission fee. (1 hour)*

★★ LENNOX ISLAND
Route 163 off Route 12, 902/831-2653

The Mi'kmaq families now living on Lennox Island Reserve are descendants of PEI's first human inhabitants. At the southern tip of the island is a small museum with native artifacts and paintings, plus an arts-and-crafts shop nearby with silver, beaded jewelry, pottery, and carvings. Also on the island is Micmac Productions (902/831-2277), Canada's only manufacturer of fine earthenware Mi'kmaq figurines. **Details:** *Lennox Island is in the Ship to Shore region. Craft shop open June–Sept daily. (1 hour)*

★★ LUCY MAUD MONTGOMERY BIRTHPLACE
New London, 902/886-2099

One of the many *Anne of Green Gables* sites that can be visited. The author was born in 1874 in this house, which now contains period furniture and Montgomery memorabilia, including her wedding dress and personal scrapbooks containing copies of her stories and poems. **Details:** *Intersection of Routes 60 and 20 in New London (Anne's Land region). Open mid-May–early Oct daily. Nominal admission fee. (1 hour)*

★★ WOODLEIGH
Route 101, 902/836-3401

See Britain without leaving North America! Woodleigh is a collection of large-scale models of historic British buildings and castles, painstakingly hand-constructed by the late (and presumably eccentric) Lt. Col. E. W. Johnston, who was quoted as saying: "Though the temporal body may sojourn to far and distant shores, the Celtic heart can never be at rest." You'll find the Tower of London and Dunvegan Castle among other famous structures, as well as a Shakespeare section with replicas of his mother's home and Anne Hathaway's cottage in Stratford-upon-Avon. Some replicas are large enough to walk into and are furnished with authentic items imported from Britain.

Details: *Route 101 from Kensington to Route 234 (Anne's Land region). Open late May–mid-Oct daily. $8 adults, $7.50 seniors, $4.50 ages 6–12.*

FITNESS AND RECREATION

For walking and bicycling, visit the Confederation Trail (see Sightseeing Highlights); local rental companies can provide you with a bike. Hikers won't find anything really challenging, but the national park has marked trails ranging from one to eight kilometers in length. Four provincial parks—Green Park, Mill River, Strathgartney, and Brudenell—also have marked trails. Horseback riding is available at several spots on the island, including beach rides along Brudenell River; contact Brudenell Trail Rides, 902/652-2396. Outside Expeditions, North Rustico, 902/652-2434 or 800/207-3899, offers sea-kayaking expeditions along the coast. For wintertime visitors, the island's rolling hills are ideally suited for cross-country skiing.

In recent years the island has been pushing golf big-time, noting that its courses are uncrowded, well-conditioned, challenging, and inexpensive, not to mention unbelievably scenic. Some of the layouts are ranked in *SCORE Magazine's* top 50 Canadian courses, whereas others are reserved for the more casual golfer. The island has a total of 18 courses, plus new courses opening periodically, with the three crown jewels being Mill River, 902/859-8873 or 800/377-8339, Brudenell River, 800/377-8336, and The Links at Crowbush Cove, 902/961-7300 or 800/377-8337. The newest big-news course is Dundarave, 800/377-8336, which opened in the summer of 1999 next door to Brudenell River Golf Course. Also on the site is the new Brudenell Resort Golf Academy. Another new nine-hole course, Countryview Golf Club, 902/675-2800, opened in 1999 as well; it's located near the West River about 20 minutes from Charlottetown. The golf season runs from May to October.

The provincial tourist information line, 888/734-7529, can provide complete information on all these activities.

CHARLOTTETOWN

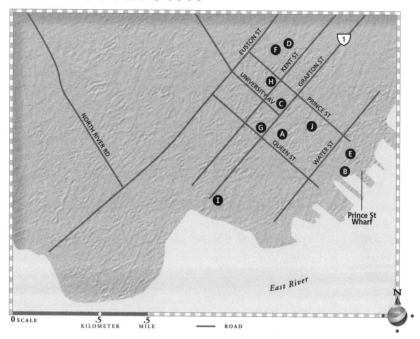

SIGHTS

Ⓐ Confederation Centre Art Gallery
Ⓑ Peake's Wharf
Ⓒ Province House

FOOD

Ⓑ Anchor & Oar House
Ⓓ Claddagh Room
Ⓔ Lobster on the Wharf
Ⓕ Olde Dublin Pub
Ⓑ Peake's Quay Restaurant

LODGING

Ⓖ Carriage House
Ⓗ Dutchess of Kent Inn
Ⓘ Heritage Harbour House Inn
Ⓙ Inns on Great George

Note: Items with the same letter are located in the same area.

FOOD

Surrounded by waters abundant with lobsters, mackerel, scallops, mussels, oysters, and clams, the entire island is clearly a seafood lover's paradise. (This is not to say you can't eat other types of meals; even the seafood restaurants tend to offer steak as well.) Partake of a lobster supper if you can—the island is famous for them. These all-you-can-eat feasts of lobster, fresh vegetables, and homemade breads are served by restaurants all over the island; you'll see advertisements for them all over the place. The island is also famous for its blue mussels and Malpeque oysters, culled from Malpeque Bay.

In Charlottetown, dining options range from the aforementioned seafood to casual pub-style dining. **Peake's Quay Restaurant**, on the waterfront, 902/368-1330, boasts the island's largest outdoor dining area and a wide variety of seafood and other dishes and is open from May to September. The specialty at **Lobster on the Wharf**, Prince Street Wharf, 902/368-2888, is self-evident, although steaks and pasta are also available. The **Anchor & Oar House**, Peake's Wharf boardwalk, 902/566-2222, dishes up barbecued seafood, hamburgers, and standard pub fare from mid-May to mid-October. The upscale **Claddagh Room**, 131 Sydney Street, 902/892-9661, offers fresh live lobster and other seafood in the historic district. By way of contrast, another restaurant at the same address, the casual **Olde Dublin Pub**, 131 Sydney Street, 902/892-6992, serves up snacks and meals, plus live music six nights a week in summer.

The two top restaurants in all of PEI are considered to be **Seasons in Thyme**, 644 Water Street, Summerside, 902/888-DINE (3463), and the **Inn at Bay Fortune**, Route 310 in Bay Fortune, 902/687-3745, both of which make brilliant use of the wonderful and abundant local ingredients such as lobster, mussels, and oysters. A cooking show called the Inn Chef, which airs on Canada's Life Network and stars inn chef emeritus Michael Smith, is filmed in the kitchen at the Inn at Bay Fortune.

Elsewhere on the island, **Mrs. Profitt's Tea Shop**, Victoria-by-the-Sea, 902/658-2503, serves lunch and traditional afternoon tea in the sedate surroundings of the Orient Hotel on Main Street in quaint Victoria-by-the-Sea. You can sample traditional home-style Acadian dishes at **Mémé Jane's Restaurant**, 6 Lady Slipper Drive, Miscouche, 902/436-9600, or **Étoile de Mer**, Le Village de l'Acadie, Mont-Carmel, 902/854-2227.

LODGING

Charlottetown features a wide variety of lodgings, from inexpensive motels through pricey inns, but the most attractive, central, and moderately priced establishments are the historic B&Bs and inns in Old Charlottetown. They include the **Carriage House**, 37 Grafton Street, 902/368-1426 or 888/207-5444, a restored, antique-filled home located one block from the Confederation Centre for the Arts, and the **Duchess of Kent Inn**, 218 Kent Street, 902/566-5826, another designated heritage home, featuring a three-story "turret" corner that's been converted to a bed-and-breakfast; both establishments are non-smoking. **Heritage Harbour House Inn**, 9 Grafton

Bridging the Gap

Part of PEI's unique character stems from its physical separation from the rest of the country. That distinction changed in 1997, however, when the Confederation Bridge between New Brunswick and PEI was completed, providing 24-hour access to a province that previously had been accessible only by air or ferry. Result: an astounding 60 percent increase in tourism to the island during the year in which the bridge was opened.

When a contest was held to name the new bridge, the most popular suggestion was Span of Green Gables, in honor of *Anne of Green Gables*. Predictably and prosaically, however, the powers that be settled on Confederation Bridge instead. All the same, a towering new statue of Anne now greets visitors as they drive off the foot of the bridge and onto the island.

You cross the Confederation Bridge from Cape Tormentine, New Brunswick, to Borden-Carleton. This structure is the world's longest continuous multispan bridge over ice-inhabited waters (whew!). It's nine miles long and takes about 10 minutes to drive across. The bridge is very high off the water, but as you drive across you have no sense of that, thanks to the three-foot-high concrete sidewalls. They block the view in addition to breaking the wind, which can whistle something fierce down the Northumberland Strait. An astonishing engineering feat, the gracefully curving span opened in mid-1997 after years of controversy. Initially, many residents worried that Prince Edward Island's special character would be irrevocably changed once the fixed link was in place. However, as construction neared completion, on time and on budget, public approval for the project increased. The fee to use the bridge is $36.50 per vehicle. Pedestrians and cyclists cross via a shuttle.

If you're arriving from Nova Scotia, you can catch a car ferry to Wood Islands from Caribou. Northumberland Ferries, 902/566-3838 or 888/249-7245, run from May to December. The crossing takes about 45 minutes, and the cost is $45 per vehicle. Borden-Carleton is less than one hour west of Charlottetown, and Wood Islands is about 45 minutes east of the capital city.

Street, 902/892-6633 or 800/405-0066, is a gracious establishment overlooking the water. The **Inns on Great George**, Great George Street, 902/892-0606 or 800/361-1118, are a cluster of five elegant 1800s Georgian-style buildings on Great George Street in Old Charlottetown.

In Brackley Beach on the north shore, 12 miles northwest of Charlottetown on Highway 15, **Windsong Farm**, Route 16, 902/672-2874, is a pre-Victorian farmhouse nestled in the countryside with antique-furnished guest rooms. **Dalvay-by-the-Sea Country Inn**, Route 6, 902/672-2048, is renowned for its dining room, but the rest of the inn is attractive, too. None of the 26 guest rooms in the gingerbready Victorian mansion has a telephone, radio, or TV, and the main activity is relaxing. The luxurious inn is located near the eastern boundary of Prince Edward Island National Park. It is partially wheelchair accessible.

As noted in the Food section, memorable dining can also be found at the **Inn at Bay Fortune**, RR4, Souris, 902/687-3745, acclaimed for its creative cuisine that uses fresh island vegetables and seafood. The upscale inn overlooks Fortune Harbour off the eastern part of the island (Bays and Dunes region). **The Doctor's Inn**, Route 167, Tyne Valley, 902/831-3057, in a charming village in the Ship to Shore region, is a 140-year-old home that's open year-round and charges moderate rates.

The **West Point Lighthouse**, Route 24, O'Leary, 902/859-3605 or 800/764-6854, is billed as Canada's first inn in a functioning Coast Guard lighthouse; it offers nine moderately priced rooms. Unlike all the other establishments mentioned here, breakfast isn't included at the lighthouse inn.

You might also want to consider staying on a farm or renting a cottage. Island farm families have opened their homes to guests for many years. They're all working farms, and most have housekeeping units or cottages on their land. As for the cottages, you have a wide variety from which to choose. The *Prince Edward Island Visitors Guide* has all the information you need. Or call 888/267-6667 for accommodations vacancy information.

CAMPING

Campgrounds and trailer parks are located throughout the province. You'll find 13 such facilities in provincial parks and 3 in Prince Edward Island National Park. More than three dozen privately run campgrounds are also available. The Anne's Land region alone has nearly 20 campgrounds. Listed here are just a few of the options. **Cavendish Campground**, Prince Edward Island National Park, 902/672-6350, is right by the ocean and offers 225 unserviced sites as well as 78 serviced ones, with daily rates of between $17 and $21.

SIDE TRIP: MAGDALEN ISLANDS

Also known as Îles de la Madeleine, these windswept but charming is-
lands in the middle of the Gulf of St. Lawrence are part of the
province of Quebec but are much closer physically to Prince Edward
Island than to Quebec. That's why they're mentioned here as well as in
the Montreal chapter.

If you have the time, the islands are well worth roaming around to
take in their long sand dunes, cliffs, lagoons, bright wooden houses,
and hospitable inhabitants. The islands have 100 kilometers of roads
and 300 kilometers of beaches, which provides an idea of what you
can expect! A magnet for savvy bird-watchers, kayakers, windsurfers,
divers (more than 400 wrecks sleep beneath the water offshore), and
other outdoorsy types, the necklace of 12 islands is a world unto itself
where time doesn't seem to matter much. It's the ideal vacation spot,
in other words.

The easiest and least expensive way to reach the Magdalen
Islands is via the ferry from the town of Souris on Prince Edward Island;
the trip takes five hours and runs daily in July and August, and six days
a week in April, May, June, and September. Call 418/986-3278,
888/986-3278 or, in Souris, 902/687-2181 for ferry reservations.

The islands are also connected by air from most Quebec cities.
Alternatively, you can take a two-day boat trip from Montreal. Call
Tourisme Quebec at 800/363-7777 for details.

Cabot Beach Provincial Park, near Kensington, 902/836-8945, where about two-thirds of the 150 or so sites are unserviced, charges between $15 and $20 daily, and offers extensive recreation and interpretive programs. Overlooking the waters of Brackley Bay, **Vacationland Travel Park**, Brackley Bay, 902/672-2317, boasts 300 serviced sites as well as a new heated swimming pool plus softball, mini-golf, and other activities.

Campgrounds in provincial parks can be booked through any of the province tourist information centers scattered around the island. National park campgrounds do not accept reservations, but visitor information centers can report vacancies. In the case of privately operated campgrounds, call direct. Consult the *Prince Edward Island Visitors Guide* for complete listings.

NIGHTLIFE

Ceilidh (KAY-lee) means party, although technically it's derived from the Gaelic word for visit. Ceilidhs are held all over the island practically every night of the week; some are gatherings of family and friends, whereas some are crowded with friends, strangers, and passersby. The parties are noisy and musical, with fiddles and Irish dancing and, usually, many drinks. You can sit back and watch, or you can jump up and become part of it. No two ceilidhs are the same, so expect surprises. Orwell Corner Historic Village east of Charlottetown holds a ceilidh every Wednesday evening in the community hall.

The island has a pretty active theater scene during peak tourist season. Many visitors consider the musical *Anne of Green Gables* a must; it's been playing to full houses for 34 years now. It's performed nightly at the Confederation Centre of the Arts, Charlottetown, 902/566-1267 or 800/565-0278, as part of the annual Charlottetown Festival. In Summerside, meanwhile, the new Harbourfront Jubilee Theatre, Summerside, 902/888-2500 or 800/708-6505, features a down-east musical with traditional song, dance, and theater. The Victoria Playhouse, Victoria-by-the-Sea, 800/925-2025, presents professional repertory productions and live music every summer. To plan a night on the town, pick up the free monthly paper, *The Buzz*, available at many outlets and tourist information centers.

SHOPPING

In addition to the usual goods, more than 80 craft outlets throughout the island offer everything from pottery and woodworking to hand-painted silk. The Dunes Studio Gallery, Route 15, Brackley Beach, 902/672-2586, housed in a magnificent complex that's a work of art unto itself, is one of the best. You can also find antique shops aplenty, and native crafts are available at the Lennox Island shop (see Sightseeing Highlights). Old Charlottetown features a variety of appealing gift and craft emporiums, including a shop that sells nothing but *Anne of Green Gables* wares.

9
HALIFAX

Replete with historic buildings and tree-lined streets, Halifax sits on one of the largest natural harbors in the world. This seafaring city of 115,000 seems tailor-made for walking; from the Citadel, its most-visited tourist site, the picturesque downtown area spreads toward the waterfront, itself lined with heritage buildings that now house bars, boutiques, and restaurants.

As a major East Coast port, Halifax was a hive of activity during the two world wars because it was a base from which troops sailed for Europe. During World War I, in 1917, a munitions ship and a relief ship collided in the harbor, creating the largest man-made blast in history before the atom bomb.

Now a busy international port and the largest city in Atlantic Canada, Halifax is also the cultural center of Nova Scotia, offering a wide variety of music, art, and theater. It further boasts that it has the highest ratio of educational facilities per capita of any city in North America, and because it is a university town, numerous secondhand bookstores and a lively nightlife abound. Considering its size, Halifax also offers an unusually wide array of interesting dining options, running the gamut from fresh seafood to lively pubs and exotic ethnic eateries.

A PERFECT DAY IN HALIFAX

Any visit to Halifax has to include a trip to the Halifax Citadel, simply because it offers such a terrific view of the city and harbor beyond. Nearby, the

HALIFAX

glorious Halifax Public Gardens are ideal for a morning stroll, followed by a wander along Spring Garden Road to check out the trendy shops. After lunch at one of the waterfront restaurants, take the commuter ferry across the harbor to the city of Dartmouth—an inexpensive way to enjoy a harbor vista. Back on the Halifax waterfront, wander through Historic Properties and finish up at the fascinating Maritime Museum of the Atlantic, where the most popular draw these days is the exhibition about the *Titanic*.

ORIENTATION

The central part of the city occupies a fat peninsula of land girded by Bedford Basin to the north, a long slender inlet called the Northwest Arm to the southwest, and Halifax Harbor and the Atlantic to the south. Across the Narrows, which link Bedford Basin and Halifax Harbor, lies the city of Dartmouth. Commuter ferries cross regularly between the two cities.

Walking is the way to go in Halifax; the major sights are all in a fairly compact area in the center of the city. Begin at the Citadel and work your way down toward the waterfront. If you get lost in central Halifax and can't see a street name, walk to the nearest corner and look down: the names of streets are carved into the sidewalk at each corner. On the other hand, parking here isn't the problem that it is in some other Canadian cities. If you want to drive, parking is available at both the Citadel and at Historic Properties.

Two provincial tourist information centers operate year-round in Halifax: one in the Red Store Building in Historic Properties, the other in the International Visitor Center at the corner of Barrington and Sackville Streets. Tourism Halifax also runs a year-round information center in the International Visitor Center.

SIGHTSEEING HIGHLIGHTS

★★★★ HALIFAX CITADEL
Citadel Hill, 902/426-5080, http://parkscanada.pch.gc.ca

SIGHTS

- Ⓐ Art Gallery of Nova Scotia
- Ⓑ Black Cultural Centre
- Ⓒ Discovery Center
- Ⓓ Halifax Citadel
- Ⓔ Historic Properties
- Ⓕ Maritime Museum of the Atlantic
- Ⓖ McNabs Island
- Ⓗ Nova Scotia Museum of Natural History
- Ⓘ Old Burying Ground
- Ⓙ Pier 21
- Ⓚ Point Pleasant Park
- Ⓛ Public Gardens
- Ⓜ St. Paul's Anglican Church

This star-shaped fortress provides not only a history lesson but also a dramatic view of the city and harbor below. Halifax was, for years, the bastion of British imperial control in North America. The present fortress, constructed between 1828 and 1856, is actually the fourth citadel on this site. The previous fortifications date back to 1749, when Halifax was founded. The hill was never attacked. When the British garrison finally departed in 1906, the site was handed over to the Canadian militia. It was manned by Canadian forces during both world wars and, during World War II, served as a temporary barracks for troops heading overseas. It was declared a National Historic Site in 1956.

One of the biggest events in Canada in the year 2000 is expected to be the Tall Ships gathering in Halifax, to be held from July 19 to 24. More than 150 vessels will take part in the event, a transatlantic race that will visit Cádiz, Bermuda, and Boston before arriving in Halifax. For details, point your browser at www. tallships2000.ns.ca.

In summer, soldiers in nineteenth-century uniforms drill on the parade grounds, and a bagpiper is usually on hand. The firing of the noon gun is worth seeing. The Citadel also includes sentries, vaulted barracks, a musketry gallery, and the privately operated Army Museum. For the best view of the city and the Town Clock, go up on the ramparts. The Town Clock, almost as much a Halifax landmark as the Citadel, was a gift to the city in 1803 from Prince Edward, son of King George III, who was manic about punctuality. It served as the garrison clock and is so big that it blocks part of the view of the city.

Details: *Walk uphill from the waterfront, and climb the Town Clock steps; the bridge entrance is to your right. If you're coming by car from Highway 102 or 103, take Exit 1A and proceed to downtown Halifax. The site entrance is located near the corner of Sackville and Brunswick Streets. Open mid-May–mid-Oct 9–5, open to 6 June 15–Aug 31. Guided tours of the Citadel leave every half-hour between 9:30 and 5 from near the entrance. $6 adults, $4.50 seniors, $3 ages 6–16, $14.75 families. Parking $2.75. (2 hours)*

★★★★ **HISTORIC PROPERTIES**
1869 Upper Water Street, 902/429-0530
This attraction is a picturesque three-block waterfront complex of boutiques, restaurants, and pubs housed in 10 restored wood and

stone buildings that date back to the early 1800s and are purportedly Canada's oldest waterfront buildings. With cobblestone courtyards, a waterside boardwalk, whimsical storefronts, fine restaurants, and plentiful outdoor cafés, it's a nice area just to stroll even if you're not in a shopping mood. Historic Properties is also the departure point for harbor cruises. Take one; you get to see much more of the cityscape, including Point Pleasant Park at the southern end of the city and McNabs Island in the harbor. Evening cruises are available as well. If you don't have time for a cruise, at least take the ferry across to Dartmouth and back. The ferry terminal is south of Historic Properties, and the seven-minute round-trip provides a good view of the skyline and some of the harbor.

Details: *Historic Properties is on the waterfront. (2 hours)*

★★★★ **MARITIME MUSEUM OF THE ATLANTIC**
1675 Lower Water Street, 902/424-7490
www.ednet.ns.ca/educ/museum/mma

Ever since the blockbuster film *Titanic* came out in December 1997, the permanent exhibit on the famous doomed vessel has been the main attraction at this museum, including one of the only intact *Titanic* deckchairs in the world (see Sidebar). This fascinating facility has many other interesting things to see, however, such as an exhibit called *Halifax Wrecked: The Story of the Halifax Explosion,* featuring photographs, artifacts (a comb and pencil belonging to schoolkids, for instance), and a 17-minute video about the disastrous event. Altogether, the museum's collection comprises more than 20,000 maritime artifacts. The options range from a set of extraordinary ship models to some real life-size boats, including Queen Victoria's royal barge, a beautiful *Bluenose*-class sloop, and a couple of dories (small boats used aboard fishing schooners because they were easily hoisted and lowered and could carry two men, their gear, and the catch). Upstairs, a display called *The Age of Steam* has models of everything from Arctic patrol vessels and Great Lakes freighters to magnificent Cunard liners. (Company founder Samuel Cunard was born in Halifax.) Berthed at the dock outside the museum is the C.S.S. *Acadia,* a onetime hydrographic survey vessel that is now a museum ship. The *Bluenose II,* the replica of the famous original *Bluenose* depicted on the Canadian dime, also docks at the museum's wharf when she's in Halifax.

Details: *Between Prince and Sackville Streets. Open June–mid-Oct*

Mon–Sat 9:30–5:30 but open to 8 on Tue, Sun 1–5; mid-Oct–May 31 Tue 9:30–8, Wed–Sat 9:30–5, Sun 1–5. In summer, $4.50 adults, $3.50 seniors/students, $1 ages 5–17; free rest of the year. (2 hours)

★★★★ PUBLIC GARDENS
Spring Garden Road and South Park Street

The peaceful and picturesque Public Gardens are just the ticket for an afternoon stroll. First created more than 150 years ago, this site is one of the few surviving examples of a formal Victorian public garden in the heart of a modern city. The gardens, lush with roses, hibiscus, dracaenas, and other varieties, are laid out around a lovely Victorian bandstand, where musical performances are given on summer Sunday afternoons.

Details: *The gardens lie just southwest of Citadel Hill. Open May–Nov, dawn to dusk. Free. (1 hour)*

★★★ McNABS ISLAND
902/490-5946 (Halifax Harbor)

Nearly 20 kilometers (about 12 miles) of bicycle trails wind past old forts and abandoned homesteads on historic McNabs Island, just inside the entrance to Halifax Harbor. In the past, small numbers of military and civilian families lived on the island, which was part of the city's defense system. Nowadays, it's a nature lover's retreat—no motorized vehicles are permitted on the island and no services of any kind are provided (so pack a picnic lunch). McNabs is famous for its Hangman's Beach, so named because one hundred years ago the British used to punish errant soldiers by tarring them and hanging them, leaving them swinging above the beach as a warning to sailors coming in and out of town. The ruins of Fort McNab are another historic highlight.

Details: *A ferry for the island departs regularly from Cable Wharf on the Halifax waterfront in summer. (2 hours)*

★★★ NOVA SCOTIA MUSEUM OF NATURAL HISTORY
1747 Summer Street, 902/424-7353 or 902/424-6099
http://nature.ednet.ns.ca

Dedicated to conserving remnants of the province's natural history, this museum offers a wide variety of displays housed in separate galleries devoted to geology, botany, marine life, birds, insects, and reptiles. Exhibits include skeletons and models of whales, a fossil of a

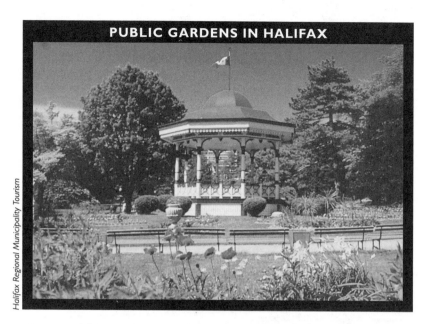

Halifax Regional Municipality Tourism

mastodon bone unearthed in 1835, a play area called the Bone Zone, life-size models of the earliest dinosaurs in Canada, Mi'kmaq quill work, and Acadian cultural materials. Naturalists are on duty to explain and assist.

Details: *Mon–Sat 9:30–5:30 but open to 8 on Wed, Sun 1–5:30; Oct 16–May 31 closes at 5, closed Mon. $3.50 adults, $3 seniors, $1 kids, $8 family. (1–2 hours)*

★★★ **PIER 21**
1055 Marginal Road, 877/474-3721, http://Pier21.ns.ca
An estimated one in five Canadians can trace some relationship to this Halifax immigration shed—no wonder Pier 21 is billed as "Canada's Ellis Island." Between 1928 and 1971, more than 1.5 million immigrants, refugees, war brides, and British evacuee children passed through Pier 21, making it the first place they set foot on the soil of their new homeland. Thousands of Canadian troops also passed through the shed on their way to battle in Europe, and again upon their return at the end of World War II. Opened as a National Historic Site in 1999, and considered one of the most significant sites in the country, Pier 21's high-tech interactive exhibits are designed so that visitors can experience not just the bureaucratic process of

going through immigration at the start of a new life in a new country but a keen sense of the accompanying feelings as well.

Details: *On the waterfront. Mid-May–mid-Oct 9–8; mid-Oct–mid-May 9–5. $6 adults, $5 seniors and students, $2.75 children under 14. (2 hours)*

★★★ ST. PAUL'S ANGLICAN CHURCH
1749 Argyle Street, 902/429-2240

Constructed in 1750, St. Paul's is the oldest standing building in Halifax as well as the oldest Protestant church in Canada. Its greatest claim to fame is the third window on the right on the upper level after you enter the church. You'll notice immediately that there seems to be a silhouette of a man's profile etched on the pane. Local lore has it that a piece of flying debris crashed through this window during the Halifax Explosion and left a hole whose outline duplicates the profile of the parson of the day, who was killed in the explosion. A piece of wood above the door in the north wall was also embedded there during the tragedy and was left where it landed as a mute memorial. The church is at the edge of the Grand Parade, a onetime parade ground in the middle of the city that has ample green space and often hosts live entertainment in summer.

You can learn about the colorful privateers and other characters who once populated the waterfront on nighttime "spirit walks" conducted by Dtours (902/455-9977). The Halifax Ghost Walk tours begin at 8:30 p.m. at the Old Town Clock on Citadel Hill (902/469-6716).

Details: *Between Barrington and Argyle Streets on the Grand Parade; to get there, walk down Prince or George Street to Argyle Street. (15 minutes)*

★★ ART GALLERY OF NOVA SCOTIA
1741 Hollis Street, 902/424-7542
www.agns.ednet.ns.ca

The permanent collection includes mainly Nova Scotian artists but gives some space to Canadian, British, and European works as well. The art gallery is particularly known for its extensive, colorful folk-art section, located on the mezzanine level. Temporary exhibits change every 6 to 12 weeks. Recently expanded, the gallery now includes space dedicated to the Nova Scotia College of Art and Design and an enlarged shop selling the work of Nova Scotian artisans.

Details: At the corner of Cheapside, near Historic Properties. Open Tue–Fri 10–6 but open to 9 on Thu, Sat–Sun 12–5. Nominal admission fee; free for children under 12. (2 hours)

A handy publication for travelers who enjoy fine dining is a booklet titled "Taste of Nova Scotia," available from Nova Scotia's tourist information line: 902/425-5781 from Halifax, 800/565-0000 from the rest of Canada.

★★ BLACK CULTURAL CENTRE
1149 Main Street, Dartmouth, 902/434-6223 or 800/465-0767, www.nstn.cabcc.html

The Halifax region has a black presence that dates back centuries. Slaves who sailed with the early explorers were here before Plymouth was settled. Others arrived because the British promised them freedom from slavery in return for loyalty during the American Revolution. Still others were relocated here in 1796 from Jamaica, where they had rebelled against British rule. Some came via the Underground Railroad, the dangerous route used by slaves seeking freedom in Canada in the years prior to the Civil War.

This museum and cultural and educational center—the first of its kind in Canada—is low-key and low-tech but contains many surprises for visitors, most of whom are learning for the first time about Nova Scotia's lengthy and rich black heritage.

Details: Dartmouth, Halifax's twin city, is just a short ferry ride from the waterfront. Open May–Sept Mon–Fri 9–5, Sat 10–4. Nominal admission fee. (2 hours)

★★ DISCOVERY CENTER
1593 Barrington Street, 902/492-4422
www.discoverycentre.ns.ca

This hands-on science center will divert the kids with more than 80 interactive exhibits that make learning fun whether the topic is bubbles, electricity, optical illusions, or light and sound.

Details: Mon–Sat 10–5, Sun 1–5. $5 adults, $3 ages 2–18. (2 hours)

★★ OLD BURYING GROUND
Barrington Street, 902/429-2240

The oldest burial ground in Halifax has gravestones dating as far back as 1752 and provides an intriguing glimpse into the city's early history. The cemetery was declared a National Historic Site in 1991 and is being gradually restored as an outdoor museum and park.

Details: *Corner of Spring Garden Road and Barrington Street. (15 minutes)*

★★ POINT PLEASANT PARK

One of the city's loveliest green areas, Point Pleasant Park encompasses both shoreline and woods. With an unimpeded view of the Atlantic Ocean and miles of walking and cycling paths, it's a perfect place for a picnic, a walk, or a swim off Black Rock Beach. No cars are permitted inside the park, but ample parking is available at both the eastern and western entrances. In July and August, the park is also the setting for the Shakespeare by the Sea Theatre Festival, with two plays performed outdoors and viewers paying by donation ($5 recommended).

Details: *Located at the southern tip of Halifax. (2 hours)*

FITNESS AND RECREATION

McNabs Island and Point Pleasant Park are good for cycling, jogging, walking, or swimming. Bicycles are available from various rental places around town, and cyclists can find easy riding on Dartmouth's hard-surface Multi-Use Trail. More than one dozen golf courses are scattered around the Halifax region; a listing of them is published in *The Greater Halifax Regional Guide*. Several public tennis courts are available at no charge, generally from 8 a.m. until dusk; for locations, call 902/490-4723.

Approximately one dozen beaches are within easy driving distance of central Halifax; one of them, Lawrencetown Beach on Route 207 near Dartmouth, is known for its surfing, and another, Crystal Crescent Beach south of Halifax, is known for its fine white sand and frigid turquoise waters. For canoeing and kayaking, rentals are available from St. Mary's Boat Club, 902/490-4688. Canoe Nova Scotia, 902/425-5450 ext. 316, can provide general information, and ardent kayakers can head for the islands near Prospect. The Shubenacadie Canal, beginning in Halifax Harbor and running up to the north coast of the province, is a good bet for boaters.

Scuba divers can explore more than 300 shipwrecks that lie on the floor of

Titanic Tourism

Halifax has been inextricably linked with the tragedy of the *Titanic* ever since the ship struck an iceberg in the Atlantic late on April 14, 1912, and sank a few hours later. Because it was the nearest major port to the sinking, Halifax played a pivotal role in the saga. Vessels were dispatched from the city to search for bodies, and 150 victims were later laid to rest in Halifax, making it the site of the largest number of *Titanic* graves in the world. In the days after the disaster, the international media dubbed Halifax "the City of Sorrows."

But it took James Cameron's epic film *Titanic*, released in late 1997, to really put Halifax on the *Titanic* tourism map. Around the time the movie was released, the Maritime Museum of the Atlantic dug through its collection and put together a permanent display titled *Titanic: The Unsinkable Ship and Halifax, Nova Scotia*. Result: attendance at the museum jumped by 150 percent in 1998.

Meanwhile, visitors began going to the Fairview Lawn Cemetery, where 121 of the *Titanic* dead lay buried under three rows of plain granite markers. Teenage girls started leaving flowers at the foot of one grave marked "J. Dawson" because they thought he might be the model for Jack Dawson, the character played by Leonardo DiCaprio in the film (he wasn't). Soon, pamphlets detailing *Titanic*-related sites in the city were published, and The Warehouse restaurant was using its private dining room to serve a meal similar to the one first-class passengers dined on the night the ship sank.

In addition to the Maritime Museum of the Atlantic (see Sightseeing Highlights) and the Fairview Cemetery (Windsor Street and Kempt Road), other *Titanic*-related sites include the Mount Olivet Cemetery (7076 Mumford Road), the Baron de Hirsch Cemetery (Connaught Avenue at Windsor Street), and churches that held memorial services in the wake of the tragedy.

Strangely enough, Halifax was connected to the sinking of another liner operated, like the *Titanic*, by White Star. The *Atlantic* sank after hitting shoals in Terence Bay in April 1873. It was carrying about 1,000 passengers, 562 of whom died in what was then the worst single-vessel marine disaster in history. Those bodies not claimed by family members were buried in two Halifax-area cemeteries.

HALIFAX

LOWER WATER ST

PRINCE ST

ARGYLE ST
GRAFTON ST
MARKET ST

DUKE ST

GEORGE ST

QUEEN ST

BLOWERS ST

E G
C F
A
M
D
B
H

McNabs Island

Halifax Harbor

Georges Island

UPPER WATER ST
DUKE ST
PRINCE ST
ARGYLE ST
BLOWERS ST
HOLLIS ST

To J

I

O
YOUNG AV

MORRIS ST
INGLIS ST
SOUTH PARK ST
SPRING GARDEN RD

N K

BELL RD
SACKVILLE
ROBIE ST
SOUTH ST

Northwest Arm

AGRICOLA ST
EDGEWOOD ST

BARRINGTON ST

To P S

WEST ST

L

QUINPOOL RD

CONNAUGHT AV

BAYERS RD

To Hwy 102
To Q R

N
Z

0 SCALE

1.5 KILOMETERS
1.5 MILES

ROAD

the outer harbor; several local operators offer guided dives of the wrecks, which range from small sailing craft to a British frigate. Wet suits are imperative in these cold waters. Contact the Nova Scotia Underwater Council, 902/425-5450 ext. 325, for information about dive sites, dive shops, and so on.

FOOD

Seafood is naturally the way to go in Halifax. Noteworthy seafood places include **Five Fishermen**, 1740 Argyle Street, 902/422-4421, offering a mussel bar plus lobster, trout, and other fresh seafood in a 175-year-old building at the corner of George Street, and **Salty's**, Historic Properties, Upper Water Street, 902/423-6818, a two-level place at the end of the Historic Properties Pier with pub-style dining downstairs and seafood aplenty upstairs. For seafood or steak, try the **Upper Deck**, Historic Properties, 902/422-1289. For Bourbon Street jazz along with your seafood, head for **Crawdad's Crab Shack & Oyster Bar**, 1599 Grafton Street, 902/422-500.

Halifax also offers many other types of restaurants. The **Granite Brewery**, 1222 Barrington Street, 902/423-5660, serves bitters, stouts, and other beers along with pub-style food in the warm atmosphere of historic Henry House. The **Lone Star Café**, 1599 Grafton Street, 902/422-8524, offers a variety of Tex-Mex dishes. The **Middle Deck Pasta Works**, Historic Properties, 902/425-1500, has Italian dishes and a casual atmosphere with a view of the harbor from Privateers Warehouse. Pasta, fresh salads, and seafood are also on the menu at **Sweet Basil Bistro**, 1866 Upper Water Street, 902-425-2133. **Cafe Mokka**, 1588 Granville Street, 902/492-4036, offers divine pastries and desserts and is a good bet for brunch. If you can't

---

FOOD

Ⓐ Alfredo Weinstein & Ho
Ⓑ Cafe Mokka
Ⓒ Crawdad's Crab Shack & Oyster Bar
Ⓓ Five Fishermen
Ⓔ Granite Brewery
Ⓕ Lone Star Café
Ⓖ Middle Deck Pasta Works
Ⓗ Salty's

FOOD (continued)

Ⓘ Sweet Basil Bistro
Ⓖ Upper Deck

LODGING

Ⓙ Delta Barrington
Ⓚ Halliburton House Inn
Ⓛ King Edward Inn
Ⓜ Prince George Hotel
Ⓝ Queen Street Inn Tourist Home

LODGING (continued)

Ⓞ Sheraton Halifax
Ⓟ Waverley Inn

CAMPING

Ⓠ Colonial Camping
Ⓡ Shubie Park
Ⓢ Woodhaven Park

Note: Items with the same letter are located in the same area.

decide what type of food you want, check out **Alfredo Weinstein & Ho**, 1739 Grafton Street, 902421-1977, which as its name suggests serves up Italian, Chinese, and deli dishes.

LODGING

Staying in Halifax's attractive historic inns is a good bet for their moderate prices (which include breakfast), their atmosphere, and their central locations—all within strolling distance of the city's major attractions. The **Waverley Inn**, 1266 Barrington Street, 902/423-9346 or 800/565-9346, is a charming, antique-furnished Victorian establishment. The **King Edward Inn**, 5780 West Street, 902/422-3266 or 800/565-5464, is an Edwardian-style inn. The **Halliburton House Inn**, 5184 Morris Street, 902/420-0658, an elegant four-star establishment, also has a fine dining room. For the more budget-minded, the **Queen Street Inn Tourist Home**, 1266 Queen Street, 902/422-9828, is in an old stone house downtown, but payment is requested in cash only.

Several upscale properties are located right in the heart of the action, including the **Sheraton Halifax**, 1919 Upper Water Street, 902/421-1700 or 800/325-3535. The **Prince George Hotel**, 1725 Market Street, 902/425-

DISASTER #2

Aside from the sinking of the *Titanic,* the historic event that most people connect with Nova Scotia's capital city is the famous Halifax Explosion of December 6, 1917. On that wartime morning, the French munitions ship *Mont Blanc* barely bumped the Belgian relief ship *Imo* in the Halifax harbor and exploded with the most powerful manmade blast in history before the atom bomb. The ship's anchor flew almost two miles. The blast shattered windows as far away as Truro, some 100 kilometers (60 miles) to the northeast, and was heard on Prince Edward Island. It also emptied the harbor beneath the *Mont Blanc's* keel, creating a tidal wave that roared up city streets. When the horror was over, more than 1,600 people were dead and 9,000 injured. One-fifth of the seaport, which had a population of 50,000 at the time, was devastated.

SIDE TRIP: THE MARINE DRIVE

The Marine Drive, one of Nova Scotia's many scenic routes, runs from Halifax along the length of the southeastern coast (the so-called Eastern Shore) and around Chedabucto Bay to Antigonish. This drive is coastal all the way, zigzagging along bays, inlets, headlands, beaches, and coves for about 340 kilometers (200 miles). It is a particularly unspoiled part of the province, with no big tourist resorts or amusement parks to mar the landscape.

Noteworthy stops include the Black Cultural Center in Westphal and the Railway Museum in Musquodoboit Harbour. A smokehouse at Tangier produces smoked salmon, mackerel, and eels. Sherbrooke Village, a restored riverside pioneer village that's part of the provincial museums system, is a short side trip from the Marine Drive.

1986 or 800/565-1567, and the **Delta Barrington**, 1875 Barrington Street, 902/429-7410 or 800/268-1133, both offer the full range of amenities and room rates to match.

The 300-page visitors guide published by the Nova Scotia Department of Tourism and Culture contains several pages of accommodations listings for Halifax. A handy brochure from Tourism Halifax, "Guide to Bed and Breakfast and Country Inns of Metropolitan Halifax-Dartmouth," lists more than 30 B&Bs and inns. The province's tourist information line doubles as a booking service called Check In. You can reserve hotels, motels, inns, bed-and-breakfasts, resorts, campgrounds, and car rentals simply by calling 800/565-0000, or, if you're already in Halifax, 902/425-5781. Tourism Halifax's phone number is 902/490-5948, or check out their Web site at www.region.halifax.ns.ca.

CAMPING

Several campgrounds are within easy driving distance of Halifax-Dartmouth. **Shubie Park**, 902/435-8328, on Route 318 in Dartmouth, offers swimming, fishing, nature trails, a play area, and a tennis court; rates begin at $15. **Woodhaven Park**, 902/835-2271, is a wooded campground on Hammonds Plains Road; sites cost $16 and up. **Colonial Camping**, 902/865-4342, in Upper Sackville, is on a river and offers swimming, boating, a playground, minigolf, and rates beginning at $14.

SIDE TRIP: GLOOSCAP TRAIL

The Glooscap Trail on Nova Scotia's central North Shore runs along the Bay of Fundy, which means you can see the highest tides in the world as you drive it.

According to Mi'kmaq legend, Glooscap was the god who created the land and the tides hereabouts. The Five Islands in Minas Basin, for instance, were said to be created when an enraged Glooscap threw some huge clumps of earth out across the bay.

The travelway is also known for the semiprecious stones, including agate and amethyst, found in the beaches and cliffs near Parrsboro. To learn more, stop in at the Fundy Geological Museum in Parrsboro. Also noteworthy is the Joggins Fossil Centre on Main Street in Joggins, featuring the world's largest collection of 300-million-year-old Joggins Fossils as well as other fossils from around the world. What are Joggins Fossils? They come from cliffs overlooking Chignecto Bay that have yielded the fossilized remains of everything from an ancient forest to amphibians, reptiles, and plants. The town is now lobbying to have the United Nations recognize the cliffs as a World Heritage Site.

NIGHTLIFE

Halifax is a port city, so consider a pub crawl. Pick up a copy of a *Halifax Pub Guide* from one of the tourist offices and start crawling. The Lower Deck, 902/425-1501, in Privateer's Warehouse, Historic Properties, is popular for drinking as well as eating since a singer leads the crowd in maritime folk songs from 9 nightly. Indeed, Halifax is known for its live music, from Celtic to jazz to swing to rock, which may have something to do with the 25,000 university students who live there.

Culture vultures also have abundant choices, with professional concerts and drama offered by the Neptune Theater, the Dalhousie University Arts Center, and Symphony Nova Scotia. Check the *Halifax Herald* for up-to-date listings.

The Sheraton Casino Halifax, 902/425-7777, is in the Sheraton Hotel but is expected to move to a new location on the waterfront any day now. It contains hundreds of slot machines, blackjack tables, and roulette wheels.

SHOPPING

Some of Halifax's smartest shops are found in the Shops of Granville Mall on Granville Street and Barrington Place Shops on Barrington Street. Spring Garden Road, too, offers designer labels along with sidewalk cafés, pubs, and jazz clubs. The Brewery Market Complex between Lower Water and Hollis Streets is an historic stone structure that now houses shops and restaurants; it's also the site of a lively farmers' market every Saturday, complete with colorful stalls and street-performing musicians. Antiques shops, bookstores, and jewelry shops are dotted along Argyle, Blowers, and Grafton Streets.

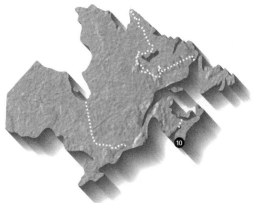

10
THE NOVA SCOTIA COAST

Nova Scotia calls itself "Canada's Oceanside Playground," and indeed, you can drive the coast from Halifax practically all the way around the province. This chapter covers two of the most scenic routes. The Lighthouse Route follows the south coast from Halifax almost to Yarmouth, at the province's western tip, through such picturesque coastal towns as Peggy's Cove, Mahone Bay, and Lunenburg. Ocean vistas and the beauty of these towns place this route among the province's most popular tourist draws. The Evangeline Trail leads northeast from Yarmouth, along the Acadian Shore of the Fundy coast, through Annapolis Royal and the Annapolis Valley. Blessed with more sunny days and milder weather than most other parts of the Maritime provinces, the fertile Annapolis Valley is dotted with small, peaceful villages boasting glorious old Victorian houses. Annapolis Royal, particularly lovely, retains its unspoiled small-town atmosphere and beauty despite its tourist popularity. The valley is also apple-growing country; in May and June, the apple trees blossom to a marvelous pink, and the annual five-day Apple Blossom Festival is held throughout the valley during the late-May height of the blossoms.

Evangeline, by the way, is the fictional young Acadian woman immortalized by American poet Henry Wadsworth Longfellow in his haunting *Evangeline: A Tale of Acadie,* later translated into 130 languages. The story tells how she was separated from her betrothed, Gabriel, when the Acadians were deported from Nova Scotia. The lovers reunited only at the end of their lives, as Gabriel lay dying.

NOVA SCOTIA COAST

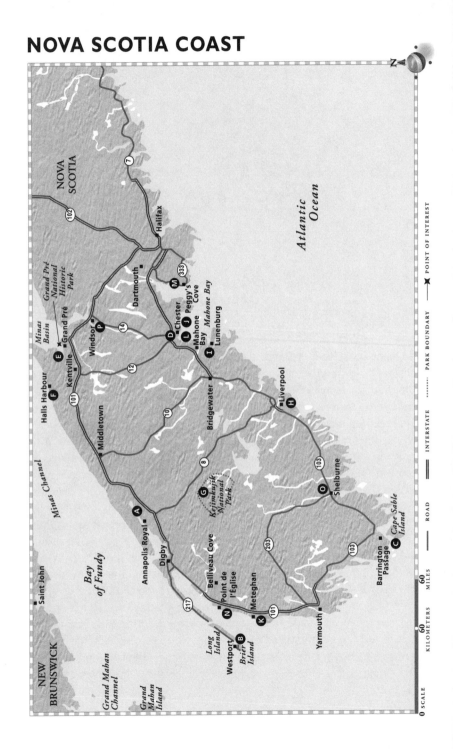

MORE NOVA SCOTIA FACTS

Nova Scotia is only 560 kilometers (340 miles) long and never more than 130 kilometers (78 miles) wide, but its serrated coastline runs for 7,400 kilometers (4,600 miles) past harbors, inlets, bays, long beaches, and rugged cliffs. Its physical beauty has made tourism a major industry. In fact, the province is really one big tourist trap, but not in a negative way. Although it is markedly geared toward tourism, Nova Scotia still manages for the most part to remain tasteful.

Nova Scotia drew settlers mainly from Britain, although an influx of German Protestants led to the founding of German-flavored Lunenburg (see Sightseeing Highlights), famous for both its shipbuilding and its annual Octoberfest. Thousands of New Englanders and, later, Loyalists also came to Nova Scotia from south of the border, including many African Americans. The indigenous people, the Mi'kmaq, were decimated by European diseases and territorial clashes and now number about 10,000.

A PERFECT DAY ON THE NOVA SCOTIA COAST

Get to Peggy's Cove as early in the day as possible to beat the crowds. After that there's no rush—devote the rest of the day to meandering this lovely route at whatever pace you choose. Oak Island is probably the only place along the coast that's not particularly scenic, but it's fascinating because of its

---

SIGHTS

- Ⓐ Annapolis Royal
- Ⓑ Brier Island
- Ⓒ Cape Sable Island
- Ⓓ Chester
- Ⓔ Grand Pré National Historic Site
- Ⓕ Hall's Harbour
- Ⓖ Kejimkujik National Park
- Ⓗ Liverpool
- Ⓘ Lunenburg (Bluenose II, Fisheries Museum of the Atlantic)
- Ⓙ Mahone Bay
- Ⓚ Meteghan

SIGHTS (continued)

- Ⓛ Oak Island
- Ⓜ Peggy's Cove
- Ⓝ Point de l'Église
- Ⓞ Shelburne
- Ⓟ Windsor

FOOD

- Ⓑ Big Red's
- Ⓒ Charlotte Lane Café
- Ⓞ Claudia's Diner
- Ⓕ Grand Banker Seafood Bar & Grill
- Ⓙ Innlet Café
- Ⓗ Lane's Privateer Inn
- Ⓘ Old Fish Factory Restaurant

LODGING

- Ⓓ Captain's House Inn
- Ⓘ Compass Rose Inn
- Ⓗ Lanes Privateer Inn
- Ⓞ Loyalist Inn
- Ⓘ Lunenburg Inn
- Ⓙ Sou'Wester Inn

CAMPING

- Ⓞ Islands Provincial Park
- Ⓘ Lunenburg Board of Trade Campground
- Ⓘ Ovens Natural Park Family Campground

Note: Items with the same letter are located in the same area.

fabled buried treasure and the massive (but so far fruitless) efforts of various people to get at it. Stop in Lunenburg for lunch and a wander through the old part of town, declared a UNESCO World Heritage Site a few years ago. The Giant's Causeway on Brier Island is utterly compelling, and the drive along Digby Neck that takes you there is particularly pleasant. Annapolis Royal is another favorite, especially the peaceful Royal Historic Gardens and the waterfront promenade overlooking the river.

ORIENTATION

From Halifax, follow Highway 333 to Peggy's Cove. After that, follow the road signs for the Lighthouse Route (silhouette of a lighthouse) to Yarmouth. Yarmouth is the province's largest seaport east of Halifax and the terminal for the ferry service from Bar Harbour and Portland, Maine. The average driving speed on the Lighthouse Route is about 70 kilometers an hour (42 mph), so you'll pretty much have to take your time, but you'll undoubtedly be inclined to linger often along the way anyway. Much the same goes for the Evangeline Trail, which follows Highway 101 along the Fundy shore and runs through the center of the Annapolis Valley and into the outskirts of Halifax. Follow the scenic-route signs depicting a church—several towns on the route boast amazing churches—and you can't go wrong. For a change of scenery, try the side roads that lead to fishing villages along the Minas Channel shoreline. In fact, the shoreline is never more than 15 kilometers (9 miles) due north.

SIGHTSEEING HIGHLIGHTS

★★★★ ANNAPOLIS ROYAL
902/532-5769, www.valleyweb.com

St. George Street, parallel to the waterfront in Annapolis Royal, claims to be the oldest town street in Canada and is lined with restored buildings housing small historical museums, shops, and restaurants. Pick up a walking-tour pamphlet from the local tourist information bureau in the railway station at the base of Victoria Street. Running parallel to St. George Street behind King's Theater, a waterfront promenade overlooks the Annapolis River and the village of Granville Ferry, where the falling Fundy tides leave vessels berthed at the wharf, high and dry. Annapolis Royal is on the Evangeline Trail.

Annapolis Royal Historic Gardens, Upper St. George Street, 902/532-7018, reflect the heritage of the area. This site features a formal Victorian garden, a vast rose collection, a Governor's Garden that re-creates a garden of the colonial period, and even an Acadian section with a replica of a 1671 Acadian cottage surrounded by a willow hedge, apple trees, and a "potager" or vegetable garden. For latter-day gardeners, one section of the grounds is devoted to in-

Families might want to stop in at Upper Clements Park on Route 1 outside Annapolis Royal, 902/532-7557. It's open from mid-May to mid-October—daily in July and August and on weekends the rest of the year. Admission is just $2.30 per person, but you then pay either $1.15 per ride, $9 for 10 ride tickets or $15 for 20 tickets.

novations and trends in gardens and gardening techniques. The setting, alongside the Allains River, is absolutely lovely. The Gardens are open mid-May to mid-Oct, 8 to dusk.

Displays at **Fort Anne**, St. George Street, 902/532-2321, http://parkscanada.pch.gc.ca, a National Historic Site, recount the struggle between the French and English in the area. When French explorers Samuel de Champlain and Sieur de Monts first came across the Annapolis River basin in 1604, they named the area Port-Royal. Within a couple of years, a small band of French farmers had settled there, making it the first European settlement in Canada. Port-Royal changed hands several times as the French and British battled over Nova Scotia. It was eventually renamed Annapolis in honor of Queen Anne. Later, after the Acadians were expelled, the area was resettled by New Englanders and Loyalists, and the two names merged to become Annapolis Royal. The fort is open mid-May to mid-Oct 9–6.

Details: Annapolis Royal is on the Evangeline Trail. (4–5 hours)

★★★★ **BRIER ISLAND**
902/839-2853 or 902/681-1645, www.valleyweb.com
Visiting Brier Island requires a side trip from the Evangeline Trail that's well worth it. Renowned for its natural beauty and its great whale- and bird-watching, the island is also home to the Giant's Causeway: tall, strange rock pillars that extend from the shore hundreds of meters into the sea like ragged rows of marching columns. Also worth checking out is Balancing Rock, a towering rock that

stands at the edge of a sharp drop and looks for all the world as if it's about to pitch over into the water. Getting to Balancing Rock used to involve a hardy hike through patches of skunk cabbage and over a ridge, but now you can easily traverse a one-kilometer trail with steps, boardwalks, and a path. When you tire of scrambling over the rocks, several local operators offer whale- and bird-watching tours.

Details: *About 65 kilometers (40 miles) from Digby, at the tip of a long, thin peninsula called Digby Neck. Follow Route 217 from Digby, catch a ferry from East Ferry to Tiverton on Long Island, and, at the far end of Long Island, catch another ferry from Freeport across to Westport, the only community on Brier Island. A tourist bureau is located in Tiverton, 902/839-2853. (4 hours)*

★★★★ **LUNENBURG**
902/634-8100, www.ncsl.com/lunenburg
Lunenburg is the famous shipbuilding center where both the original *Bluenose*—the schooner depicted on the Canadian dime—and the replica *Bluenose II* were built. The town was honored in 1995 when the United Nations designated its Old Town portion a World Heritage Site. Indeed, this exceedingly picturesque place on the Lighthouse Route boasts some breathtaking and beautifully restored buildings. Pick up a walking-tour pamphlet from the local tourist information center, housed in a lighthouse replica on Blockhouse Hill, a public park that provides a panoramic view of the town and harbor.

Lunenburg's German heritage is reflected during Octoberfest, with activities for all ages. Other events worth checking out are the Lunenburg Folk Harbor Festival, usually the second weekend of August, and, a couple of weeks later, the Nova Scotia Fisheries Exhibition and Fishermen's Reunion.

For many years Lunenburg was one of Canada's great fishing and shipbuilding ports. Located on the waterfront, the **Fisheries Museum of the Atlantic**, 902/634-4794, http://museum. ednet.ns.ca, brings that heritage alive through all sorts of activities, demonstrations, and talks. You can learn to tie knots, knit fishermen's mittens, mend fishing nets, and listen to talks about everything from lobsters to whales to rum-running. You'll also see the world's largest collection of *Bluenose* artifacts, and you can board the restored *Theresa E. Connor,* the last Canadian schooner to fish Newfoundland's Grand Banks, which is moored alongside the museum.

Built in 1921, the original *Bluenose* was the undefeated champion of the North Atlantic fishing fleet and winner of four international schooner races. The replica **Bluenose II**, 902/634-1963 or 800/763-1963, www.bluenose2.ns.ca, serves as Nova Scotia's sailing ambassador and spends much of the summer visiting ports around the province and farther afield. From its home port in Lunenberg, the boat provides two-hour harbor sailings for $20 per person.

Details: *Visitor information center is located on Blockhouse Hill Road. Open May–Oct. (4 hours)*

★★★★ **PEGGY'S COVE**
902/624-6466, www.ssta.com

Peggy's Cove is a tiny fishing village renowned for its picturesque setting and rustic buildings. The only way to see this attraction properly, without elbow-to-elbow crowds, is to get there first thing in the morning: get in and out before 9, when the tour buses start arriving. Park in the lot at the edge of the village and walk down the slope. Peggy's Cove sits in a calm little inlet, and when you get into the center of the village you'll understand why it's one of the most-photographed parts of Nova Scotia. Take a few shots; they'll come out looking like picture-perfect postcards because that's exactly how Peggy's Cove looks. Then continue along the road toward the lighthouse, which sits on a point and doubles as a post office during tourist season. The coastline here consists of huge, gently rounded granite boulders with surf splashing against them. It's a powerfully stark scene; take some time to walk over the rocks and sit awhile contemplating the sea. But wear sneakers and be careful! Every once in a while, when the weather is stormy, someone on the rocks at Peggy's Cove is swept out to sea. Of all the local souvenir shops, the one worth searching out is Beales Bailiwick. It offers wares from oil-cloth coats and pewter to pretty pottery, mohair sweaters, and high-quality sweatshirts and T-shirts.

Peggy's Cove, alas, was the closest community when a Swissair flight dropped into the ocean in September 1998, killing everyone on board. Hundreds of residents of Peggy's Cove and other communities took park in the search-and-recovery effort. The province is planning to erect a memorial overlooking St. Margaret's Bay, where the jet crashed.

Details: *About a half-hour's drive southwest of Halifax via Route 333. (2 hours)*

GRAND PRÉ NATIONAL HISTORIC SITE

Tourism Nova Scotia

★★★ CHESTER
902/275-4616, www.ssta.com

An elegant old resort town where lots of wealthy Americans used to spend their summers, Chester has some lovely old mansions, including the Sword and Anchor Inn, built in the early 1800s. It also has professional summer theater at the Chester Playhouse. The town has long attracted sailors and yachters, especially for the busiest week of the year, Chester Race Week in mid-August, Atlantic Canada's largest sailing regatta.

Details: *On the Lighthouse Route. (1 hour)*

★★★ GRAND PRÉ NATIONAL HISTORIC SITE
902/542-3631, http://parkscanada.pch.gc.ca

This site commemorates the expulsion of the Acadians, one of the most shameful events in Canada's history. Prior to the expulsion, which ran from 1755 to 1763 and saw 10,000 French-speaking maritimers forced into exile by the British, Grand Pré was a thriving Acadian community. The site contains formal gardens, a commemorative church, and a statue of the fictional heroine Evangeline, who looks back toward the land she is being forced to leave.

A growing number of artisans are settling in the town of Grand Pré, so it's a good place to browse for arts and crafts. Grand Pré is also the center of Nova Scotia's wine industry; the Grand Pré Winery offers tours, tastings, and a wine and gift boutique. **Details:** *Grand Pré is on the Evangeline Trail. The National Historic Site is open mid-May–mid-Oct 9:30–5:30. (2 hours)*

★★★ HALL'S HARBOUR
902/681-1645, www.valleyweb.com

This picturesque little fishing village on the Evangeline Trail slopes steeply down to the shore where the tides rise and fall to an astounding extent. When the tide is out, fishing boats are grounded far below wharf level, and stranded fish flop about in the small pools of water left behind until the tide returns. You can also go for a walk on a gravel beach bordered by 25-meter (80-foot) cliffs. **Details:** *A short side trip from the Evangeline Trail. To get there, take Route 359 from Kentville. (1 hour)*

★★★ KEJIMKUJIK NATIONAL PARK
902/682-2772, http://parkscanada.pch.gc.ca

One of Nova Scotia's two national parks, this park lies inland. Kejimkujik is a wooded, gently rolling wilderness area dotted with lakes, rivers, and hiking trails. A family campground is situated on the site. Canoeing is a particularly popular activity; rentals are available. In summer, park naturalists give lectures and lead guided walks and canoe trips. **Details:** *Route 8 between Liverpool on the south shore and Annapolis Royal to the north. Visitor Reception Centre and Campground Kiosk open June 19–Sept 7 8:30–9; Sept 8–June 18 8:30–4:30. Nominal admission fee. (3 hours)*

★★★ LIVERPOOL
902/354-5421, www.ssta.com

Liverpool, on the Lighthouse Route, is designated as the Port of Privateers, in honor of the period from 1750 to 1812 when it was perfectly legal to scour the seas looking for victims. Local merchants would launch fleets of fighting ships that pirated goods from vessels sailing from the North Atlantic to the Caribbean. One merchant, Simeon Perkins, even hired militiamen to guard the town against other marauders. Nowadays, if you go through Liverpool on a tour

Cape Breton Island

Besides the Cabot Trail (see Scenic Route on page 187), Cape Breton Island offers a number of attractions. One is the Fortress of **Louisbourg**, 902/733-2280, http://fortress.uccb.ns.ca, a living-history museum and the largest historical reconstruction project in North America. One-quarter of the town has been rebuilt, and you can visit period buildings, from homes to soldiers' barracks to a noisy waterfront tavern. From June to early September, the fortress is brought to life by costumed soldiers, merchants, sea captains, and other "residents" who re-create the summer of 1744 and regale visitors with stories, dances, music, and the "latest" local gossip. The weather tends to be cool and damp, even in summer, so bring a sweater and raincoat and wear comfortable walking shoes. Admission is $11 for adults, $8.25 for seniors, and $5.50 for children.

Louisbourg lies at the south end of the **Marconi Trail**, a rugged coastal route that begins in Glace Bay. Several other scenic routes are worth checking out. The **Ceilidh Trail** leads north along Route 19, from the Canso Causeway to Margaree Harbour on the Cabot Trail, running along the coast most of the way. All over Cape Breton Island and the rest of Nova Scotia, but particularly along this route, you'll see the phrase "Ciad Mìle Fàilté"—Gaelic for "One Hundred Thousand Welcomes." The region was originally settled by Scottish highlanders. The beaches, clifftop views, sheep on hillsides, and landscapes are eerily reminiscent of Scotland. Stop in at Mabou Provincial Park for a panoramic vista of the Mabou Valley. In Glenville, north of Mabou, drop by the Glenora Distillery, the only one in North America that makes single-malt whiskey. It's open for tours and offers an inn and restaurant.

The **Fleur-de-lis Trail** leads south from the Canso Causeway, along the southern rim of Bras d'Or Lake, all the way to Louisbourg; it's mainly Acadian country. Pondville Beach Provincial Park boasts a sandy beach. At

bus, you may find yourself "hijacked" by musket-toting militiamen to give you a taste of what life in Liverpool was once like.

At least one required stop in town is the **Simeon Perkins House**, 105 Main Street, 902/354-4058. Admission is free. Built in 1766, the house is now a provincial museum. In addition to eighteenth-century furniture, the house contains a copy of Perkins's di-

Marble Mountain, a museum tells the story of the marble-quarrying industry, and the village has a marble-chip beach. Île Madame to the south, accessible by causeway, has a strong Acadian heritage and several shoreline picnic areas. The Bras d'Or Lakes Scenic Drive circles the huge lake, often described as an inland sea, that lies at the heart of the island. In July, the tiny village of Big Pond is the site of a major Cape Breton folk concert. Big Pond is also the hometown of famous Cape Breton singer Rita MacNeil; Rita's Tea Room in town displays her awards and records. In the town of Iona, the **Nova Scotia Highland Village** is a living-history museum, featuring 10 historic buildings. Costumed guides show visitors how the early Scottish settlers lived and worked.

One of Cape Breton Island's most outstanding features is its Gaelic culture. The only Gaelic college in America, the Gaelic College of Celtic Arts and Crafts, is located in St. Ann's. You'll notice fiddles, bagpipes, and music wherever you go. Singer Rita MacNeil, fiddler Ashley MacIsaac, and the Rankins are just some of the Cape Breton musicians who have gained national and international fame. Every night of the year, there's a *ceilidh*, or party, going on somewhere.

As of May 2000, a new luxury Via Rail train, the Bras d'Or, will run between Halifax and Sydney on Cape Breton Island. The first-class train will feature a glassed-in dome providing panoramic views, and passengers will be entertained by a costumed guide and dine on foods traditional to the region. The trip will take 10 hours, including off-train activities. For details, contact Via at **888/842-7245**.

For more information on Cape Breton Island, contact Tourism Cape Breton at **800/565-9464**.

aries, which he kept painstakingly for 40 years. His writings provide succeeding generations with a vivid record of daily life in a colonial town. For some reason, he was particularly detailed about any illness in the family. Next, take a stroll along some of Liverpool's tree-lined streets, where fine old houses dating from the Loyalist influx still stand. Stop in at the Fort Point Lighthouse, which has recently been extensively restored and sits in an attractive waterfront park.

Details: The local tourist information center is in Centennial Park. Liverpool's major annual festival is Privateer Days, held around the end of June, when life in 1780 is reenacted. (1 hour)

★★★ MAHONE BAY
888/624-6151, http//fox.nstn.ca/~mahonebay
Mahone Bay is famous for its three churches (Anglican, Lutheran, and United), which stand in a row at the head of the town's harbor and form one of the most photographed scenes in the province. Perhaps less well known but equally interesting is the nearby heritage cemetery; take the time to wander through it. You can also visit and photograph Blue Rocks, black-slate ledges stretching into the sea that were eerie enough to serve as a location for the Stephen King thriller *Dolores Claiborne* in 1994. Otherwise, Mahone Bay, which calls itself "one of the prettiest towns in Canada," is a terrific place in which to stroll, shop, and eat because its streets are lined with distinctive craft shops, art galleries, and cafés.

Details: On the Lighthouse Route. (2 hours)

★★ CAPE SABLE ISLAND
902/624-6466, www.ssta.com
Cape Sable Island, Nova Scotia's southernmost point, is linked by a 1,200-meter (3,925-foot) causeway to Barrington Passage, a tiny village on the mainland south of Clark's Harbour. The island's other claim to fame is that over the years, hundreds of ships have run afoul of the submerged shoals here; the cape has long been known to sailors as one of the graveyards of the Atlantic. In the tiny community of Centreville on Cape Sable Island, the Archelaus Smith Museum, 902/745-3361, exhibits items salvaged from vessels shipwrecked in the area. Admission is free.

Details: On the Lighthouse Route. (1 hour)

★★ METEGHAN
902/645-2389 (Visitor's Center), www.valleyweb.com
Just before the village of Meteghan, stop in at Smugglers Cove Provincial Park, which offers a lovely vista of St. Mary's Bay. Meteghan, a small but busy port, is an Acadian town, and one of its historic homes is now a museum called La Vieille Maison (the Old

House), 902/645-2389. Drop in to get a taste of nineteenth-century Acadian life, complete with Acadian guides in traditional costumes. A very curious story is also attached to Meteghan. In 1854 a mysterious man apparently materialized on the beach at Sandy Cove, across the bay from Meteghan. He was dressed in clean clothes and had a supply of water and biscuits, but his legs had been amputated above the knees. He was unable to speak and never revealed his origins. He was named Jerome by local residents, who cared for him until his death 58 years later; he is buried in Meteghan.

Details: Meteghan is on the Evangeline Trail. The visitor's center is in La Vielle Maison; open May–Sept. (1 hour)

★★ OAK ISLAND

Oak Island, five minutes outside Mahone Bay on the Lighthouse Route, has a fascinating history. Legend has it that Captain Kidd's treasure is buried in a pit here, but the head of the Triton consortium that has so far invested $3 million in exploration on Oak Island thinks it may hold Sir Francis Drake's booty from plundered French and Spanish ships. For decades, serious treasure hunters have been trying to figure out how to solve the mystery of the so-called Money Pit. It contains an elaborate system of shafts and tunnels that were apparently designed to cave in or flood with seawater when disturbed. So far, nobody has succeeded in this great treasure hunt, although searchers have spent millions of dollars trying to uncover the mystery, and at least six people have died.

Seasonal tourist information bureaus are located in Annapolis Royal, Chester, Liverpool, Lunenburg, Mahone Bay, Meteghan, Shelburne, and Windsor. For tourist information and lodging reservations throughout Nova Scotia, call 800/565-0000.

Details: The island is not open to the public, but a small museum on the island causeway offers details on the mystery. (1 hour)

★★ POINTE DE L'ÉGLISE (CHURCH POINT)
902/769-2808 or 902/769-2832

Pointe de l'Église on the Evangeline Trail is home to one of the most remarkable of all the churches scattered along the trail. St. Mary's Church, one of the largest wooden churches in North America, was built between 1903 and 1905. The spire reaches 56 meters (183 feet) into the air and is weighted down inside with tons of rocks that act as ballast in the strong winds that blow in off St. Mary's Bay.

Details: Guided tours of the church are available in summer. The church is located adjacent to the campus of Université Sainte-Anne, the province's only French-language university. (1 hour)

★★ SHELBURNE
902/875-4557 (Visitor's Center)
www.ssta.com
For a time after it was first settled by Loyalists in 1783, Shelburne was the third-largest town in North America. Eventually, many Loyalists moved on, but the town's tourist literature encourages visitors to trace their roots because so many colonists funneled through Shelburne. You never know. Many of the town's houses date from Loyalist times, including the **Ross-Thompson House**, 9 Charlotte Lane, 902/875-3141, built in 1784 and now a provincial museum. Part of the museum is a restored Loyalist store displaying period merchandise. Settlers George and Robert Ross originally opened the store in the 1780s and sold salt, tobacco, molasses, and dry goods to the other settlers. Admission is free. You'll find both a tourist information center and the Shelburne County Genealogical Society on Dock Street. Lined with restored eighteenth-century homes, the street has been used as a backdrop in several Hollywood movies, including the Demi Moore megabomb *The Scarlet Letter.* The movie did precious little for tourism in the town but left some quirky artifacts in its wake, such as the public gallows on Dock Street. Near Shelburne, The Islands Provincial Park, connected to the mainland by a causeway, offers picnic tables and a campground. Shelburne hosts a big lobster festival in early June.

Details: Shelburne is located on the Lighthouse Route. (2 hours)

★★ WINDSOR
902/798-2690 (Visitor's Center)
www.valleyweb.com/windsor
Windsor is a good place to view the tidal bore, the tumbling wave that moves upriver with the advancing tide from the Bay of Fundy. It can vary from a few inches to several feet in height and is most dramatic as it enters certain rivers that empty into the bay. Along this shore, the bore is most pronounced in the Meander River near Windsor.

Windsor is also home to the **Shand House**, 389 Avon Street,

902/798-8213. This magnificently gingerbreaded late-Victorian home is now a provincial museum furnished with just about everything ever acquired by the Shand family, including trophies won by Clifford Shand in high-wheeled bicycle races.

Finally, Windsor calls itself "the Giant Pumpkin Capital of the World." How big are these gargantuans? Would you believe 600 pounds?

Details: *The visitor's center is at 31 Colonial Road. (2 hours)*

FITNESS AND RECREATION

Kejimkujik National Park, Route 8, 902/682-2772, http://parkscanada. pch.gc.ca, offers numerous hiking trails as well as canoeing and other outdoor activities (see Sightseeing Highlights). Ovens Natural Park, near Riverport on the Lighthouse Route, is known for its dramatic seacliff nature trail that leads to several seacaves. From Chester, you can take a ferry to the Tancook Islands at the mouth of Mahone Bay and explore the many walking trails on both islands.

Golfing options include Granite Springs, 902/852-4653, near Peggy's Cove, the Liverpool Golf Club, 902/683-2485, and Digby Pines Resort, 902/245-4104. Beaches are found all along the coast, notably at Lockeport, which boasts five in and around town. You can rent a kayak in Mahone Bay and boat along the coast on your own, or you can take part in a group tour. The Annapolis Valley is ideal for cycling because it's so flat.

FOOD

In Lunenburg, the **Old Fish Factory Restaurant**, 68 Bluenose Drive, 902/634-3300, is right on the waterfront and offers a broad menu of fresh seafood and non-seafood items, served along with an outstanding view of the harbor. **Big Red's**, 80 Montague Street, 902/634-3554, offers family fare such as pizza and salads, and the **Grand Banker Seafood Bar & Grill**, 82 Montague Street, 902/634-3300, has an extensive menu of hearty meals and lighter snacks, plus a cozy neighborhood bar.

In Shelburne, the cozy **Charlotte Lane Café**, 13 Charlotte Lane, 902/875-3314, serves seafood, pasta, and salads, and **Claudia's Diner**, Water Street, 902/875-3110, features hearty home cooking and is famous for miles around for its lobster chowder. In Mahone Bay, try the **Innlet Café**, Kedy's Landing complex, 902/624-6363, which offers fresh seafood, salads, and sandwiches, plus a view of the famous three churches from its location at the head of the bay. In Liverpool, **Lane's Privateer Inn**, 27 Bristol Avenue,

ANNAPOLIS ROYAL

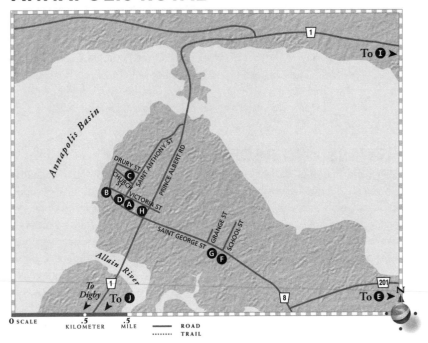

FOOD

Ⓐ Garrison House Inn
Ⓑ Leo's Café
Ⓒ Ye Old Town Pub

LODGING

Ⓓ Bread and Roses
Country Inn

LODGING (continued)

Ⓔ English Oaks B & B
Ⓐ Garrison House Inn
Ⓕ King George Inn
Ⓖ Queen Anne Inn
Ⓗ Turret Bed & Breakfast

CAMPING

Ⓘ Dunromin Campsite
and Trailer Court
Ⓙ Fundy Trail
Campground

Note: Items with the same letter are located in the same area.

902/354-3456, boasts no less than three dining rooms serving seafood, steak, pasta, and fish and chips.

In Annapolis Royal, **Ye Old Town Pub**, 9 Church Street, 902/532-2244, features fish and chips, clam and chips, and 16-ounce burgers for lunch and dinner. For more upscale dining, try the **Garrison House Restaurant**, 350 St. George Street, 902/532-5750, which has three intimate dining rooms and serves exquisite fare based on fresh local seafood and vegetables. At the other end of the scale, **Leo's Café**, 222 St. George Street, 902/532-7424, offers sandwiches and homemade soups.

LODGING

Many delightful heritage inns and B&Bs are located in towns all along the Lighthouse Trail, virtually all of them in the moderate price range. In Lunenburg, try the exquisite old **Lunenburg Inn**, 26 Dufferin Street, 902/634-3963, or another equally charming heritage property, the **Compass Rose Inn**, 15 King Street, 800/565-8509. In Shelburne, the **Loyalist Inn**, 160 Water Street, 902/875-2343, is in the heart of the action and also has a dining room. In Liverpool, **Lanes Privateer Inn**, 27 Bristol Avenue, 902/354-3456 or 800/794-3332, is a 200-year-old property overlooking the Mersey River. In Mahone Bay, the **Sou'Wester Inn**, 788 Main Street, 902/624-9296, once a Victorian shipbuilder's home, features a verandah overlooking the water. In Chester, try the **Captain's House Inn**, 29 Central Street, 902/275-3501, yet another property that once belonged to someone involved in the maritime industry.

Several charming old Victorian inns in Annapolis Royal offer moderately priced rooms. The **Queen Anne Inn**, 494 Upper St. George Street, 902/532-7850, a registered heritage property with antique furnishings, is situated up the road from the Annapolis Royal Historic Gardens. The **Garrison House Inn**, 350 St. George Street, 902/532-5750, boasts a wonderful restaurant in addition to charming rooms. The **Bread and Roses Country Inn**, 82 Victoria Street, 902/532-5727, is a restored Victorian brick mansion. The **King George Inn**, 548 Upper St. George Street, 902/532-5286, is a Victorian sea captain's home and a registered heritage property with antique furnishings and a library. For those on a tighter budget, a number of B&Bs in the area have very reasonable rates. Try **English Oaks B&B**, off Route 201, 902/532-2066, a modern house on lovely riverside property just outside town, or **Turret Bed & Breakfast**, 372 St. George Street, 902/532-5770, yet another registered historic property.

CAMPING

The **Lunenburg Board of Trade Campground**, 902/634-8100, is adjacent to the tourist information center on Blockhouse Hill Road; rates begin at $16. Eight miles southwest of Lunen-burg on Route 332, **Ovens Nat-ural Park Family Camp-ground**, 902/766-4621, is right by the ocean and has a licensed restaurant; rates start at $18. Three miles west of Shelburne on Route 3, you can stay at the campground in **Islands Prov-incial Park**, 902/875-4304, with sites starting at $14. Graves Island Provincial Park, 902/275-4425, is two miles east of Chester and has rates beginning at $14.

You can reserve hotels, motels, inns, bed-and-breakfasts, resorts, camp-grounds, and car rentals simply by calling 800/565-0000, the province's information and reservation service.

Several campgrounds are avail-able around Annapolis Royal. **Dunromin Campsite and Trailer Court**, 902/532-2808, a wooded and open campground with a gro-cery store, laundromat, boating facil-ities, swimming area, and play area, is minutes west of town on Route 1; rates begin at $13.50. **Fundy Trail Campground**, 902/532-7711, is on the Bay of Fundy, 12 miles north of Route 1, and has a recreation hall, laundromat, canteen, pool, and walking trails as well as wilderness sites on a freshwater brook. It's near a theme park and features family days; rates begin at $15.

SHOPPING

Many of the picturesque towns along the Lighthouse Route contain quaint shops selling a wide variety of gifts, souvenirs, and other goods. In Mahone Bay, the Teazer (named after a ghost ship) is popular for souvenir shopping. Stop in at Suttles & Seawinds, located in a giant pink house on Main Street, which sells clothes and quilts—it's worth a visit just to see the inside of the house. For pewter goods, try Amos Pewterers, also on Main Street. In Lunenburg, many of the renovated buildings now house appealing shops and galleries. Along the Evangeline Trail, Grand Pré is known for arts and crafts, and the quaint shops in Annapolis Royal sell a wide range of gifts.

Scenic Route: The Cabot Trail

Cape Breton Island sits at the northeastern edge of Nova Scotia, attached to the rest of the province by a short causeway. Its most famous attraction is the Cabot Trail. One of the most beautiful scenic routes on the continent—if not in the world—it can literally take your breath away. The trail follows the Gulf of St. Lawrence shoreline around the magnificent Cape Breton Highlands National Park and along the Atlantic coast. The scenery is rapturously beautiful, all cliffs and crashing waves and remarkable vistas. Fortunately, the route is dotted with lookouts where you can pull off the road to absorb the panorama without causing an accident. Little wonder that readers of Condé Nast Traveler identified Cape Breton Island as having the best island scenery in the world in the most recent annual readers' poll.

The loop route is about 300 kilometers (180 miles) long, with the park accounting for roughly 100 kilometers (60 miles) of the drive. It can be done in a day or a week, depending on how much you dawdle, but it generally takes two days. It doesn't particularly matter which direction you travel, although the bigger of two park information centers is at the western entrance outside Cheticamp, inviting clockwise travel. Baddeck is a good base for your Cape Breton Island visit; it's centrally located and, as the gateway to the Cabot Trail, offers many tourist facilities. Once you've crossed the

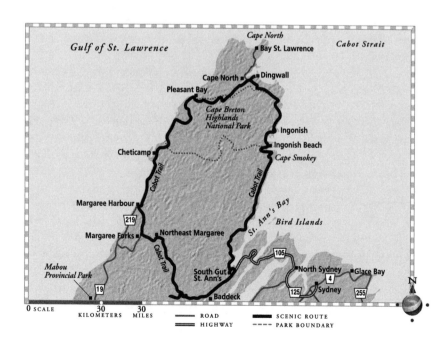

Canso Causeway to the island, follow Highway 105 (the TransCanada) from Port Hastings to Baddeck.

The major sight to see in Baddeck is the **Alexander Graham Bell National Historic Park**, Chebucto Street (Highway 205), 902/295-2069, http://parkscan-ada.pch.gc.ca. Bell first visited the Baddeck area in 1885 and eventually returned to settle there. On a headland overlooking Baddeck Bay, he built a home that he named Beinn Breagh—"beautiful mountain" in Gaelic. He died there in 1922 and was buried on the summit of his beautiful mountain. The home is not open to the public; Bell's descendants still live there. But the Alexander Graham Bell National Historic Park houses a museum devoted to the life and work of the Scottish-born genius. Besides inventing the telephone, he conducted aviation research leading to the first-ever flight in the British Empire, when, in 1909, his Silver Dart flew over Baddeck Bay. The museum displays the Silver Dart and other such Bell inventions as a huge HD-4 hydrodrome (a forerunner of hydrofoil boats), a vacuum jacket (an early version of the iron lung), and, of course, early telephone equipment.

The scenery around these parts looks a lot like the Scottish highlands, and when you think of Scotland you naturally think of golf. You can tee off at the **Highlands Links**, 902/285-2600 or 800/441-1118, in Ingonish Beach, considered by leading golf publications as among the finest in North America. The island's newest course, the **Bell Bay Golf Club**, 902/295-1333 or 900/565-3077, is also located in Baddeck.

Now it's on to Cape Breton Highlands National Park. Assuming you're starting from the western entrance, you might want to spend an hour or so in Cheticamp, an Acadian fishing village whose streets are lined with shops and restaurants with French signs. Stop in at Les Trois Pignons (the Three Gables), a museum and cultural center where one of the galleries houses hooked rugs, something Acadian artisans have elevated to an art form. Just north of town, stop in at the information center for **Cape Breton Highlands National Park**, 902/285-2691 or 902/224-2306, http://parkscanada.pch.gc.ca. The park itself is a realm of sandy beaches and plunging cliffs along the coast, and dizzying canyons when the road swings eastward across the top of the peninsula. Twenty-eight hiking trails range from 20-minute strolls to challenging treks. At French Lake, you can take a walk along the Bog Trail, a short, wheelchair-accessible path into the heart of bog life. Elsewhere, you can visit Mary Ann Falls, one of the prettiest and most accessible waterfalls in the park. Signs along the route indicate lookouts and nature trails. In summer, the Cabot Trail is like a hilly ocean of green dropping steeply to the water below. In autumn, when the leaves change, it's truly incredible—some people swear this season is the best time to visit.

You never know what you'll find around the next corner. At one lookout not far north of Cheticamp, for example, a moving inscription is dedicated to all the Canadians who have died overseas in the service of their country "who will never know the beauty of this place or the changing of the seasons." Wildlife is abundant, including deer, bobcat, mink, moose, eagles, and dozens of bird species.

You exit through the eastern access to the park, the town of Ingonish. Together with the adjoining communities of Ingonish Center, Ingonish Beach, South Ingonish Harbour, and Ingonish Ferry, Igonish provides everything from restaurants to whale-watching tours. The town is also the site of **Keltic Lodge**, 902/285-2880 or 800/565-0444, a lovely old resort set atop cliffs overlooking the ocean. Don't miss Cape Smokey, a towering headland south of Ingonish. Cape Smokey Provincial Park provides a magnificent lookout over the ocean and coastline. Drive carefully; Cape Smokey Road has many hairpin turns.

A variety of whale- and bird-watching cruises are available from different places along the Cabot Trail. For instance, whale-watching cruises leave from Cheticamp, Pleasant Bay, Bay St. Lawrence (north of Cape North), and Dingwall (between Cape North and Ingonish on the eastern coast). Tours to the Bird Islands are available from South Gut St. Ann's. Bird Islands, two small islands off St. Ann's Bay, are the nesting site of thousands of seabirds, including Atlantic puffins, cormorants, gulls, and razorbills.

11
ST. JOHN'S

Newfoundland sits at the easternmost edge of Canada and is known as The Rock; you'll understand why once you see it. Because of its location, it doesn't attract huge numbers of tourists—in short, it's deliciously unspoiled. Travelers who are interested in things other than amusement parks and beaches should make a real effort to visit this province. It's different from the rest of Canada—different from anywhere else in North America, in fact. The landscape ranges from forests to barrens, the rugged coast is steep, rocky, and wild, and the people are warm and wry. "When you live in this province," one St. John's native quips, "all you've got going for you is your sense of humor."

St. John's, the capital city, lies on the east coast of the Avalon Peninsula. One of the oldest cities in North America, it rambles up steep hills surrounding the harbor. The downtown core is on relatively level land, but as soon as you venture further afield, you're climbing precipitous, squiggly streets lined with colorful wooden row houses interspersed with Victorian mansions. The hills, the harbor, and the houses are what make this historic port city of 174,000 so picturesque.

MORE NEWFOUNDLAND FACTS

Explorer John Cabot, sailing for England, is believed to have landed in 1497 on what is now Bonavista Bay. It was the first recorded landfall on this

ST. JOHN'S

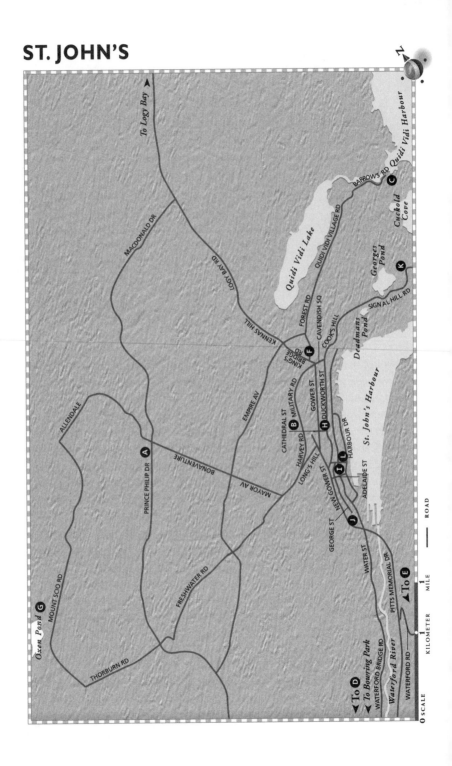

continent since the Vikings had briefly camped on Newfoundland's Great Northern Peninsula five centuries earlier. True, Christopher Columbus had sailed five years prior to Cabot, but he stuck to the Caribbean and points south on his voyages. It was Cabot who marked the start of permanent European settlement of North America. He claimed this "New Founde Land" for England and took back word of an incredible fishery—reportedly, so many fish crowded the waters around Newfoundland that Cabot's ship, the *Matthew*, could barely make headway—which in turn triggered an influx of Europeans and the spread of the English language across the continent.

Cabot's arrival also had sad repercussions for the Beothuk, the indigenous people then living on the huge island that became known as Newfoundland. Some historians think that these people prompted the pejorative expression "Red Indians" because they painted their bodies, their canoes, and other items with liberal amounts of red ochre. Because they were the first aboriginal people encountered on the continent by Europeans, this custom may well have been responsible for the term. Far more devastating to the Beothuk, however, were the diseases brought by the Europeans. Many Beothuk were also slaughtered outright by the new arrivals. According to the *Canadian Encyclopedia,* the last known Beothuk died of disease in St. John's in 1829.

This province actually has two parts—Newfoundland, a vast island, and Labrador, on the mainland to the northwest separated from the island of Newfoundland by the Strait of Belle Isle. Labrador, the much larger of the two but far less populated, lies north of the province of Quebec. It's remote and undeveloped, except for small ports along the coast and a few towns inland, and is home to the largest caribou herd in the world. Officially, the province is called Newfoundland and Labrador, but everyone calls it Newfoundland.

A PERFECT DAY IN ST. JOHN'S

If it's not foggy, start at Signal Hill, with its wonderful view of the city and harbor. Then wander the waterfront and maybe do some browsing in the Murray

SIGHTS

- Ⓐ Art Gallery of Newfoundland
- Ⓑ Basilica Cathedral
- Ⓒ The Battery
- Ⓓ Bowring Park
- Ⓔ Cape Spear National Historic Site
- Ⓕ Commissariat House
- Ⓖ Memorial University Botanical Gardens
- Ⓗ Newfoundland Museum
- Ⓘ Newfoundland Science Centre
- Ⓙ Newman Wine Vaults
- Ⓚ Signal Hill
- Ⓛ Waterfront

Premises, a restored mercantile complex on Water Street bordering the harbor. For lunch, stop at one of the wonderful fish-and-chips places on Freshwater Road. Then head out to the Cape Spear National Historic Site, only 10 minutes from downtown. The most easterly point in North America is also home to Newfoundland's oldest lighthouse and offers a close-up view of the forbidding North Atlantic. Back in the city, walk through the Memorial University Botanical Gardens, and then head down to George Street for dinner and some live music long into the night.

ORIENTATION

St. John's was destroyed by fire several times in the nineteenth century. The worst blaze, which raged for 24 hours in 1892 and razed more than half the town, has come to be known as the Great Fire. The town was rebuilt each time in a rather haphazard manner, so this city is anything but planned. Except for the heart of downtown, finding your way around can be very confusing. Arm yourself with a good map and don't hesitate to ask for directions. It's very hilly, so wandering around becomes a form of exercise in itself. Outside the downtown core, the best way to get around is by car. Harbour Drive runs along the harborfront, with Water (reputedly the oldest commercial street on the continent) and Duckworth Streets parallel to it. Signal Hill Road is situated off the eastern end of Duckworth Street. At its western end, Duckworth runs into New Gower Street.

SIGHTSEEING HIGHLIGHTS

★★★★ SIGNAL HILL
Signal Hill Road, 709/772-5367, http://parkscanada.pch.gc.ca
Signal Hill, a National Historic Site, is the best place to start a tour of St. John's because it affords a magnificent view over the city, the harbor, and the Atlantic (when not fogged in). A majestic rock guarding the narrow harbor entrance, Signal Hill lies around a curve of the shoreline east of the harborfront area. Gibbet Hill, to the right of the interpretive center, has a rather ghoulish history. In the 1700s, anyone who broke the law was hanged there and left for a week as a deterrent to would-be criminals. From all over town, people could see the bodies swinging up on Gibbet Hill. After a week of dangling in chains, the bodies were stuffed into barrels, weighted, and dumped into Dead Man's Pond. The English and French fought several times for

---

WEATHER WATCH

You can never be sure of the weather in Newfoundland. Sometimes, St. John's may be blanketed in fog during your entire visit, whereas the rest of the Avalon Peninsula will be warm and sunny. Wandering around the city in such weather is an agreeable if faintly eerie experience. This inclimate weather doesn't happen all the time, but when it does it can last for days. Even in early November, you may encounter a bad snowstorm. Any time you venture outside of St. John's, you're likely to experience firsthand the vagaries of Newfoundland weather, ranging in a single day from cold rain and fog to warm sunshine. Part of what makes Newfoundlanders so hardy is the weather in their area of the world. They talk a lot about it, and no wonder.

When Queen Elizabeth visited the town of Bonavista on June 24, 1997, to join in huge celebrations marking the 500th anniversary of explorer John Cabot's landfall in North America, the temperature was hovering around freezing. That's unseasonable even for Newfoundland, but as someone said later, the wonky weather made it a particularly Newfoundland-style event. In general, don't expect hot weather in Newfoundland even in July and August. It happens occasionally, but so do rain and fog and cool temperatures, so travel with appropriate clothing.

control of Signal Hill, and the last battle of the Seven Years' War was fought here in 1762. It was also on Signal Hill that Guglielmo Marconi, in 1901, received the world's first transatlantic radio transmission. It was the letter S; Marconi said it stood for "Success." Signal Hill also hosts the Queen's Battery, fortifications dating from the Napoleonic Wars, and the imposing Cabot Tower, a monument built in 1897 to commemorate the 400th anniversary of the European arrival in Newfoundland. In July and August, the Signal Hill Tattoo performs twice a day from Wednesday through Saturday, at 3 and 7 p.m., weather permitting.

Details: *The access road, Signal Hill Road, runs off the end of Duckworth Street. The interpretive center, about halfway up Signal Hill*

Road, has exhibits spanning one thousand years of Newfoundland history, from the Viking era to the province's entrance into Confederation in 1949. Open mid-June–Labor Day 8:30–8; the rest of the year 8:30–4:30. Nominal admission fee. (2 hours)

★★★★ **WATERFRONT**

To get a real sense of this historic port city, stroll along the waterfront. The harbor will doubtless be crowded with vessels from all over the world and with small fishing boats. Several boat tours depart from sites along the wharf, which runs the length of Harbour Drive. Four rest stops on the wharf feature interpretation panels about the harbor's history. Then pick up some walking-tour pamphlets and wander Water Street and Duckworth Road, which are lined with restaurants, cafés, and stores. Stop in at the **James J. O'Mara Pharmacy Museum**, a heritage site depicting a working pharmacy circa 1895, at 488 Water Street. George Street is the hub of the city's nightlife and is lined with restaurants and bars; walk up Adelaide Street to see it. Then continue another block along Adelaide to New Gower. Mile 0, the point where the TransCanada Highway begins, is located there at City Hall.

> ***Details:*** *(2 hours)*

★★★ THE BATTERY

Stroll through the past in this quaint fishing village that has been functioning since the seventeenth century and is now within city limits, making it a unique St. John's neighborhood that retains the look and feel of a bygone era. It's called the Battery because city residents once used gun emplacements in the village to fight off an attack on St. John's by three Dutch pirate ships. It's been known by that name ever since.

Details: The Battery stretches along the bottom of Signal Hill toward the Narrows, the entrance to the harbor. (2 hours)

★★★ BOWRING PARK
Waterford Bridge Road, 709/576-6134

If you're with children, make time for this large park, which boasts a replica of the famous *Peter Pan* statue in London's Kensington Gardens. The park was given to the city by the Bowrings, a wealthy business family. Legend has it that Sir Edward Bowring persuaded the sculptor of the original statue to make the replica in memory of his godchild, Betty Munn, who died in a disaster at sea in 1918. The park features picnic sites, a swimming pool, and a playground.

Details: In the west end of the city. Various guided tours of the park, including a hiking tour and a children's tour that involves trivia and games, are offered at a nominal charge. (1–2 hours)

★★★ CAPE SPEAR
709/772-4444, http://parkscanada.pch.gc.ca

Here, at the easternmost point of North America, you're a lot closer to Ireland than you are to Manitoba. The oldest lighthouse in Newfoundland stands on a rocky cliff at Cape Spear. It was built in 1835, remained in use until 1955, and is now a museum; it's also what makes Cape Spear a National Historic Site. The scenery hereabouts is rugged and beautiful, and you can enjoy picnic grounds and hiking trails throughout. The clifftops also provide an excellent vantage point from which to spot whales and icebergs. In July and August, bunkers built at the site during World War II as part of a coastal defense battery now serve as an evening venue for Voices from Cape Spear, a popular local music event.

Details: Roughly 10 kilometers (6 miles) from downtown St. John's; head west on New Gower Street and take the first exit after crossing the Waterford River. Visitor center open mid-May–mid-Oct 10–6. Site is wheelchair accessible. Nominal admission fee. (1–2 hours)

★★★ MEMORIAL UNIVERSITY BOTANICAL GARDENS
306 Mount Scio Road, 709/737-8590
www.stemnet.nf.ca/vsc/botgard.html
Newfoundland's only botanical gardens cover 45 hectares (110 acres) of land at Oxen Pond in C. A. Pippy Park, the vast park north of downtown. The grounds include an extensive rock garden, peat and woodland beds, a cottage garden, a perennial garden, a heritage garden, and a heather and rhododendron garden. A nature reserve offers trails leading through a variety of habitats, such as boreal forests and bog.

Details: North of downtown. Gardens open July–Aug daily 10–5; closed Mon–Tue in spring and autumn. Guided tours Sun at 3. Nominal admission fee. (1–2 hours)

★★★ NEWFOUNDLAND MUSEUM
285 Duckworth Street, 709/729-2329
www.delweb.com/nfmuseum/stjohns.htm
This museum depicts one thousand years of Newfoundland and Labrador history, beginning with the Vikings who set up a temporary camp on the Great Northern Peninsula five hundred years before explorer John Cabot's arrival. An archaeology/ethnology gallery illustrates the cultures and traditions of the Beothuk, Newfoundland's now-extinct indigenous people, as well as those of still-existing peoples such as the Mi'kmaq and the Labrador Inuit. Other exhibits detail the lifestyles of European settlers and fishermen. Part of the museum is devoted to wildlife, and the Tales from the Vault gallery features temporary exhibits on all manner of themes culled from the facility's vast collection. The museum is also the setting for assorted lectures, special programs for kids, the occasional concert, and so on.

Details: Tue, Wed, Fri 9–5, Thu 9–9, Sat–Sun 10–6. Closed Mondays. Free. (2 hours)

★★★ NEWMAN WINE VAULTS
440 Water Street, 709/739-1892
www.avalon.nf.ca/heritage/newman.htm
The only surviving intact historic wine vault in the province, the Newman Wine Vaults were built in the early 1800s to age the renowned Newman's port. Legend says that a New-man's ship bound for Lon-don in 1677 was driven off course and sought shelter in St. John's for the winter, storing the ship's cargo of wine in caves

there. When the ship returned to Lon-don, the port's flavor seemed much improved. After that the company sent its port to Newfoundland to age in the wine cellars there. The vaults are currently being restored by the Newfoundland Historic Trust to serve as an interpretation space about the colorful history of the liquor trade in Newfoundland.

Details: July–Aug Mon–Fri 10–4. On Water St. Nominal admission fee. (1 hour)

★★ ART GALLERY OF NEWFOUNDLAND
Allandale Road and Prince Philip Drive, 709/737-8209

The province's major public art gallery showcases Canadian and Newfoundland works, with the permanent collection's primary focus on art from 1960 on. In particular, the paintings, sculpture, photography, drawings, and prints by Newfoundland artists reflect the development of the visual arts in the province since it joined Confederation—only 50 years ago. Everything from major works by nationally recognized artists to hooked mats made by outport women is on display. The gallery is housed in the Arts and Culture Centre, which also holds theaters and libraries.

Driving at night in the Newfoundland countryside is strongly ill advised. The roads are winding and badly marked, often with no outside lines and only faint center lines. Furthermore, sheep and moose may wander across the road, and you won't see them in the dark until you're practically on top of them.

Details: Tue–Sun noon–5, Fri evenings 7–10. Free. (1 hour)

★★ BASILICA CATHEDRAL
Military Road, www.delweb.com/rec

Built of Newfoundland and Irish bluestone and granite, the beautiful Romanesque Basilica Cathedral of St. John the Baptist was consecrated in 1855 and dominates the St. John's skyline to this day. The ornate Italianate ceiling is highlighted in gold leaf, and the stained-glass windows were crafted by Irish, French, and English artists. Capped with twin towers, the basilica sits on a high hill on the northern side of the harbor and is a prominent feature of the skyline in a city that has no skyscrapers. A museum on the premises of this National Historic Site holds exhibits of the cathedral's history.

Details: Guided tours mid-June–late Aug, Mon–Sat 10–5. In winter, call 709/754-2170 to make an appointment. (1 hour)

★★ COMMISSARIAT HOUSE
King's Bridge Road, 709/729-6730

This gracious, restored Georgian house was constructed between 1818 and 1821 and served as the home of the assistant commissary general. The house is now a provincial historic site, furnished to the 1830 period, with costumed guides on hand to show visitors around and answer questions.

Details: Mid-June–mid-Oct 10–5:30. Free. (1 hour)

★★ NEWFOUNDLAND SCIENCE CENTRE
5 Beck's Cove, the Murray Premises, 709/754-0823
www.nsc.nfld.com

This place is a good bet if you're traveling with kids. The center, while small, offers entirely new exhibits up to three times a year. All exhibits include plenty of hands-on, interactive displays.

Details: On the harborfront between Bishop's Cove and Beck's Cove. Mon–Fri 10–5, Sat–Sun noon–6. $4.50 adults, $3.50 seniors and students, free children under 5. (1 hour)

FITNESS AND RECREATION

Enormous C. A. Pippy Park, 709/737-3655, at the city's northern limits, presents the best opportunity for hiking, walking, or jogging in the city. The park also has picnic sites, two golf courses, and cross-country skiing in winter. Bowring Park, 709/576-6134, has a swimming pool and tennis courts. Canoeing, kayaking, and sailboarding are popular activities on Quidi Vidi Lake. The Grand Concourse offers some 40 kilometers (25 miles) of trails and walkways within the city limits. The Rennie's River Trail, part of this urban trail system, begins at C. A. Pippy Park and winds through the heart of St. John's to Quidi Vidi Lake, and the Lake-to-Lookout Walk and the Cuckold Cove Walk connect from Quidi Vidi Lake to Signal Hill. Needless to say, the trails on Signal Hill, 709/772-5367, offer spectacular views of the Atlantic. Popular cycling areas are on the outskirts of the city, including Route 30 to Logy Bay, Route 20 to Torbay, Route 40 to Portugal Cove, and Route 50 to St. Philips.

A little farther afield, the new East Coast Trail, 709/334-2977 or 709/738-

SIDE TRIP: SAINT-PIERRE AND MIQUELON

Officially, the French islands of Saint-Pierre and Miquelon have nothing to do with Newfoundland, or, for that matter, with Canada. They're included here, however, because they're located only 25 kilometers (15 miles) off the south coast of Newfoundland in the Gulf of St. Lawrence, and ferry service connects with them from a town called Fortune. Several crossings a day are made in summer; the trip lasts just under one hour. Fortune is about 350 kilometers (210 miles) from St. John's along the TransCanada and Route 210. You can also fly to Saint-Pierre and Miquelon from Sydney or Halifax in Nova Scotia, or from Montreal.

The tiny islands of Saint-Pierre, Miquelon, and Langlade, left over from the days of New France, form a little French outpost where you pay in francs and chat with gendarmes. It's like visiting France without having to cross the Atlantic. Saint-Pierre is where most of the residents live, whereas Miquelon and Langlade, connected by a sandbar, are home mainly to wild deer and large seal colonies, plus some 80 species of birds. In July and August, ferry service runs from Saint-Pierre to Miquelon several times a week. The island isthmus connecting Langlade and Miquelon reputedly conceals the remains of hundreds of ships that went aground in storms over the past centuries.

The major industry on these islands has always been fishing. The only other economic activity is tourism, which has been growing in recent years. The climate is windy, damp, and generally harsh.

For more information, call 800/565-5118 or contact the French Government Tourist Office, 1981 McGill College Avenue, Suite 490, Montreal, Quebec H3A 2W9, 514/288-4264 or 514/987-9761. You can also contact the French Government Tourist Office in Toronto at 416/593-6427, and in New York City at 212/757-1125.

HIKE (4453), runs for 360 kilometers (216 miles) from Topsail Beach on Conception Bay, around St. Francis at the northern tip of the bay, and then all the way down the coast to Cape Race at the lower end of the Avalon Peninsula, passing St. John's, Cape Spear, Ferryland, and so on. The trail is not actually complete yet because it involves linking existing hunting paths and

ST. JOHN'S

To Logy Bay

Quidi Vidi Lake

Quidi Vidi Harbour

BARROWS RD

Cuckold Cove

MACDONALD DR

LOGY BAY RD

QUIDI VIDI VILLAGE RD

George's Pond

SIGNAL HILL RD

KENNA'S HILL

FOREST RD

CAVENDISH SQ

COOK'S HILL

Deadmans Pond

E **A**
Q
C
D
H
K
G
P
M
F **I**
J

KING'S BRIDGE RD

CATHEDRAL ST

MILITARY RD

GOWER ST

DUCKWORTH ST

HARBOUR DR

St. John's Harbour

EMPIRE AV

ALLENDALE

PRINCE PHILIP DR

BONAVENTURE

MAYOR AV

HARVEY RD

LONG'S HILL

NEW GOWER ST

ADELAIDE ST

GEORGE ST

O **B**

WATER ST

R

MOUNT SCIO RD

FRESHWATER RD

Oxen Pond

N

THORBURN RD

WATERFORD BRIDGE RD

PITTS MEMORIAL DR

WATERFORD RD

To Bowring Park

Waterford River

0 SCALE   1 KILOMETER   1 MILE   —— ROAD

coastal rights-of-way into a single trail system with access from any of the 30 communities along the way, but you can already hike large chunks of it.

Terra Nova National Park, 709/533-2801, http://parkscanada.pch.gc.ca, on Bonavista Bay (roughly a three-hour drive from the city), offers scenic hiking trails along the fjords, coves, and cliffs of the coast, and through forests and around freshwater lakes kilometers inland. A magnificent 18-hole golf course is set amid spectacular scenery, and long, empty sandy beaches along the southern shore of Bonavista Bay invite quiet contemplation. The park is about 300 kilometers (180 miles) northwest of St. John's.

The Avalon Wilderness Reserve, 709/729-5679, a vast protected region that lies about an hour southeast of St. John's in the center of the Avalon Peninsula, is the place to go if you're a hardy outdoorsy type. The single road into it is located just before Shore's Cove as you're traveling south on Route 10. The reserve has rolling barrens, a panoramic viewpoint, and thousands of roaming caribou; nowhere else in North America does such a large population of caribou dwell so close to a city. The area attracts mainly hikers, canoeists, wilderness campers, photographers, and anglers.

The sailing is reportedly excellent off Holyrood at the southern end of Conception Bay. Speaking of the ocean, several tour operators based in St. John's offer sea-kayaking expeditions along the coast, including Whitecap Adventures, 709/726-9283, and Wilderness Newfoundland, 709/747-6353.

FOOD

Cod tongues, saltfish, savoury, partrideberries, peppermint nobs, lemon creams—Newfoundlanders and Labradorians enjoy many unique foods.

FOOD

- **A** Bon Apetit Bistro
- **B** Bruno's Fine Foods
- **C** Cabot Club
- **D** Casa Grande
- **E** Chucky's Fish & Chips
- **F** Classic Café
- **G** Crooked Crab & Savage Lobster
- **H** Harbourfront Pub and Eatery

FOOD (continued)

- **I** Hungry Fisherman
- **J** Pastaria
- **K** The Westminster

LODGING

- **L** Battery Hotel and Suites
- **M** A Bonne Esperance House
- **N** Compton House
- **O** Delta St. John's

LODGING (continued)

- **P** A Gower Street House
- **Q** Hotel Newfoundland
- **Q** Prescott Inn

CAMPING

- **R** Pippy Park Trailer Park

Note: Items with the same letter are located in the same area.

The Newfoundland Ferry

Marine Atlantic, boasting a modern fleet that includes Canada's two largest superferries, MV *Caribou* and MV *Joseph and Clara Smallwood,* provides passenger and vehicle service year-round between North Sydney, Nova Scotia, and Port aux Basques on the west coast of Newfoundland. Additional service in summer links North Sydney and Argentia on Newfoundland's Avalon Peninsula on the east coast.

The Avalon Peninsula incorporates St. John's and a varied landscape of rocky shore and windswept tundra. The west coast is the site of Gros Morne National Park, one of Atlantic Canada's most scenic areas. Exploring both coasts is the ideal plan. You could take the ferry to Port aux Basques, travel through Gros Morne and beyond, then drive across to the east coast, explore St. John's and the Avalon Peninsula, and return to North Sydney via the ferry from Argentia. It would probably take a minimum of a week; it's a 900-kilometer (540-mile) drive across the province from Port aux Basques to St. John's.

The ferry schedule can vary slightly from one summer to another. The ferry to Argentia is a 14-hour crossing. One-way rates in 1999 were $124 per car plus $55 per adult passenger, $50 for seniors, and $27.50 for children ages 5 to 12. Because it's an overnight trip, you may want to book a cabin for an extra $125 or a dormitory sleeper for $20. The huge cruiseship-style ferry has large lounges, a casino with slot machines, a cafeteria, a dining room, a playroom for kids, and lots of comfortable chairs scattered throughout the vessel.

Influenced by Irish and English cooking, and by the plentiful fresh fish and seafood on hand, local chefs have also developed such exotic dishes as cultured scallops, partridgeberry mustard, and moose stroganoff. (The Newfoundland wine industry, based on local wild berries, is tiny but growing.) A new provincewide program called A Taste of Newfoundland and Labrador is designed to assist the public in identifying restaurants that offer traditional foods (seafood, wild berries, and game) and new and unique dishes using the finest local ingredients. Restaurants identified by the program's logo have been strictly evaluated for menu, cuisine, service, and surroundings. When you see the logo, you can pretty much assume you're in for a treat.

For a small city, St. John's boasts a wide range of decent restaurants in the

In the opposite direction, in some years the ferry brings you into North Sydney late at night, so be sure to book accommodation there ahead of time. The North Sydney–Sydney area isn't much to see, but it has ample roadside accommodations and eateries to cater to all the tourists passing through. For information and bookings, call the Nova Scotia tourist information line at 800/565-0000.

The ferry from North Sydney to Port aux Basques runs daily virtually year-round, with several ferries on most days between mid-April and late September. One-way rates in 1999 were $62 per vehicle plus $20 per adult, $18 for seniors, and $10 for children ages 5 to 12. The crossing takes about five hours.

It's important to call well ahead of time to find out the ferry schedule, finalize your itinerary, reserve passage on the ferry, and, depending on the time of sailings, book accommodations at both ends of the ferry crossing. Some years the schedule brings you into Argentia late at night, in which case you should book lodging in Placentia, the town nearest the Argentia ferry slip. Or you could drive to St. John's: the most direct route is via Route 100 north and then the TransCanada east. Total distance is 113 kilometers (70 miles), which will take perhaps 90 minutes to drive.

Call Marine Atlantic at 902/794-5814 or 800/341-7981 to reserve, or check out their website at www.marine-atlantic.ca.

downtown area—almost every one of which serves seafood. At the **Hungry Fisherman**, the Murray Premises, Water Street, 709/726-5791, the menu is broad but the real attraction is seafood. **Chucky's Fish & Chips**, 10 Kings Road, 709/579-7888, specializes in snowcrab and other seafood, and the menu at **Crooked Crab & Savage Lobster**, 98 Duckworth Street, 709/738-8900, features, you guessed it, assorted crab and lobster dishes.

The elegant **Cabot Club**, Hotel Newfoundland, Cavendish Square, 709/726-4980, is among the top fine-dining experiences in town, with seafood and international specialties in a gorgeous setting overlooking the harbor. The **Bon Apetit Bistro**, 73 Duckworth, 709/579-8024, offers more casual French cuisine and a great view of the harbor.

You have several options for pub grub, including **The Westminster**, 210 Water Street, 709/738-3018, an Old English-style pub and eatery, and the **Harbourfront Pub and Eatery**, 190 Duckworth Street, 709/576-0040, which offers a range of fresh seafood and Newfoundland cuisine, plus all-day breakfasts.

Newfoundland doesn't have a huge selection of ethnic eateries but good bets include **Casa Grande**, 108 Duckworth, 709/753-6108, specializing in Mexican fare; **Bruno's Fine Foods**, 248 Water Street, 709/579-7662, specializing in Italian food; and **Pastaria**, 32 George Street, 709/722-4444, offering gourmet pizza and pasta.

Or you can satisfy your hunger pangs at any hour of the day or night at the **Classic Café**, 364 Duckworth Street, 709/579-7888, which specializes in traditional Newfoundland cuisine and seafood.

LODGING

Historic city that it is, St. John's has many heritage-style inns and B&Bs with moderate rates. The **Prescott Inn**, 19 Military Road, 709/753-7733, stands in a row of Victorian houses downtown and features an extensive collection of local art as well as Newfoundland crafts and literature for guests to view. Gourmet breakfasts are included in the cost of a room. Another heritage home, **A Gower Street House**, 180 Gower Street, 709/754-0047, also features a large art collection and nice ocean views. A third Victorian-style establishment in the downtown area, **Compton House**, 26 Waterford Bridge Road, 709/739-5789, offers amenities such as antique furnishings, a sun deck, a library, and a sitting room with a big-screen TV. Gardens, a sun deck, and hearty breakfasts complement the Victorian atmosphere of **A Bonne Esperance House**, 20 Gower, 709/726-3835.

When you arrive on Newfoundland soil, set your watch ahead 30 minutes. Newfoundland's time zone is half an hour ahead of the Atlantic zone and 90 minutes ahead of the Eastern zone. When it's 5 p.m. in Toronto and 6 p.m. in Halifax, it's 6:30 p.m. in Newfoundland.

One of the ritziest hotels in town is the landmark **Hotel Newfoundland**, Cavendish Square, 709/726-4980 or 800/866-5577. In addition to smoking and non-smoking floors, floors with special amenities for business travelers, harborview rooms, and the like, the hotel offers several restaurants, a whirlpool, and a sauna. Another upscale establishment, the **Delta St. John's**,

A WORD ABOUT WORDS

A word about the Newfie accent: It takes some getting used to. It's a mixture of English and Irish dialects that have mingled into a quite distinct language. But don't worry—you'll be able to understand most of it right away and virtually all of it after a couple of days. You'll learn that b'y means "boy" and away means the mainland, as in "When I lived away, I noticed that the beer labels were different." If someone says, "We have a time on tonight," it means that a dance, party, or some other sort of social gathering is planned.

The names of some communities and geographical features attest to Newfoundlanders' sense of humor—Backside Pond, Blow Me Down, Chase Me Further Pond. Newfoundland's rugged beauty notwithstanding, the best thing about the province is its people. Spend as much time as possible getting to know them. You won't have to go out of your way to make friends; in Newfoundland, everybody says hello—and usually much more.

120 New Gower Street, 709/739-6404 or 800/563-3838, features similar facilities minus ocean views but plus a pool. For exceptional harbor views, the **Battery Hotel and Suites**, 100 Signal Hill Road, 709/576-0040 or 800/563-8181, is a good bet for business travelers.

CAMPING

The best bet for camping is the **Pippy Park Trailer Park**, C. A. Pippy Park, 709/737-3669, which has 156 serviced sites and 24 tenting sites, plus a convenience store. Rates start at $9 a night, and reservations are recommended in July and August. The park features all manner of diversions, including hiking trails, miniature golf, and a playground.

NIGHTLIFE

Newfoundlanders are self-proclaimed party animals, and St. John's is renowned for its lively nightlife and thriving live music scene, which encompasses everything from jazz and rock to toe-tapping jigs and reels. The center of it all is

SIDE TRIP: CONCEPTION BAY

Some of Newfoundland's most striking coastal scenery lies along a vast bay to the west of St. John's. Accented with brooding cliffs and dotted with dozens of small outports on which wooden houses cling to the hillsides, Conception Bay is ideal for exploring at your own pace, taking time to absorb the atmosphere of life along the rugged Newfoundland shore. This region also offers fascinating glimpses into the province's colorful history.

Arctic explorer Robert Abram Bartlett, who commanded ships in the polar expedition of Commodore Peary, was born in 1875 in the charming village of **Brigus,** where his former home is open to the public. Another Conception Bay community, **Harbour Grace,** once head-quartered the infamous pirate Peter Easton. (Centuries later, Harbour Grace was the departure point for famed aviatrix Amelia Earhart's successful 1932 flight to Northern Ireland, which made her the first woman to fly solo across the Atlantic.) A little farther north along the west coast of the bay, a seventeenth-century Irish princess, whose story is the stuff of fairy tales, is buried in a private garden in **Carbonear.** During the reign of Elizabeth I, English pirate Gilbert Pike fell in love with the Irish princess after rescuing her from a ship where she was being held prisoner after being kidnapped. The princess wed (and reformed) Pike, and the couple decided to make a new life for themselves in the New World, ending up in nearby Bristol's Hope.

Hibbs Cove, where the small, rock-ringed harbor is rimmed with square wooden houses, is so picturesque (yet so typical of Newfoundland outports) that artists and photographers are often drawn to it. **Baccalieu Island,** one of Newfoundland's amazing bird colonies, lies just off the tip of the western arm of the bay.

George Street, which is lined with pubs, dance bars, and restaurants; just wander until something strikes your fancy. In summer, outdoor concerts and other organized events take place on George Street. More pubs can be found on Water Street, one of the oldest thoroughfares in North America. This winding downtown street has been the center of commercial activity in the city for more than 400 years and is still lined with a variety of interesting stores, restaurants, and pubs; the latter offer musical entertainment that ranges from traditional Irish music to the latest country and rock fads.

BIRD-WATCHING

Imagine cliffs so crammed with birds that the noise is almost unbearable. Newfoundland boasts that it has one of the greatest concentrations of seabirds in the world—40 million of them, allegedly. Luckily for bird-watching visitors, some of the most spectacular bird colonies lie within one hour or so of St. John's. The Witless Bay Ecological Reserve is home to the largest Atlantic puffin colony in North America; the Cape St. Mary's Ecological Reserve protects a spectacular oceanside gannet nesting area; and Baccalieu Island in Conception Bay is home to the largest known colony of storm petrels in the world—reputedly more than 7 million birds. You can visit them on your own or take one of the many guided tours available out of St. John's.

WHALE-WATCHING

The province offers prime whale-watching. Seventeen species frequent the waters of Newfoundland and Labrador, and the best time to see them is summer, when they're migrating northward. The most common species are the humpback, minke, and fin whales, with less-frequent sightings of white-sided dolphins, harbor porpoises, belugas, sperm whales, and common dolphins. But the humpbacks rule. Some 5,000 of them—the largest congregation of migrating humpback whales in the world—cruise Newfoundland and Labrador waters each year. You can often spot whales from shore, but the best hope of seeing them is out on the ocean. Companies offering whale-watching tours out of St. John's include Adventure Tours-Scademia, 709/726-5000 or 800/77WHALE; Dee Jay Charters, 709/753-8687; and J&B Schooner Tours, 709/753-SAIL (7245).

ICEBERG-WATCHING

If you're visiting in late spring or early summer, the other large bodies you'll probably see floating in the waters off Newfoundland are icebergs. Most bergs that reach the Newfoundland coast have drifted south from Greenland—a trip that takes a year or two for the biggest bergs. When and where they show up varies from year to year. In 1999, hundreds were around the northern tip of the island by mid-May, with lots drifting into bays, inlets, and coves. They occasionally drift southward as late as August, but as a rule the best time to see them in the St. John's area is June. Some years the currents and winds have sent them along a route that's too far offshore to see with the naked eye; other years, thousands loom in the ocean for as far as the eye can see. If icebergs are indeed about, then you'll either see them from shore (lots of people head to the town of Twillingate on the north central coast of the island because huge icebergs are a fairly common sight there in springtime) or you'll see them as a bonus to any whale-watching tour you take. The enormous success of the movie *Titanic* has served only to boost iceberg-viewing as a tourist activity in the last few years.

Scenic Route: The Avalon Peninsula

Newfoundland is very much a nature-lover's destination, and some of its best nature-viewing is to be found on the Avalon Peninsula, an H-shaped land mass that juts from the southeast corner of Newfoundland and encompasses a richly diverse landscape in a relatively small area. You'll come across windswept coastal villages, barren heathlands where caribou wander, and a noisy seabird sanctuary on three rocky islands offshore. Don't miss a cruise out to the sanctuary, which may reward you with sightings of whales and/or icebergs as well as vast numbers of Atlantic puffins. Cape St. Mary's' wondrous Bird Rock, where more than 20,000 birds nest, is another must-see, as is Salmonier Nature Park. All this natural splendor is just an hour or two from St. John's. All you have to do is head south on Route 10 and continue as it turns into Route 90 at the bottom of what Newfoundlanders call the Southern Shore.

Start with a whale- and bird-watching cruise out to the **Witless Bay Ecological Reserve,** *three islands that attract scores of seabirds in summer. You can book passage aboard O'Brien's Whale & Bird Tours, 709/753-4850 or 877/639-4253; Gatherall's Boat Tours, 709/334-2887 or 800/419-4253; Mullowney's Puffin &*

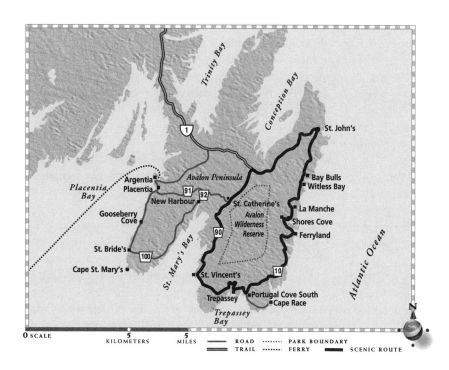

Whale Tours, 709/334-3666; or any of several other boat tours listed in the Newfoundland & Labrador Travel Guide. Whichever company you choose, you should have a terrific time. Not only do you get to see unbelievably dense colonies of Atlantic puffins (the provincial bird), razorbills, murres, kittiwakes, and other species (the nesting season runs from mid-June to late July), but you'll probably also spot whales and maybe even see towering icebergs. Moreover, you'll be treated to some down-home Newfoundland-style hospitality on board, complete with music, songs, stories, dancing, and nature lore. The cruises depart from Bay Bulls. Remember to dress warmly and bring your camera and binoculars.

Recover your landlegs by walking the trails in scenic **La Manche Provincial Park**, featuring a spectacular waterfall and birds, moose, beavers, and mink aplenty. The park is also the site of the remains of a village that was destroyed by a severe storm in 1966, which washed away boats, buildings, and a bridge. Miraculously, no lives were lost, although residents had to resettle elsewhere.

Continuing south, stop in to see the **Colony of Avalon Archaeology Site** at Ferryland, where archaeologists are uncovering the oldest known remains of seasonal fishing stations set up by Portuguese, French, and English mariners back in the 1500s. A more permanent presence wasn't established until 1621, when Sir George Calvert (later Lord Baltimore) founded the colony of Avalon here. After a few harsh winters and some battles with the French, he transferred his colony to Virginia, where he established Maryland. Encampments of native Beothuk people (now extinct) are also being excavated at Ferryland. A visitor's center has information about what's been found at the dig.

The world's richest find of Precambrian fossils—records of marine creatures that flourished more than 500 million years ago—lies at the southern tip of the peninsula. **Mistaken Point Ecological Reserve** is off Route 10, 16 kilometers southeast of Portugal Cove South. A little farther along the same road, past Mistaken Point, is the Cape Race lighthouse. Now the coastline gets wilder and the inland landscape increasingly tundra-like. When the road veers away from the sea, you'll feel as if you are driving across the moors, especially if it's misty, as it often is in these parts. Chances are you'll see a herd of caribou roaming the eerie barrens.

Follow Route 90 to **Salmonier Nature Park**, 709/229-7888, home to a variety of animals that have been wounded or otherwise injured and cannot be released back to nature. Visitors to this beautiful, peaceful park explore via a boardwalk that winds through woodlands and past ponds and streams. (The boardwalk not only protects the site but also makes the park accessible to people in wheelchairs or those with young kids in strollers.) Each animal species resides in a large area that resembles its natural habitat as closely as possible. The beavers, for example, live in a vast pond.

Wildlife includes a snowy owl, a peregrine falcon, and a bald eagle, as well as lynx, moose, mink, arctic fox, caribou, and other species. Wear comfortable shoes and take binoculars and a camera. Insect repellent will also come in handy if the weather is warm. The park, 12 kilometers (7 miles) south of the TransCanada on Route 90, is open from early June until Labor Day. Admission is free.

Then backtrack to St. Catherine's and turn onto Route 91 and then Route 92 south to get to the remarkable **Cape St. Mary's Seabird Ecological Reserve**. Located at the end of an 11-kilometer (7-mile) road that leads south from Route 100, the sanctuary features a lighthouse where you can pick up information on the bird colony and a trail that leads along the clifftops to Bird Rock. It's an awesome sight—many thousands of huge, golden-headed gannets and other birds crowded onto near-vertical, 150-meter (490-foot) cliffs with waves crashing below. An estimated 53,000 birds blanket the cliffs at Cape St. Mary's in summertime, making it one of the best spots in the province to see a seabird colony up close. If you go all the way, it's a 30-minute walk to Bird Rock, but you can get a good view after about 10 minutes of walking. Dress warmly; the weather can be cold and foggy, and it's always very windy. You will probably see sheep wandering around the clifftops, so leave your dog in the car or keep it on a leash. Take binoculars, and keep an eye out for pods of whales feeding in the water below, especially in July. A picnic table is located near the lighthouse, but it may be too gusty to enjoy a meal. The sanctuary is open to the public from mid-May to late October; for more information, call 709/729-2429.

From there, continue following the coast road, which leads past tiny villages nestled in "dokes"—long, wooded river valleys that all seem to end in calm blue lagoons separated from the sea by stretches of sandy beach. The hilltops offer great opportunities for photography. Eventually you'll find yourself back on the TransCanada; head east back into St. John's.

12
WESTERN
NEWFOUNDLAND

Newfoundland's west coast is a natural wonder, a panoply of cavernous fjords, dense forests, tufted heathlands, and ancient mountains that run from Port aux Basques in the south to L'Anse aux Meadows at the northern tip of the Great Northern Peninsula. The Viking Trail, a scenic route along the coast, links two UNESCO World Heritage Sites—the magnificent Gros Morne National Park at its base and L'Anse aux Meadows at its tip. With a geologic history as old as the planet, the Great Northern Peninsula is endlessly fascinating.

Gros Morne's varied landscape, including turquoise glacial lakes, freshwater fjords, waterfalls, inlets, sea stacks, sandy beaches, and mountains, is perfect for exploring on foot or by boat. Several colorful fishing villages are also located in this national park, one of the most awesome in the country.

L'Anse aux Meadows is the only authenticated remains of a Viking-period Norse settlement in North America. In addition to reconstructions of the sod huts in which the settlers lived, it affords an inspiring view of the ocean that brought the hardy Vikings to this coast so long ago. You can explore several hiking trails, as well as use the picnic facilities, at this National Historic Site.

MORE NEWFOUNDLAND HISTORY

One thousand years ago, in the spring of the year 1000, Lief Ericsson established the first European settlement in North America at L'Anse aux Meadows.

WESTERN NEWFOUNDLAND

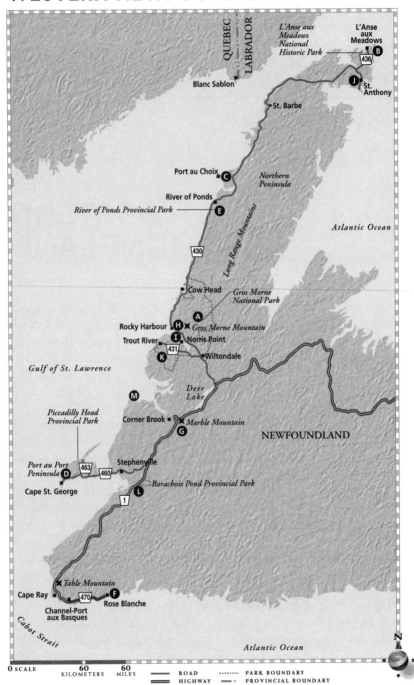

QUEBEC

LABRADOR

L'Anse aux Meadows National Historic Park

L'Anse aux Meadows

B

436

J St. Anthony

Blanc Sablon

St. Barbe

Port au Choix **C**

Northern Peninsula

River of Ponds

River of Ponds Provincial Park **E**

430

Long Range Mountains

Atlantic Ocean

Cow Head

Gros Morne National Park

A

Rocky Harbour **H** ✕ *Gros Morne Mountain*

Trout River **I** Norris Point

431 ● Wiltondale

K

Gulf of St. Lawrence

Deer Lake

M

Piccadilly Head Provincial Park

Corner Brook ■ ✕ *Marble Mountain*

G

NEWFOUNDLAND

Port au Port Peninsula **D**

463 460

Stephenville

Cape St. George

Barachois Pond Provincial Park

1 **L**

✕ *Table Mountain*

Cape Ray ■

470 **F**

Rose Blanche

Channel-Port aux Basques

Cabot Strait

Atlantic Ocean

N

0 SCALE
60
KILOMETERS
60
MILES
——— ROAD ········ PARK BOUNDARY
═══ HIGHWAY ─·─· PROVINCIAL BOUNDARY

It was more than five hundred years before Columbus and Cabot hit these shores. The Vikings, of course, were extraordinary travelers, ranging across Europe and the Middle East at a time when most people barely knew what the other side of the nearest hill looked like. Ericsson had heard stories told by Bjarni Herjolfsson about the time in 986 when Herjolfsson was blown off course on his voyage to Greenland and saw three new lands but did not go ashore. When Ericsson grew up, he set out to find those lands, now known as Baffin Island, Labrador, and Newfoundland. In Newfoundland, believed to be the "Vinland" of the Icelandic sagas, Ericsson built a sod hut village. The community lasted only a few years, however; outnumbered by the aboriginal inhabitants with whom they fought, the newcomers soon returned to Greenland and Iceland.

Throughout the year 2000, the entire province is planning to mark the 1,000th anniversary of the Viking settlement with a series of special events. Naturally, the focus of the celebrations will be the re-created sod huts that now stand at the site of that long-ago community, which will probably be the only National Historic Site in the country to throw a New Year's Eve party as the new millennium dawns. A major multimedia touring exhibit about the Vikings is also being billed as one of the anchor events of Canada's millennium celebrations in 2000, although details as of this writing were still sketchy. For information on the Viking Millennium, call the provincial tourist information line at 800/563-6353.

SIGHTS

- Ⓐ Gros Morne National Park
- Ⓑ L'Anse aux Meadows
- ⒸPort au Choix
- ⒹPort au Port Peninsula
- ⒺRiver of Ponds Provincial Park
- ⒻRose Blanche
- ⒼTable Mountain

FOOD

- ⒽEarle's Convenience Store
- ⒽFisherman's Landing
- ⒽHarbour Seafoods

FOOD (continued)

- ⒿLightkeepers' Café
- ⒿNorsemen Café
- ⒿTryco

LODGING

- ⒿBayside Housekeeping Units
- ⒿBottom Brook Cottages
- ⒿEvergreen Bed and Breakfast
- ⒿGros Morne Cabins
- ⒿHaven Inn
- ⒿSugar Hill Inn

LODGING (continued)

- ⒿTerry's Bed and Breakfast
- ⒿWildflowers Bed & Breakfast

CAMPING

- ⒾBarachois Pond Provincial Park
- ⓂBlow Me Down Provincial Park
- ⒶGros Morne National Park (5 campgrounds)
- ⒷPistolet Bay Provincial Park

Note: Items with the same letter are located in the same area.

A PERFECT DAY IN WESTERN NEWFOUNDLAND

Gros Morne National Park is the indisputable highlight in this part of the world, and you can experience several enjoyable activities here. One is to take a cruise along Western Brook Pond, an immense lake surrounded by towering cliffs—a setting that invariably recalls Norway. Another is to stop in the town of Trout River for the magnificent views of the coast and then head from there to the Tablelands, a plateau that has some of the oldest and oddest rocks in the world. If it's nice weather, stop by St. Paul's Inlet to see if any harbor seals are sunning themselves on the rocks. The hike along the James Callaghan Trail to the peak of Gros Morne Mountain is arduous, but the view at the end is positively exhilarating. One particularly tranquil picnic spot is on South East Hill near Neddy Harbour: One of the highest points of road elevation in the province, it provides a panoramic view of the East Lomond Valley and the Long Range Mountains.

ORIENTATION

The Viking Trail (Route 430) snakes all the way up the west coast from Deer Lake through Gros Morne National Park to L'Anse aux Meadows, a distance of about 463 kilometers (278 miles). It continues along Route 510 in southern Labrador, as far as Red Bay, where the Basques operated a whaling station in the sixteenth century. If you're arriving on Newfoundland's west coast via the ferry from North Sydney, Nova Scotia, factor in another 267 kilometers (160 miles) from Port aux Basques to Deer Lake. You'll obviously need a minimum of two days, and you could easily spend 10 days exploring the peninsula. If you're driving from St. John's, it's 638 kilometers (383 miles) from there to Deer Lake. The only other way to get to Newfoundland's west coast is to fly; small airports are located in Stephenville, Deer Lake, and St. Anthony.

SIGHTSEEING HIGHLIGHTS

★★★★ GROS MORNE NATIONAL PARK
709/458-2417, www.grosmorne.pch.gc.ca
Gros Morne, a UNESCO World Heritage Site since 1988, may be the single most compelling reason to see Newfoundland's west coast. Located northwest of Deer Lake, it has an outstanding and remarkably varied landscape. Barren rock ridges, tundra-like plateaus, densely forested foothills, glacier-carved fjords, boggy coastal plains,

grasslands, lakes, huge sand dunes, and picturesque villages are all found within the 2,000-square-kilometer (772-square-mile) park. Scientists theorize that billions of years ago the floor of the ocean ruptured, sending lava and chunks of ocean bed up onto the edge of North America. Rocks from deep inside the earth also ended up along the edge of the continent; they are now to be found on the Tablelands, a plateau in the southwest corner of the park.

Other areas of the park were carved out by succeeding ice ages—towering canyons, deep lakes, serpentine gorges, bogs, and lowlands. You will have marvelous opportunities to spot wildlife, including caribou, arctic hares, black bears, lynx, moose, and offshore seals and whales. You could easily spend a week exploring the park. For example, you could take a boat tour of a fjord called Western Brook Pond, which runs for 16 kilometers (10 miles) through 600-meter (2,000-foot) cliffs that have some of North America's highest waterfalls cascading over them. Or, if you're feeling hale and hearty, you could hike the 16-kilometer (10-mile) James Callaghan Trail to the peak of Gros Morne Mountain, a challenging outing that would take a day but offers an unsurpassed view of the entire park. You could laze on one of the many beaches along the coast, or spend hours exploring the picturesque fishing villages inside the park. You could spend days on the various hiking trails.

Details: *The visitors center is 3 kilometers (2 miles) south of Rocky Harbour in the heart of the park and is wheelchair accessible. Several of the trails in the park are wheelchair accessible as well, such as the Berry Hill Pond Trail, 10 kilometers (6 miles) north of Rocky Harbour. Park admission per day: $3.25 adults, $2.50 seniors, $1.75 children. Four days: $9.75 adults, $7.50 seniors, $5 children. (full day minimum)*

★★★★ L'ANSE AUX MEADOWS
709/623-2608, http://parkscanada.pch.gc.ca

This site is where the only authentic Viking establishment in North America was discovered. As far back as 1914, Newfoundlander William A. Munn suggested that Norse landings had occurred on this spot, but the remains were not discovered until 1960 when the Norwegian explorer and writer Helge Ingstad and his wife, archaeologist Anne Stine, searched the area. Stine excavated the site through much of the 1960s, after which Parks Canada took over. Eight or nine turf houses, some boat sheds, a primitive forge, and other small buildings were turned up. Archaeologists found slag from

SIDE TRIP: LABRADOR

The most isolated part of Newfoundland, Labrador is for those who want a vacation that's out of the ordinary. Labrador lies north of Quebec, and most of it is a wilderness of towering mountains, wide rivers, and broad lakes. Traditionally, Labrador has attracted hunters and anglers more than tourists, and if you love the wild, unspoiled outdoors, it's worth a visit.

The native Innu (Indian) and Inuit (Eskimo) people have survived in Labrador for thousands of years. The first Europeans to settle the coast were Basque mariners who set up a huge whale-oil processing center at **Red Bay** in the sixteenth century. An interpretive center explains the hard life of those who toiled to bring whale oil to Europe at the end of the Middle Ages. Other noteworthy sites in Labrador include the **Labrador Heritage Museum** in Goose Bay, which depicts the history of the land and the people, and the oldest known aboriginal burial mound in North America. Located at **L'Anse Amour**, the 7,500-year-old site contains the remains of a 12-year-old child.

Getting to and around Labrador takes some planning. In summer, a car ferry makes the short crossing from St. Barbe on the peninsula's west coast to Blanc Sablon in Quebec, right next to the Labrador border; from there, the road takes you to Red Bay. Car ferries are also available to Goose Bay in Labrador from Lewisporte in north-central Newfoundland; they stop at St. Anthony on the Great Northern Peninsula and in Red Bay. For information on the **St. Barbe–Blanc Sablon ferry**, call 709/931-2309 (Labrador office) or 418/461-2056 (Quebec office); for information on the **Lewisporte–Goose Bay ferry**, call 800/563-6353. Otherwise, sizable airports are located at Goose Bay, Wabush, and Churchill Falls, and coastal communities are served by smaller airfields. From Baie Comeau, Quebec, you can drive to Labrador City and Wabush in western Labrador. Seasonal coastal boats operate along the north Labrador coast as far as Nain; the number to call is 800/563-6353.

The provincial tourism experts say you should plan your visit well in advance; once there, visitors should never venture into unknown territory without an experienced guide. For more information, contact the province's toll-free tourist information line at 800/563-6353.

the forge, cooking pits, iron rivets, and other material. Radiocarbon dating of the organic material uncovered confirmed that the settlement dated from the early eleventh century. Archaeologists believe the Norse were here during a relatively short time between A.D. 990 and 1050.

Declared a UNESCO World Heritage Site in 1978, the site also contained evidence that Groswater, Maritime Archaic, and Dorset people lived in the area before the Norse. Visitors can wander through a re-creation of three turf houses unearthed at the site. Displays in the park's interpretive center include the floorboard of a Norse boat and iron rivets excavated at the site. In summer, costumed animators portray trader Bjorn, his wife, and his crew cooking and chatting with visitors and going about the daily business of a Viking encampment. Visitors can also attend a reenacted Viking feast and other events.

Details: The site is 42 kilometers (25 miles) from St. Anthony on Route 436. The park grounds are open year-round, the visitor's center from mid-June–Labor Day, 9–8. $5 adults, $4.25 seniors, $2.75 children, $10 family. Visitors can find a full range of services in the town of St. Anthony. (3 hours)

★★★ PORT AU PORT PENINSULA
Route 460, 709/644-2050

A side trip from the TransCanada west along Route 460 leads to the westernmost point of Newfoundland, Cape St. George, at the tip of the small, triangular Port au Port Peninsula. Turn west at Stephenville. The peninsula has 130 kilometers (78 miles) of rocky coastline and the highest proportion of French-speaking residents of any part of Newfoundland (15 percent). Battered by wind and water, the limestone and dolomite cliffs along the peninsula create some dramatic scenes. Picadilly Head Provincial Park, with camping, hiking trails, picnic tables, lookouts, and a playground, is located on the northeast shore. The town of Cap Saint-George is considered the heart of French Newfoundland, and one of the best times to visit is during the annual Une Longe Veillée folk festival. Held each August to celebrate French heritage, the festival attracts performers from all over Newfoundland, Atlantic Canada, Quebec, and Saint-Pierre and Miquelon.

Details: There is a regional visitor information center in Cape St. George. (2 hours)

★★★ TABLE MOUNTAIN
709/648-9244

Table Mountain is in the Long Range Mountains, part of the ancient Appalachian escarpment, and it's a geological oddity that sends winds whooshing down to the forest below. Sometimes the winds are so strong that they disrupt highway traffic. They were even known to topple railway cars back when Newfoundland had a train system. In fact, a man known as the "human wind gauge" lived in the valley below the mountain and for years was under contract to the railway. He would determine whether the area was safe for the train to traverse on any given day, or whether the wind was so strong it might derail the train. Table Mountain is accessible by a trail (10 kilometers) that leads to a lookout offering a panoramic view.

Detail: *Table Mountain is about eight kilometers northeast of Stephenville. (1 hour)*

★★ PORT AU CHOIX
709/861-3522, http://parkscanada.pch.gc.ca

An interpretive center at the Port au Choix National Historic Site displays skeletons, tools, ornaments, and other artifacts unearthed from a 3,500-year-old burial site here. The site was discovered by accident in 1967 by some construction workers as they dug foundations for a building. The next year, archaeologists found three ancient cemeteries and more than one hundred skeletons of the Maritime Archaics, hunters and gatherers who plied the coastal resources between Maine and Labrador more than four thousand years ago. Also on display are relics from another major archaeological site in this area discovered in the 1950s. It turned up the remains of a Dorset Inuit community that lived on nearby Pointe Riche around A.D. 100.

Details: *Nominal entrance fee. (1 hour)*

★★ RIVER OF PONDS PROVINCIAL PARK
709/225-3130

A display at this park includes whale bones that are an estimated seven thousand years old. Found at nearby sites, the bones offer proof that this part of Newfoundland's west coast was once under the ocean. The park includes a freshwater lake ringed by beaches and a forest. Visitors can camp, swim, hike, canoe, or fish.

Details: *About 60 kilometers (36 miles) north of the edge of Gros Morne. (1 hour)*

★★ ROSE BLANCHE
Route 470, 709/956-2863

The rugged coastal scenery along the 45-kilometer (27-mile) drive between Port aux Basques and Rose Blanche is what makes this short sidetrip worthwhile. Small fishing villages cling to the rocky shores in this region of brooding cliffs and crashing waves. Rose Blanche, a small fishing village, lies to the east of Port aux Basques. Nearby, a boardwalk about one kilometer long leads to a beautiful natural waterfall, Barachois Falls. The Rose Blanche lighthouse provides a good view of the Cabot Strait, at the bottom of which reportedly lie the wrecks of approximately 40 ships. The light in the lighthouse was apparently designed by the family of Robert Louis Stevenson.

Details: (1 hour)

FITNESS AND RECREATION

Western Newfoundland is heaven on earth for active, outdoorsy people. You can scramble over the rocks of the Long Range Mountains, rent canoes in Barachois Pond Provincial Park, 709/643-3474, or windsurf at Cape Ray Sands at the southern end of the peninsula. Practically anywhere you happen to find yourself, you can hike until you drop. In Gros Morne National Park, which contains 22 trails, several of the less strenuous trails are wheelchair accessible. At the other end of the scale, it takes eight days to hike the Cormack Trail, which runs from Petites on the south coast to St. George's on the west coast. Or maybe you'd like to tackle the mother of all hiking trails in Newfoundland. It's called T'Railway Provincial Park, 709/256-8833, and it runs for 883 kilometres (about 535 miles) from Port aux Basques across the interior of the province all the way to St. John's!

Three rivers in the St. George's Bay area—the Robinson's, Crabbes, and Barachois—are renowned for their excellent salmon angling, but if you're from outside the province you need a licensed guide with you; just ask at a visitors information center for a list of guides. Pistolet Bay Provincial Park at the northern tip of the peninsula is renowned for its canoeing. Several boat services ply the coast, allowing visitors to embark on outport adventures. If you're in the region in winter (decidedly the off-season), you can ski at Marble Mountain, 709/637-7611, www.skimarble.com, near Corner Brook. Marble Mountain is the highest ski mountain in Atlantic Canada and gets the most snowfall in all of eastern North America—a lofty 4.8 meters (16 feet) every winter.

Golfers might want to check out St. Andrew's Na Creige Golf Course, Route 407, 709/955-3322, a new nine-hole course just 20 minutes from the ferry at Port aux Basques. The Humber River Golf Club, Route 1, Deer Lake, 709/635-5955, is another nine-hole course that's laid out along the river.

FOOD

In Rocky Harbour, the biggest town in Gros Morne National Park, **Fisherman's Landing**, Main Street, 709/458-2060, is a complex that offers a restaurant as well as entertainment ranging from go-carts to mini-golf. Or you can get your fill of seafood at **Harbour Seafoods**, Main Street, 709/458-2821, and finish off your meal with an ice cream cone from **Earle's Convenience Store**, Main Street, which offers 44 flavors of soft ice cream plus homemade hard ice cream.

In Norris Point, **Tryco**, Main Street, 709/458-2486, is both a pub and a restaurant that serves a range of dishes to suit any taste. In L'Anse aux Meadows, the **Norsemen Café**, 709/623-2018, offers seafood and other traditional Newfoundland fare on the harborfront. In St. Anthony, you can chow down at the **Lightkeepers' Café**, Fishing Point Road, 709/454-4900, housed in a former lightkeeper's residence from which you may see whales and icebergs floating past; this restaurant is so popular that reservations are recommended.

LODGING

For such a wild landscape, plenty of tourist facilities exist along this route. Hotels and B&Bs are situated in small communities as well as in larger centers such as Corner Brook and Deer Lake. Accommodations are also available in several of the villages inside Gros Morne National Park, chiefly Rocky Harbour (where the emphasis is on efficiency units at low to moderate prices) and Norris Point. Staying inside the park allows you to explore at your leisure. Because it's about halfway up the peninsula, it also makes a good base for daytrips up and down the Viking Trail.

Here are some lodging suggestions in Rocky Harbour. **Bayside House-keeping Units**, Lloyds Lane, 709/458-2749, which offers efficiency apartments, is a good bet for families because it has playgrounds and allows pets. Similarly, **Bottom Brook Cottages**, Main Street, 709/458-2236, features two-bedroom efficiency units and playground and picnic areas. **Gros Morne Cabins**, Main Street, 709/458-2020, consists of 22 self-contained log chalets overlooking the ocean. If you'd prefer B&B accommodations, try **Ever-green Bed and Breakfast**, Evergreen Lane, 709/458-2692, or **Wildflowers Bed & Breakfast**, Main Street North, 709/458-3000.

In Norris Point, the luxurious **Sugar Hill Inn**, 115-129 Sexton Road, 709/458-2147 or 888/299-2147, offers gourmet cuisine and fine wines in the heart of the national park. **Terry's Bed and Breakfast**, Main Street, 709/458-2373, offers a picnic and playground area as well as a view of Bonne Bay.

If you're basing yourself nearer to L'Anse aux Meadows and the northern section of the peninsula, the largest establishment in St. Anthony is the **Haven Inn**, Goose Cove Road, 709/454-9100 or 877/428-3646. It stands on a hill overlooking town, has recently undergone renovations, and offers a good variety of rooms and suites.

Parks Canada offers a Viking Trail Pass that provides admission to Gros Morne National Park, L'Anse aux Meadows National Historic Site, and Port au Choix National Historic Site. For example, a daily pass costs $23 for adults and is valid for seven consecutive days. The fee is $20 for seniors 65 and up and $9 for children up to age 16.

For detailed listings in these and other towns, consult the *Newfoundland and Labrador Travel Guide*. But note that wherever you stay, it's vital that you book well ahead if you're traveling in summer.

CAMPING

Most of the numerous provincial parks along the coast offer camping facilities, mainly either semi-serviced or unserviced. Rates begin around $10 a night. The campground at **Barachois Pond Provincial Park**, 709/649-0048, at the base of the Long Range Mountains, is one of the largest and most popular in the provincial park system, and it's also one of the very few that are wheelchair accessible. Campgrounds are also available at **Blow Me Down Provincial Park**, 709/681-2430, and **Pistolet Bay Provincial Park**, 709/551-1457.

Five attractive campgrounds are situated in **Gros Morne National Park** alone; note, however, that no electrical hookups exist. Rates run around $15 a night. For reservations, call 800/563-6353. For details on each of the campgrounds, contact the park at 709/458-2066. An additional five backcountry campsites are available for $10 per night.

APPENDIX

Consider this appendix your travel tool box. Use it along with the material in the Planning Your Trip chapter to craft the trip you want. Here are the tools you'll find inside:

1. **Planning Map.** Make copies of this map and plot out various trip possibilities. Once you've decided on your route, you can write it on the original map and refer to it as you're traveling.

2. **Mileage Chart.** This chart shows the driving distances (in kilometers and miles) between various destinations throughout the region. Use the chart in conjunction with the Planning Map.

3. **Special Interest Tours.** If you'd like to plan a trip around a certain theme—such as hiking, skiing, or golf—one of these tours may be right for you.

4. **Calendar of Events.** Here you'll find a month-by-month listing of major area events.

5. **Resource Guide.** This guide lists various regional chambers of commerce and visitors bureaus, state offices, bed-and-breakfast registries, and other useful sources of information.

PLANNING MAP: Eastern Canada

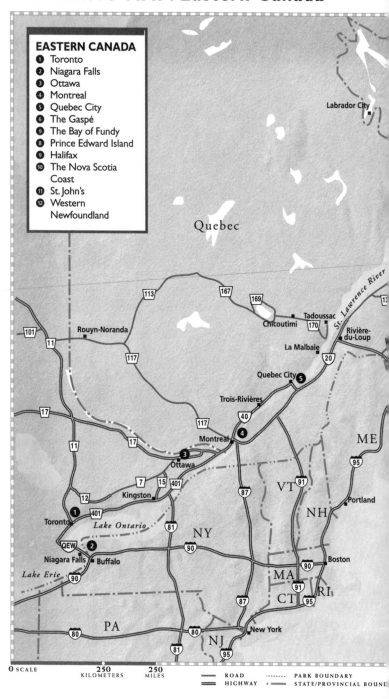

EASTERN CANADA
1. Toronto
2. Niagara Falls
3. Ottawa
4. Montreal
5. Quebec City
6. The Gaspé
7. The Bay of Fundy
8. Prince Edward Island
9. Halifax
10. The Nova Scotia Coast
11. St. John's
12. Western Newfoundland

Labrador City

Quebec

113
167
169
101
Rouyn-Noranda
Chicoutimi
170
Tadoussac
13
11
St. Lawrence River
117
Rivière-du-Loup
La Malbaie
20
117
Quebec City 5
Trois-Rivières
17
40
11
17
117
Montreal 4
ME
95
3
Ottawa
7
15
401
91
VT
12
Kingston
87
NH
1
401
Portland
Toronto
Lake Ontario
81
NY
QEW
2
90
Niagara Falls
Buffalo
Boston
90
Lake Erie
90
MA
91
87
CT
95
RI
PA
80
80
New York
NJ
81
95

0 SCALE   250 KILOMETERS   250 MILES

─── ROAD   ⋯⋯⋯ PARK BOUNDARY
═══ HIGHWAY   ▪─▪ STATE/PROVINCIAL BOUND

Goose Bay

Battle Harbour

Newfoundland

St. Anthony

430

Gros Morne
National Park

12

Windsor

Corner Brook

Newfoundland

70

St. John's

1

11

Île Anticosti

90

10

210

Argentia

de la
sie

132

Gulf of St. Lawrence

6

Gaspé

Peninsula

Cape Breton
Highlands
National
Park

Cabot Strait

Channel-Port-
aux-Basques

11

Prince
New Edward
unswick Island

8

Cape Breton
Island

North Sydney

105

Baddeck

11

2

1

4

8

16

Charlottetown

ericton 2

104

Truro

7

7

102

Nova
Scotia

Saint John

101

9

Annapolis
Royal

Halifax

Digby

103

1

Kejimkujik
National Park

10

armouth

Cape Sable

Atlantic Ocean

N

EASTERN CANADA MILEAGE CHART (KM/MILES)

	Niagara Falls	Toronto	Kingston	Ottawa	Montreal	Quebec City	Gaspé	Fredericton	Saint John	Charlottetown	Halifax	Lunenberg	Annapolis Royal	St. John's	Placentia
Toronto	180/112														
Kingston	462/287	206/128													
Ottawa	576/358	398/247	192/119												
Montreal	704/437	589/366	383/238	203/126											
Quebec City	962/597	837/520	646/401	481/299	262/163										
Gaspé	1748/1086	2079/1291	1887/1172	1723/1070	1504/934	1241/771									
Fredericton	1596/991	1380/857	1187/737	997/619	805/499	578/359	742/461								
Saint John	1699/1055	1423/921	1290/801	1100/683	906/563	681/423	845/525	103/64							
Charlottetown	1963/1219	1771/1100	1501/932	1362/846	1117/694	947/588	1111/690	369/229	317/197						
Halifax	2065/1283	1850/1149	1663/1033	1465/910	1280/795	1045/649	1212/753	470/292	422/262	224/139					
Lunenberg	2169/1347	1953/1213	1766/1097	1568/974	1383/859	1148/713	1319/819	576/358	526/327	327/203	103/64				
Annapolis Royal	2204/1369	2050/1273	1832/1138	1652/1026	1449/900	1187/737	1351/839	609/378	559/347	380/236	206/128	129/80			
St. John's	3181/1976	3027/1880	2809/1745	2629/1633	2426/1507	2164/1344	2328/1446	1586/985	1536/954	1249/776	1323/822	1428/887	1496/929		
Placentia	3091/1920	2937/1824	2719/1689	2539/1577	2336/1451	2074/1288	2238/1390	1496/929	1446/898	1159/720	1233/766	1336/830	1404/872	116/72	
Port au Choix	2764/1717	2610/1621	2392/1486	2212/1374	2009/1248	1747/1085	1911/1187	1169/726	1119/695	838/517	906/563	1009/627	1078/670	847/543	808/502

SPECIAL INTEREST TOURS

With *Eastern Canada Travel•Smart* you can plan a trip of any length—a one-day excursion, a getaway weekend, or a three-week vacation—around any special interest. To get you started, the following pages contain five special-interest itineraries geared toward a variety of interests. For more information, refer to the chapters listed—chapter names are in boldface, and chapter numbers appear inside black bullets. You can follow a suggested itinerary in its entirety, or shorten, length, or combine parts of each, depending on your starting and ending points.

Discuss alternative routes and schedules with your travel companions—it's a great way to have fun even before you leave home. And remember: Don't hesitate to change your itinerary once you're on the road. Careful study and planning ahead will help you make informed decision as you go, but spontaneity is the extra ingredient that will make your trip memorable.

GARDEN LOVER'S TOUR

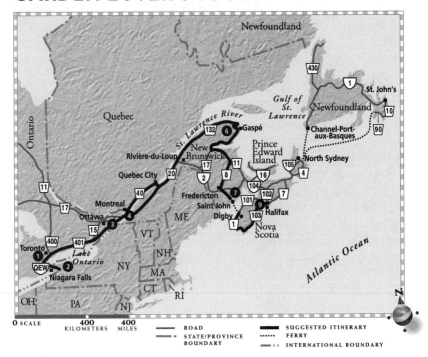

The growing season in Canada may be relatively short, but come April glorious gardens burst into bloom from the Niagara peninsula to Nova Scotia.

❶ Toronto (Royal Botanical Gardens)
❷ Niagara Falls (Niagara Parks Botanical Garden)
❸ Ottawa (Kingsmere)
❹ Montreal (Montreal Botanical Gardens)
❻ Gaspé (Les Jardins de Métis)
❼ Bay of Fundy (Kingsbrae)
❾ Halifax (Halifax Public Gardens)

Time needed: 2 weeks

GOLFER'S TOUR

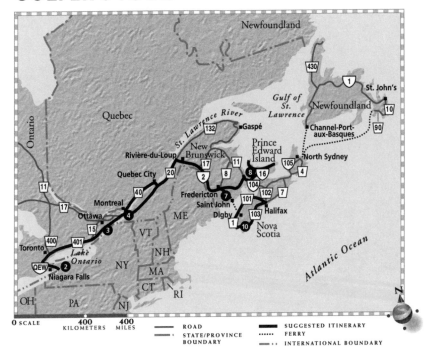

Golf courses in Eastern Canada are open at least six months of the year, and greens fees are relatively low. Prince Edward Island in particular is gaining renown as a golf destination.

❷ Niagara Falls (Whirlpool Public Golf Course)
❸ Ottawa (Upper Canada Golf Course)
❹ Montreal (Lac Carling, Le Diable, Le Géant)
❼ Bay of Fundy (Algonquin Golf Course)
❽ Prince Edward Island (Brudenell River Resort, Green Gables Golf Course, the Links at Crowbush Cove, Mill River)
❿ Nova Scotia Coast (Highland Links)

Time needed: 2 weeks

HIKER'S TOUR

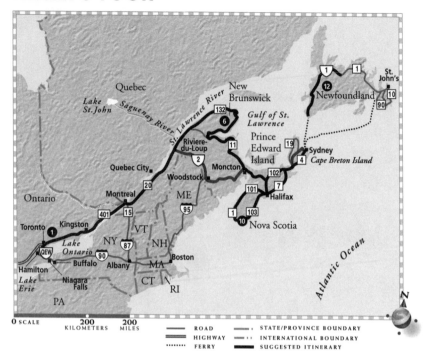

Canada is a hiker's paradise, with trails for every ability curling through a variety of awesome landscapes. The most famous trails are all somewhat off the beaten track.

❶ Toronto (Bruce Trail)
❻ Gaspé (Chic-Chocs)
❿ Nova Scotia (Cabot Trail)
⓬ Western Newfoundland (Gros Morne National Park)

Time needed: 2 weeks

SKIER'S TOUR

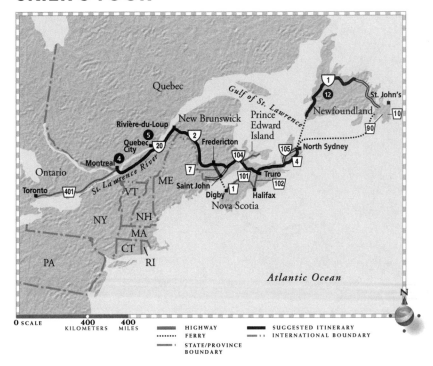

Skier's can't go wrong in Montreal, and the Quebec City area boasts several outstanding resorts, with mountains of snow virtually guaranteed.

- **❹ Montreal** (Mont Tremblant)
- **❺ Quebec City** (Le Massif de Petite-Rivière-Saint-François, Mont Sainte Anne, Stoneham)
- **⓬ Western Newfoundland** (Marble Mountain)

Time needed: 1 week

WHALE-WATCHING TOUR

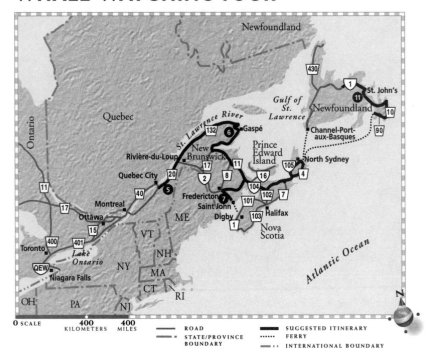

The Saint Lawrence River, the Bay of Fundy, and the Newfoundland coast are among the premier whale-watching destinations in the world. You can see the magnificent mammals aboard cruises and from shore.

- **⑤ Quebec City** (Saguenay/St. Lawrence River)
- **⑥ Gaspé** (Forillon National Park)
- **⑦ Bay of Fundy**
- **⑪ St. John's** (Avalon Peninsula)

Time needed: 1 week

CALENDAR OF EVENTS

January

Quebec Winter Carnival (Quebec City)
Highlights include night parades and a canoe race over ice floes in the St. Lawrence River.

February

La Fête des Neiges (Montreal)
This family-oriented "snow festival" takes place in the Old Port.
Winterlude (Ottawa)
Features ice and snow sculptures, ice skating on the frozen Rideau Canal, and numerous family-oriented events.

April

Shaw Festival (Niagara Falls)
Devoted to the works of George Bernard Shaw and his contemporaries, this theater festival in Niagara-on-the-Lake runs from April to October.

May

Canadian Tulip Festival (Ottawa)
An array of activities are featured during this springtime festival, including a flotilla of flower-strewn boats along the Rideau Canal.
Lilac Festival (Hamilton)
Hamilton's Royal Botanical Gardens celebrate the blooming of the delicate and deliciously scented lilac with concerts and entertainment.
Stratford Festival (Stratford)
From May through November, a wide spectrum of plays by the Bard are presented at this world-renowned festival in Stratford.

June

Benson and Hedges International Fireworks Competition (Montreal)
The competition lights up the skies over La Ronde amusement park twice a week from mid-June to mid-July.
Benson and Hedges Symphony of Fire (Toronto)
Toronto's waterfront dazzles with regularly scheduled fireworks displays from mid-June to early July.

Bridgefest (Prince Edward Island)
> A maritime festival in early June in Borden-Carleton marks the anniversary of the opening of the Confederation Bridge.

Carvan (Toronto)
> Some 50 pavilions around Toronto, representing the great cultural capitals of the world, offer lots of music and entertainment.

Charlottetown Festival (Prince Edward Island)
> From June to October, this festival presents both the long-running *Anne of Green Gables–the Musical*, and a new Canadian musical, *Emily*.

Evangeline Musical Drama (Nova Scotia Coast)
> From June through September, this classic Acadian musical is performed in the town of Church Point.

Festival International de Lanaudière (Montreal)
> Canada's largest classical music festival runs from late June through early August in Joliette, about an hour outside of Montreal.

Grand Prix du Canada (Montreal)
> North America's only Formula One world championship race.

Montreal International Jazz Festival (Montreal)
> Fabulous free outdoor concerts in the heart of downtown Montreal.

Nova Scotia International Tattoo (Halifax)
> One of the largest indoor shows in the world boasts 2,000 military and civilian participants from around the globe.

Shakespeare by the Sea (Halifax)
> From June to late September, the batteries and forts of Point Pleasant Park provide a terrific outdoor setting.

Summerside Highland Gathering and Military Tattoo (Prince Edward Island)
> Highland and step dancers, pipe-band competitions, and lots of Celtic entertainment, as well as children's activities.

July

Amber Voices from Cape Spear (St. John's)
> Regularly scheduled concerts are held from early July to early September in a natural amphitheater at Cape Spear.

Antigonish Highland Games (Nova Scotia Coast)
> The oldest continuous traditional Scottish highland games in North America unfold amid skirling bagpipes.

Bluesfest (Ottawa)
> The blues fill the air at Confederation Park.

Caribana (Toronto)
> A colorful annual celebration of Caribbean culture.

du Maurier Quebec City Summer Festival (Quebec City)
> More than 500 musicians and street performers from 25 countries fill indoor and outdoor stages with music and laughter.

Festival of Lights (Prince Edward Island)
> Charlottetown, the birthplace of the nation, celebrates the nation's birthday (July 1) with concerts, buskers, a midway, and a major fireworks display.

FrancoFolies (Montreal)
> Celebrating the work of French composers and songwriters from around the world, this festival features dozens of concerts, many of them free.

Just for Laughs Festival (Montreal)
> More than 600 comedians from 14 countries converge on Montreal.

Ottawa International Jazz Festival (Ottawa)
> Eight days of jazz come to the national capital during the third week of July, including lots of free outdoor concerts in Confederation Park.

Shakespeare by the Sea (St. John's)
> In July and August, this festival showcases the Bard in outdoor performances on the dramatic Newfoundland coastline near St. John's.

Summerside Lobster Carnival (Prince Edward Island)
> A mammoth street parade, giant midway, live entertainment, and, oh yes, lots of lobster.

August

Canadian National Exhibition (Toronto)
> Toronto's big annual fair takes place over the last week of August and the first week of September, with a midway, music, an air show, and more.

Halifax International Busker Festival (Halifax)
> Street performers from around the world come to Halifax to keep the crowds entertained in early August.

Festival Acadien de Caraquet (Bay of Fundy)
> The highlight of this 10-day festival in mid-August is a huge Tintamarre, a traditional Acadian street party.

Festival-by-the-Sea (Bay of Fundy)
> The focus is on Canadian music, dance, and culture when 300 entertainers gather in Saint John.

Lucy Maud Montgomery Festival (Prince Edward Island)
Three days of wholesome family fun in Cavendish, dedicated to the
author of *Anne of Green Gables*.
Montreal World Film Festival (Montreal)
Montreal turns into Moviedom Central the last week of August and the
first week of September.
Newfoundland and Labrador Folk Festival (St. John's)
St. John's rings with live music every day of the year, but especially
during this three-day folk music and dance festival.
Viking Encampment (Western Newfoundland)
L'Anse aux Meadows pays homage to the Vikings with a weeklong
encampment in mid-August.

September
Festival of the Fathers (Prince Edward Island)
This Charlottestown event in early September honors Canadian
Confederation with historic reenacts, Victorian walking tours, and
more.
Harvest Jazz and Blues Festival (Bay of Fundy)
Everything from jazz galas to hard-rocking blues concerts blast from
venues all over downtown Fredericton.
Niagara Grape and Wine Festival (Niagara Falls)
One hundred events ranging from tastings to cooking demonstrations
and a parade.
Toronto International Film Festival (Toronto)
With so many celebrities in town, stargazing is a favorite pastime during
this acclaimed September event.
Une Longe Veillée (Western Newfoundland)
Held in Cap Saint-George to celebrate French heritage, this folk festival
attracts performers from all over Atlantic Canada, Quebec, and Saint-
Pierre and Miquelon.

October
Celtic Colors International Music Festival (Nova Scotia Coast)
The best of Cape Breton Island's vaunted music, against a backdrop of
phenomenal fall colors in mid-October.

November

Royal Agricultural Winter Fair (Toronto)
>The world's largest indoor agricultural fair

Winter Festival of Lights (Niagara Falls)
>The falls, are illuminated with dazzling, animated light displays every evening from November through early January.

December

Christmas Lights Across Canada (Ottawa)
>Ottawa's downtown area is festooned with hundreds of thousands of twinkling lights.

RESOURCES

Each of the six provinces publishes comprehensive annual visitor guides. Quebec is the exception, in that it publishes a smaller booklet for each of the province's 19 tourist regions. Here are the provincial contacts:

Ontario Travel: Queen's Park, Toronto, ON M7A 2R9, Canada; 800/
ONTARIO (668-2746). Web site: www.travelinx.com
Tourisme Quebec: P.O. Box 979, Montreal, PQ H3C 2W3, Canada;
800/363-7777. Web site: www.tourisme.gouv.qc.ca
New Brunswick Tourism: New Brunswick Department of Economic
Development and Tourism, P.O. Box 6000, Fredericton, NB E3B 5H1,
Canada; 800/561-0123. Web site: www.tourismnbcanada.com
Prince Edward Island Tourism: Visitor Services, P.O. Box 940,
Charlottetown, P.E.I. C1A 7M5, Canada; 800/PEI-PLAY (463-4734).
Web site: www.peiplay.com
Nova Scotia Tourism: P.O. BOX 519, Halifax, N.S. B3J 2R7, Canada;
800/565-0000. Website: www.explore.gov.ns.ca
Newfoundland and Labrador: Department of Tourism, Culture and
Recreation, P.O. Box 8730, St. John's, Nfld. A1B 4K2, Canada; 800/563-
6353. Web site: www.public.gov.nf.ca/tourism

For more detailed information on individual cities, contact:
City of Charlottetown: P.O. Box 98, Charlottetown, P.E.I. C1A 7K2, Canada;
800/955-1864. Web site: www.munisource.org/charlottetown
Tourism Halifax: 1800 Argyle St., Suite 501, Halifax, NS B3J 3N8; Canada;
902/490-5946. Web site: www.halifaxinfo.com
Montreal Convention and Tourism Bureau: P.O. Box 979, Montreal, PQ
H3C 2W3, Canada; 800/363-7777. Web site: www.tourismmontreal.
org/guidea.htm
Niagara Falls Visitor and Convention Bureau, 5515 Stanley Avenue, Niagara
Falls, ON L2G 3X4, Canada, 800/563-2557. Web site: www.tourismni-
agara.com/nfcvcb
Ottawa Tourism and Convention Authority: 40 Elgin Street, Suite 202,
Ottawa, ON K1P 1C7, Canada; 800/465-1867. Web site: www.
tourottawa.org
Greater Quebec Tourism and Convention Bureau: P.O. Box 979, Montreal,
PQ H3C 2W3, Canada; 800/363-7777. Web site: www.
quebecregion.cuq.qc.ca/eng

Saint John Visitor and Convention Bureau: P.O. Box 1971, Saint John, NB E2L 4L1, Canada; (506) 658-2990. Web site: www.city.saint-john.nb.ca

Toronto Convention and Visitors Association: 207 Queen's Quay West, P.O. Box 126, Toronto, ON M5J 1A7, Canada; 800/363-1990. Web site: www.tourism-toronto.com

St. John's Economic Development and Tourism: 1 Crosby Place, St. John's, Nfld. A1C 5R4, Canada; 800/563-6353. Web site: www.city. stjohns.nf.ca

Other helpful resources include:

Air Canada: 888/247-2262 from Canada; 800/776-3000 from the United States. Web site: www.aircanada.ca

Canadian Airlines International: 800/665-1177 from Canada; 800/426-7000 from the U.S. Web site: www.cdnair.ca

Car rentals (Canada): Avis, 800/879-2847; Budget, 800/268-8900; Hertz, 800/654-3131; National/Tilden, 800/387-4747; Thrifty, 800/367-2277.

Hostelling International Canada: 800/663-5777.
Web site: www.hostellingintl.ca

Intercity bus lines: Acadian Lines, 902/454-9321; Greyhound Canada, 800/661-8747; S.M.T., 800/567-5151 from within New Brunswick or 506/859-5060 from elsewhere; Voyageur Colonial, 800/668-4438.

National parks: Parks Canada National Office, 25 Eddy Street, Hull, PQ K1A 0M5 Canada; 888/773-8888. Web site: www.parkscanada.pch.gc.ca

Via Rail: 888/842-0123 or 800/561-3949. Web site: www.viarail.ca

INDEX

Map Index

Cater Your Interests on Your Next Vacation

ABOUT THE AUTHOR

Felicity Munn was born and raised in the Saguenay region of Quebec, north of Quebec City. After earning a degree in English from Carleton University in Ottawa, she traveled extensively in Europe before alighting in Montreal, where she joined the Canadian Press as a reporter and editor. Munn went on to an eight-year stint as CP's national travel columnist, writing a weekly column and travel briefs that ran in approximately 90 newspapers across the country. She now works as a freelance writer and writes a weekly travel column for the *Toronto Sun*. She resides in Montreal.